AF260430

FORGOTTEN TRAILBLAZER

Joseph B. Chiles
and the Making of California

Forgotten Trailblazer

Copyright © Frederic C.Chiles 2018 All Rights Reserved

The rights of Frederic C.Chiles to be identified as the author of this work have been asserted in accordance with the Copyright, Designs and Patents Act 1988

All rights reserved. No part may be reproduced, adapted, stored in a retrieval system or transmitted by any means, electronic, mechanical, photocopying, or otherwise without the prior written permission of the author or publisher.

Spiderwize
Remus House
Coltsfoot Drive
Woodston
Peterborough
PE2 9BF

www.spiderwize.com

A CIP catalogue record for this book is available from the British Library.

The views expressed in this work are solely those of the author and do not necessarily reflect the views of the publisher, and the publisher hereby disclaims any responsibility for them.

ISBN: 978-1-911596-76-9

FORGOTTEN TRAILBLAZER

Joseph B. Chiles and the Making of California

by

Frederic Caire Chiles

SPIDERWIZE
Peterborough UK
2018

CONTENTS

The Decision — The pioneering background of the Chiles family. Missouri in the 1830s and 1840s as a launching ground for westward migration. The background of the decision to make the journey.

A Journey Without Maps 1841 — Setting off, the composition of the Bidwell-Bartleson Party, May 1841. Chiles's role in the party. What they found on the Great Plains, how they traveled and how they lived on the trail, crossing the territory which now makes up the states of Kansas and Nebraska.

From the Platte to the Bear — Entering the Black Hills, late June, passing Independence Rock, through South Pass to Soda Springs in late August, where the party divides, with most of the members heading for Oregon.

No Pilot Except the Setting Sun — The final stage, heading south, then west. Blundering around the Great

Salt Lake, wandering with only the setting sun as a definite guide. The party fractures, wagons abandoned in the desert, they enter the mountains in mid-October. Starving, they emerge from the mountains in early November, just ahead of the first blizzards and find their way to the rancho of Missourian John Marsh.

Youth turned toward California. Turned also the hothead, the adventurer, the gay ne'er-do-well, the invincible optimist, the gambler.

Irene Paden, *The Wake of the Prairie Schooner*

... most works of history tend to be no less revealing for the mental and aesthetic world of the author than for the subjects of which he treats. Particularly is this the case when the subject is the history of the author's own family.

George F. Kennan, *An American Family*

Introduction

In North American history, no single migration can match the scope, drama, and impact of the 500,000 people who crossed the continent between 1840 and 1870. It is one of the central facts and one of the essential myths of the United States. Even those who participated and lived through it were themselves astonished at the transformation they had witnessed. In 1840, between the Kansas River and the crest of the Sierra, the land was populated almost exclusively by native peoples. Thirty years later, almost none of it was. In their place were settlements, individual landholdings, and cities—all of them coming into being well within living memory of the average person.

While none of these ideas are contentious, more open to question is how to understand a phenomenon of such scale and complexity. A substantial bibliography of historical works has been written in an attempt to master the scope of the subject. Many of these have succeeded in their aim of helping Americans understand one of the defining occurrences of the nineteenth century. While much of the writing has addressed itself to the great sweep and its accompanying themes, it is my contention that there is still much to be learned from a careful examination of a single personality—the life and actions of an individual participant in this great drama. This was my motivation in searching out the life and career of my great-grandfather's uncle, Joseph B. Chiles, called by one historian, "the Adam of a generation of pioneers."[1]

As for descriptions of Chiles in other works, he is the man that everyone knows and yet nobody knows. In virtually every major work on the period, Chiles is mentioned. In George Stewart's *The California Trail* there are sixteen entries. He crops up in Ray Billington's *Far Western Frontier*, in William Camp's *San Francisco, Port of Gold*, in Will Bagley's *So Rugged and Mountainous*, John Cleland's *Pathfinders*, and in John Unruh's *The Plains Across*. In Nunis, *The Bidwell-Bartleson Party*, there are twenty-eight entries. Chiles was a friend of Broken Hand Fitzpatrick, Joe Walker, Kit Carson, John C. Fremont, Mariano Vallejo, John Bidwell, and most of the founding fathers of California. And yet there is no definitive and analytical work of the man who crossed the continent seven times between 1841 and 1854, a period that encompassed the beginnings of transcontinental travel and the expansion of the United States to the Pacific Coast.

---

[1] Webber, *Old Napa Valley*, St. Helena CA, Wine Ventures Publishing, 1998, p.42.

The explanation for this gap in our knowledge about this formative pioneer is doubtless related to the paucity of primary sources attributable to the man himself. Joseph B. Chiles was a man of few words. Even at the end of his adventurous life, with his exceptionally varied experience, he was reluctant to see it as anything special, deflecting credit by observing that he had not done anything that others had not done. And yet, in spite of Chiles's reticence, there is much to learn by reconstructing the context of his life. In terms of overland migrations, the Missouri frontier in the 1840s, and the conquest of Mexican California, the life of Joseph Chiles helps shine a light into various aspects of these complex stories. In illuminating the collision of cultures that faced the first Yankee emigrants to the west coast, and in tracing the impacts of explosive growth after the gold rush of 1849, the career of Chiles provides much specific information. Even though he did not feel compelled to publicize his own achievements, he was an active participant in virtually all the formative events of the years when California took its leave of Mexico and its place in the United States. Although Chiles might have been surprised to hear it, there is much to be understood about the great movement and issues of his day from a consideration of his life, and such is the aim of this work.

Sparked by a question from the next generation of Chiles's descendants about their famous relative, and at the urging of Western historian Prof. (Emeritus) Richard Oglesby, I set out to try to flesh out the broad background and context of Joseph Chiles's pioneering life, as well as to incorporate as much as possible about the realities of life on a trail for which, at the beginning, there were only the haziest of directions across almost 2,000 miles of prairies, rivers, and mountains. We have reached the 175th anniversary of that trek. It is my intention to reinterpret his story for the generation of young Americans in the twenty-first century. As they set out to explore their fast-changing, migrating world, they might find some useful and relevant lessons in the life of a man setting out into the unknown realities of the continent they now inhabit.

Acknowledgments

This book began with the encouragement of Emeritus Professor Richard Oglesby of the University of California, Santa Barbara, at whose suggestion I began my search for Joseph Chiles, the Forgotten Trailblazer, and I thank him for his judicious advice and positive thoughts. Also very helpful was Pat Keats, Director of the Library and Archives of the Society of California Pioneers. The staff of the California History Room of the California State Library contributed their enthusiasm for the project. I am also thankful for the interest and encouragement of my sister Mary Brock and my brother John Chiles, who read the manuscript with care and attention as well as carrying out research on various topics. The manuscript was also given a careful reading by Andrew Davidson, Editor in Chief of the University of Missouri Press. My brother Jim was my traveling partner, helping me recreate the 1841 route from Missouri to California. Cousin Nancy Douglas and her husband Marc were also very helpful in sharing their artefacts and opinions on various members of the Chiles family. Paul Alleway contributed his stellar design skills for the cover and maps. Finally, for invaluable encouragement on a daily basis, my thanks, as always, go to my wife, Jacky Davis.

CHAPTER 1

The Decision

By 1841, the Chiles family had been moving west for more than 200 years. Since the wealthy merchant Walter Chiles sailed his ship, the *Fame of Virginia*, from Bristol, England, in 1638 and settled on 400 acres near Charles City, generations of the Chiles family had sought to better themselves by taking advantage of opportunities that lay on their western doorstep. Walter Chiles's family prospered in Virginia, eventually possessing hundreds of acres of rich farmland in the central and northern part of the colony, worked by a significant number of slaves.[2] In the 1640s, Walter Chiles represented Charles City and Jamestown in the Virginia House of Burgesses.

The name Chiles continued to crop up in the various historic milestones in the early history of the United States as it broke away from the British Empire and took its place in the family of nations. About 125 years after Walter's arrival in Virginia, the status of Joseph Chiles's branch of the family would appear to have declined, for Walter's great-grandson John served not as a

---

[2] Gentry, D., & the *Dictionary of Virginia Biography*, Walter Chiles (1609–after July 6, 1653), (2013, August 22), In *Encyclopedia Virginia*, Retrieved from http://www.EncyclopediaVirginia.org/Chiles_Walter_1609-after_July_6_1653.

commissioned officer, but as a standing officer in the Navy of Virginia during the Revolutionary War. For his service as boatswain on the warship *Dragon*, he was rewarded with bounty lands on the frontier of south eastern Kentucky, taking the next step in the westward migration of the extended Chiles family.[3]

And it was in Kentucky that the paterfamilias of the subsequent generation of Chiles--John [Jack] Chiles—volunteered to serve as a captain in the East Tennessee Volunteer Mounted Gunmen. This unit was one of the volunteer militias raised on the frontier to fight in this minor theatre of the second war against the British Empire, the War of 1812. Under the overall command of General Andrew Jackson during his six-month enlistment, Chiles fought at the Battle of Horseshoe Bend in March 1814. In this war against the Southern Creek nation tribes of Northern Alabama, Jackson took advantage of the internecine warfare between the Northern Creeks, who backed the British, and the Southern Creeks, who initially sided with the Americans. By playing one faction against the other, he was able to displace the Creeks from

---

[3] "List of Officers, Sailors and Marines of the Virginia Navy in the American Revolution", *The Virginia Magazine of History and Biography*, vol. 1, no. 1, 1893, pp. 64–75. The British Royal Navy generally provided the template for the Continental Navy. The boatswain, in his blue frock coat with Navy buttons, was typically the most experienced deck seaman on board.

their ancestral lands and open the territory to white settlement.[4] This proved to be the beginning of a disastrous chapter in the history of the Creek nation, leading to the forced cession of Creek lands in Tennessee, Georgia, Alabama and northern Florida and their ultimate forced removal to territory west of the Mississippi.

These were much larger issues than Chiles's immediate concerns. With his six months service concluded, he settled into frontier farming life in the bluegrass country of Clark County, Kentucky. Here, the dominant crops were hemp and tobacco, often worked by slaves, as had been the case on frontiers farther to the east. Slave owning was common in this prosperous part of the frontier, but on a relatively small scale. Slaveholding, in the sense of large gangs of slaves under the control of an overseer, was something more prevalent, though by no means universal, in the Deep South. At the same time, there seems to have been pressure by the economic elites to use their greater resources to expand their holdings at the expense of farmers of more modest means. For the latter group, especially for families with many children, such as Jack Chiles, there was an economic imperative to find and relocate to a place that held out the prospect of more

---

[4] www.tn.gov/regimental-histories-tennessee-units-during-war-1812; Donald Hickey, *The War of 1812*, Urbana, Univ. of Illinois Press, pp. 146-151.

opportunity, including the availability of modest land parcels on which to grow the types of crops with which they were familiar.[5]

As his children matured, Jack Chiles did what many of his neighbors were doing—he looked west along the same latitude for a place where he hoped to find a continuity of soil types and terrain but less pressure from wealthy neighbors always looking for opportunities to expand their holdings. From the homestead of Jack and Sarah Chiles, a move west was the next logical step for them and the generation of children they raised.

The western migration of Jack Chiles's family from Clark County, Kentucky [Lexington] to a part of "Little Dixie," Jackson County, Missouri [Independence], fits the pattern of migration in those years. It took them to the western border of this new state of Missouri, where they would feel less economic pressure than had developed in the bluegrass country.[6]

Attracted by the excellent soils and relatively cheap land with good titles, like many of their fellow countrymen, they settled in Missouri with high hopes. Here they would not only be able to grow the crops to which they were accustomed, but they could foresee that they would be able to exploit the great rivers of

---

[5] John V H Dippel, *Race to the Frontier: "White Flight" and Westward Expansion*, New York, Algora Publishing, 2005. P. 183-89.

[6] Dippel, *Race to the Frontier*, p. 188.

the region to take advantage of markets in New Orleans and other parts of the Deep South. Earlier settlers to Missouri had sent back word of a "farmers paradise", one of them observing that the immigrants who followed, "… appear to be persons of considerable property and respectability, having with them slaves and considerable money."[7] News came back to Kentucky of people thriving on the basis of agriculture and trade on the Missouri and Mississippi rivers. In addition, there were commercial opportunities opening up to the northwest through the fur trade, and to the southwest with Mexico along the Santa Fe Trail.

Jackson County, Missouri was a setting that seemed to offer many advantages for a pioneering family. Its imagery was woven into the American imagination by the artist George Caleb Bingham in paintings such as *The Verdict of the People*, *The County Election*, and *Family Life on the Frontier*. These idealized images show democracy at work in the world of the sturdy yeomanry of the west.

But there was a balancing counter-narrative to these congenial and comforting images of democracy and family life in Missouri. The Panic of 1819 showed the fragility of the western

---

[7] Cited in R. Douglas Hurt, *Agriculture and Slavery in Missouri's Little Dixie*, Columbia, Univ. of Missouri Press, 1992, p. 52.

financial infrastructure. There was too little regulation of banks and headlong borrowing and lending, complicated by political meddling and reliance on distant markets over which Missouri farmers had no control. Then there were the endemic diseases of river bottomlands—malaria, cholera, and dysentery. Missouri at the time was also a rough and tumble society, marked by violence, with dueling and public brawling common occurrences. The career of Thomas Hart Benton, a US senator from Missouri nicknamed "Old Bullion," showed that a reputation for brawling with the likes of Andrew Jackson, and a willingness to shoot to kill a dueling opponent, was no bar to high office and respectability.

Another dark side of Missouri life, which almost certainly would have affected the Chiles family, was the pervasiveness of slavery. Even though small slaveholders who worked alongside their bondsmen were much more common in Missouri than in the Deep South, slavery, in all its dehumanizing aspects, was an established part of the culture. It was an institution that provided an economic advantage to the slave owners, one that they would not easily give up. For many, slavery was "a fact of life—an efficient management system and a moral right ... a matter of economic necessity."[8] Jackson County, where most of the Chiles family had settled, had among the highest percentage of slaves in the total population compared to most of the other counties in the state.[9]

Yet for all the risks and perils of life on this frontier, there were rewards to be had for the bold and experienced frontiersmen of means. The ability to move successfully was contingent on the possession of savings as the cost of the move from Kentucky to Missouri at the time was estimated to be in excess of $2,000 [$49,000 in current dollar values].[10] The cost could be higher if one had slaves to move.[11] For many families however, as one contemporary observed, "There are men in this country who become dissatisfied whenever others settle within ten miles of them; they feel cramped and want more room and without thinking much about the consequences they pull up stakes."[12]

Such was the world in which the Chiles family lived. Led by the eldest of their ten offspring, Joel Franklin Chiles, the family

---

[8] Hurt, *Agriculture and Slavery* ... p.244.

[9] Ibid., p. xii.

[10] Samuel H. Williamson, "Seven Ways to Compute the Relative Value of a U.S. Dollar Amount, 1774 to present," *Measuring Worth*, 2017, hereafter cited as Williamson, *Measuring Worth*.

[11] Diane Mutti Burke, *On Slavery's Border—Missouri's Small Slaveholding Households 1815-1865*, Athens GA,Univ. of Georgia Press, 2010, p. 34.

[12] Ibid., p.32.

began moving from Kentucky to Missouri in 1827. Most of the younger children, along with their parents, had made the six-week trip to Missouri by 1830 or 1831.[13] One source indicates that included in the move were 31 slaves, which would have marked the Jack Chiles family as fairly prosperous; it also might tell us something of Joseph Chiles's feelings about the institution of slavery and the south in general.[14]

Joseph B. Chiles, now 21-years-old and newly married to Polly Ann Stevenson, followed his other family members to Missouri in 1831. Joe and Polly began building a life together near Independence, and four children followed in quick succession. Then tragedy struck. In the winter of 1836, Polly succumbed to a "fever," leaving Joe B. with no mother for the children. His mother, Sarah, stepped in to help care for the children, but once she was established in the household, Joe B.'s native restlessness asserted itself. It was later that year, following the example set by his father in the War of 1812, that he and two of his brothers, Henry and James, answered the call for volunteers to fight in the Florida Wars in which the federal government, under pressure from white settlers in neighboring states, was

---

[13] Joanne Webb Chiles Eakin, Walter Chiles of Jamestown, Independence MO, 1983, Wee Print.
[14] Genealogy.com, Information about Joel Franklin Chiles, updated 2005.

attempting to force the Seminole Indians to migrate west of the Mississippi.[15]

Chiles fought in the column commanded by General Zachary Taylor, "Old Rough and Ready," who later became head of the US forces in the Mexican War and was elected president in 1848. On Christmas Day 1837, in the sawgrass and mud on the shore of Lake Okeechobee in south central Florida, the Missouri Volunteers took heavy casualties, including their commanding officer, Col. Richard Gentry, and Chiles's brother Henry.[16] Facing superior numbers, most of the Seminoles escaped across the large lake to fight another day, but for public consumption the encounter was hailed as a great victory for the US forces.[17] The Volunteers returned to Missouri with their heads held high and Joe B. found that he had achieved the honorific of Colonel, which stuck with him for the rest of his life.

He was back with his family, which doubtless came as a relief to his mother and children, but having now seen a bit of the wider world, his restlessness only seemed to increase, especially after he fell into long conversations with his friend, the millwright

---

[15] Lancaster, Jane F., *Removal Aftershock: The Seminoles' Struggles to Survive in the West*, 1836-1866, Knoxville, University of Tennessee Press, 1994, p. 18 ff.

[16] Mary Ellen Snodgrass, *Settlers of the American West*, Jefferson NC, McFarland and Co., 2015, p. 36.

[17] Ibid, and John and Mary Lou Missall, http://www.missall.net/thewars.html

William (Billy) Baldridge. Between them, they became convinced that somewhere in the far west was a land in need of water-powered mills and sturdy farmers. Baldridge had a growing reputation as a millwright and Chiles had all the homesteading skills to make a success in a country where the land and streams were available.

While Chiles reluctantly settled back into farming life, it was about this time that the first of three images, the only ones known to exist, was made. A daguerreotype dating from the late 1830s, it portrays a strong-featured man with a stern, angular, and clean-shaven face and receding dark red hair. His light-colored eyes confront the camera in an open, direct way, looking unswervingly at the viewer. With his wing collar and bow tie he is dressed in the fashion of the day, the image of a young but not unseasoned man, much of his life yet to live but already the acquaintance of hard times, even tragedy.

The second image, a formal portrait of Chiles and his second wife, was probably taken on the occasion of their wedding, 25 December 1853 in Independence. By this time, Chiles had achieved a significant amount of success at various ventures and land dealings, and his gray suit, bow tie, and contrasting waistcoat provide evidence of a considerable level of prosperity. His red hair has grayed at the sides and thinned on top. Standing by his side, her hand somewhat awkwardly resting on his shoulder, is Chiles's new wife, Margaret Garnhardt. Her dress, with its high, narrow waist and cameo at the throat, has the look of a prosperous lady of the period, but neither of them has hands unused to hard work. Unsmiling, they confront the viewer as confident pioneers.

The third image, a drawing made from a photograph after Chiles had gained a certain stature in California as one of the first architects of the new state, is that of a patriarch, eyes directed away from the artist, fixed on a distant horizon. His full chin whiskers befit his patriarchal status, perhaps offsetting the loss of his hair. Formal dress and a bold signature, J B. Chiles, across the bottom complete the stern image which belies a man who, from the accounts of those who knew him well, was full of charm, humor, and the musical ability to light up any room with his fiddle.

* * *

The rest of the Chiles family had settled on the western edge of the new state of Missouri, around the rough and ready town of Independence. But as they struggled to get themselves established, rampant speculation in distant places was about to plunge the frontier, the United States, and Europe into the first recognizably modern panic and depression. In terms that sound strikingly modern, the US economy experienced rapid economic expansion in the mid-1830s, funded in large measure by foreign investors, principally British, who were attracted by rising agricultural and land prices. In 1836, the directors of the Bank of England, alarmed at the decline in their reserves, indicated that they would raise interest rates, forcing the big banks in the United States to follow suit. Rising American interest rates fed into a decline in demand for cotton, the chief American export commodity.

The US economy relied at the time almost completely on the sale of raw materials, and falling cotton prices immediately affected the value of the dollar in relation to the British Pound sterling, the world's reserve currency. The US economy, which had been expanding strongly, plunged into recession, particularly in those states whose economies depended most heavily on production and export of primary products. The southern and western states were hardest hit by the Panic of 1837. As confidence plummeted, it led to bank failures and lower prices for agricultural products and the land on which they grew. Furthermore, the south also lay at the center of the growing partisan turmoil over the question of the expansion of slavery, an issue that would roil the nation in the following decades, culminating in the Civil War.

With this background, the 1840 presidential election was the first of its kind to be marked by modern electioneering practices, including catchphrases, ("Tippecanoe and Tyler too!"), manufactured excitement, and the personal involvement of the candidates. The result brought the leader of the Whig Party, hero of the Battle of Tippecanoe in the War of 1812, William Henry Harrison, to the White House along with Vice-President John Tyler, a distant Chiles relative. Harrison gave the longest inauguration speech on record in an early spring downpour, caught pneumonia, and died a month later. The first Vice-President to replace a sitting president, Tyler found himself embroiled in political infighting and constitutional questions over the transition of power. The reinvigorated opponents of the Whigs, the Democrats, created a challenging atmosphere that consumed the capital of the republic in its fifth decade.

Meanwhile, on the far western frontier of the United States, modest but portentous events were unfolding that would culminate in the next great continental expansion. Prior to 1841, only 13 Americans had permanently emigrated overland, joining a handful of missionaries who had previously made the journey in the footsteps of Lewis and Clark. With the founding of the Western Emigration Society in 1841 this was about to change, and radically so, leading ultimately to the acquisition of the

Oregon Country in 1846 and California and the Southwest in 1848. The Society grew out of the frightening effects of the financial panic of the previous decade coupled with awareness of the attractive settlement possibilities of the Oregon Territory and the even less familiar Mexican Territory. The information was the encapsulation of what some historians call the "push-factors" of negative economic circumstances combined with the "pull-factors" of limitless availability of fertile land, a salubrious climate, and an environment where everything appeared bigger and better than on the existing frontier. It is the combination of these motivations that convinced many to decide to make a risky long-range migration.

Word had been drifting back to the US frontier from these distant places, far to the west. It was said by early travelers, mountain men and trappers who had visited there, that a paradise existed along the Pacific Ocean. Letters and excited conversations spoke of rolling unfenced hills and valleys hugging the coast, and a mild climate in which any crop would thrive and disease was unknown. They also suggested that it was a country thinly populated by easy-going Mexican rancheros willing to sell part of their holdings to *Americanos* who were bold enough to cross the rugged and largely unmapped continent.

This broad and optimistic description masked the complexities of California, a place in a state of ferment. The last gasp of Spanish colonialism in the 1760s had led to the establishment of settlements combining the time-honored institutions of church and state which largely subjugated the coastal native tribes. A network of missions and *presidios*, supported by forced labor, most separated by a day's ride, stretched from San Diego in the south to Sonoma, just north of San Francisco Bay. Though fabled in story and song, the Mexican territory of California had a population of only 7,000 non-native residents, and was confined largely to the narrow coastal strip of settlements surrounding the missions and *presidios*. Aside from a small number of rancheros who claimed large land holdings in the Sacramento and San Joaquin valleys, the remainder of California was populated by the territory's 200,000 Native Americans. They were divided into more than 100 groupings, speaking more than 80 languages, but between 1769 and 1841 the natives kept the Hispanic population largely confined to the coast.

The fallout from the breakup of the Spanish Empire in the Americas, which among other things resulted in the establishment of the sovereign state of Mexico in 1821, brought the secularization of the missions and the transfer of much of the church's lands to powerful local ranchers, many of whose holdings expanded to a point almost beyond measurement. These were good years for the *Californios*, whose needs could usually be fulfilled from the bounty of their extensive ranches, and whose desires for luxuries could be met by the trading vessels sailing both from Europe and the eastern seaboard of the United States, which routinely plied the coast. The hides the rancheros rendered from the vast herds of cattle that roamed the golden hills were dried in the sun, these "California banknotes" providing ready exchange for manufactured goods that the local agricultural economy could not produce.

By 1841, Mexico was a troubled state which in its first twenty years had experienced religious strife, chronic political instability, civil war, and the loss of its northern province of Texas to American settlers, most of whom hailed originally from states of the border south, among them Missouri, Tennessee, and Kentucky. With the aim of securing its other sparsely populated northern frontier, *Alta California*, Mexico opted for a risky strategy of welcoming immigration from foreign countries. The authorities gambled that by offering generous land grants to immigrants they could make the new arrivals loyal Mexican citizens. The immigrants could obtain large tracts of land on the condition that they reside in California for two years, become naturalized citizens, and convert to Catholicism. The boundless opportunities and the availability of vast quantities of highly fertile land, coupled with the fact that the rules could not be strictly enforced by a federal government seated in far-away Mexico City, made the proposition especially attractive to farmers who had just endured the hard times that afflicted the frontier in the aftermath of the bank crash and depression of 1837.

One of those who caught word of these new places was Joseph B. Chiles. With his pioneering family background, it was not a great leap of imagination to consider this a realistic prospect. Independence, Missouri, already had strong trade links to the Hispanic Southwest through the development of the Santa Fe Trail, but the travelers' tales that circulated in the early 1840s around places like the tavern in Westport, Missouri, smacked of a different kind of opportunity, much more enticing to farmers and homesteaders like Joseph Chiles.

The tall, lanky red-haired, fiddle-playing Chiles, was fond of practical jokes, including those played upon himself. At six-feet four inches, he was considerably taller than many of his contemporaries, with the spare build of a frontiersman accustomed to hard work and turning his hand to anything that needed doing.[18] The attractions of these seductive stories of

---

[18] Giffen, pp. 1-5

California were even more enticing for Chiles who, as mentioned, had lost his wife Polly to a fever in 1836. Then the Depression of 1837 descended on the farmers of the west. The frontier was not sympathetic to single-parent families, and the year after his wife's death Chiles made the difficult decision to break up the family. His and Polly's small children, all under the age of six, were given over to the care of his brother, Joel Franklin, and his wife Azubah. Eager for an outlet for his undoubted energy and desire for adventure, it was at this time that Chiles joined the Missouri Volunteers. Once his enlistment was up, Chiles, now aged 31, returned home to Missouri. He had lost any illusions about the romance of warfare, but he was nonetheless reinvigorated and ready for further adventures. His imagination was particularly fired by the conversations with his millwright friend, William "Billy" Baldridge. While Chiles was away in Florida, Baldridge had been in correspondence with John Marsh, a Missourian who had been living in California for five years. "Doctor" John Marsh, a Harvard graduate, published letters in the St. Louis *Argus*, hoping to lure his fellow countrymen to the west coast. Marsh not only extolled the virtues of California, but proposed a route which promised sufficient pasturage and available drinking water all the way from St. Louis to the Pacific. In time, Marsh convinced

Chiles's friends, Baldridge and John Bartleson, that the hardships one might endure on the trail would be well worth the trouble.

Years later Chiles recalled, in the formal mode of address he reserved for interviewers sent by the likes of Hubert Howe Bancroft, "Mr Baldridge had for some time given considerable attention to the subject [of California] and had been corresponding with Dr Marsh whose descriptive letters of California and its climate and resources had awakened in him a great desire to see the country …"[19] They got news of a meeting in the Westport Tavern, a few miles west of Independence, where they could talk with a mountain man and fur trader who had actually visited California.

Chiles, Baldridge and Bartleson listened in the Common Room of the tavern as trapper and mountain man Antoine Robidoux described the country that lay to the west of the distant mountains. He had been brought to the tavern by John Bidwell, who had met him earlier in the year. Bidwell had been so impressed by Robidoux's description of California that he set up the meeting and invited him to address the assembled company. The trapper described California, "as one of perennial spring and boundless fertility," said Bidwell. "He told about oranges … [and]

---

[19] J. B. Chiles, *A Visit to California in 1841*, MS, Bancroft Library, Berkeley CA.

… every conceivable question that we could ask him was answered favorably."[20]

Clearly, Robidoux was in his element and his audience was rapt. Bidwell noted later, "Generally the first question that a Missourian asked about a country was whether there was any fever and ague. I remember his answer distinctly. He said there was but one man in California that had ever had a chill there, and it was a matter of so much wonderment to the people of Monterey that they went eighteen miles into the country to see him shake."[21] This was most likely something that would have resonated with Chiles, who recently had lost his wife to that common non-specific frontier malady. With the healthfulness of the climate settled to the audience's satisfaction, the Frenchman waxed eloquent on the friendliness of the *Californios* and even that of the local Indians.

To Bidwell, Chiles, and the rest of those who listened to Robidoux, "his description of the country made it seem like a paradise."[22] They appointed a corresponding secretary and a committee to organize a party that would go west to California. A

---

[20] John Bidwell, *Echoes of the Past*, ed. Milo Quaife, Chicago 1928 pp. 1-2

[21] Ibid, cited in John Bidwell, *Across the Plains*, pub. C. 1843, publisher unknown, cited http://scienceviews.com/bidwell/johnbidwell2.html.

[22] Ibid.

pledge was drawn up, committing the signatories to purchase suitable equipment and rendezvous at nearby Sapling Grove the following May. They called themselves the Western Emigration Society.

Chiles and the others were fired with enthusiasm. Robidoux's depiction of plentiful farmland with friendly people in a land where sickness was virtually unknown was even more persuasive than the letters from John Marsh. Nevertheless, no one in the group harbored any doubt that they would face hardships *en route* to California. As of 1841, no organized party had attempted a direct approach to California over the mountains. Marsh, however, told Baldridge and Bartleson that there was indeed one such viable route, even if it was one which was somewhat short on detail. It was not a path with which Marsh himself was directly familiar, but was based on knowledge that he had gleaned from passing fur trappers and mountain men who stopped by his ranch. Today we would call it hearsay.

According to Marsh, the Western Emigration Society should initially take the Oregon Trail from western Missouri, discovered and developed by fur trappers like Robert Stuart, who located South Pass in 1812-13, and by Jedediah Smith, who "re-discovered" the pass in 1824. They should continue along the Oregon Trail until they reached Fort Hall, in the central Rocky

Mountains.[23] Here they should diverge: and rather than follow the trail northwest towards Oregon, they should go west and south on a route that would lead to the Mary's [Humboldt] River in what is now north-central Nevada and on to the lake into which it flowed. From the lake, the path lay southwest until they reached a range of high mountains. According to Marsh, there was a pass through the mountains, then a river that flowed south. They should follow the river until they came to a wide valley where the river joined the great "San Waukeen." (He was of course referring to the San Joaquin River in present-day San Joaquin County, east of present-day San Francisco.) From there it would be a simple task to find his rancho in the shadow of Mt Diablo, southeast of San Francisco Bay.

It sounded persuasively simple, and a look at today's maps shows it to be largely misleading in terms of the difficulties involved, but for a man on his own like Chiles, confident of his trail making and pioneering skills, the lure of California, coupled with what seemed like a viable route to get there, proved irresistible. Although a disappointed Baldridge had to withdraw

---

[23] Philip Ashton Rollins, ed., *The Discovery of the Oregon Trail, Robert Stuart's Narratives of his Overland Trip Eastward from Astoria in 1812-13*; Lincoln, Univ. of Nebraska Press, 1935. See also David Dary, *The Oregon Trail*, New York, Knopf, 2004.

from the overland party for business and family reasons, Chiles along with nine friends who constituted the "Chiles Mess"—John Bartleson, Michael Nye, Charles Hopper, Robert Rickman, Charles Weber, James John, Charles Weaver, H. Peyton, and George Shotwell—made plans to meet up with John Bidwell and the other members of the new Western Emigration Society, which would head west from Sapling Grove, just to the southwest of Independence, on 9 May 1841.

Almost 500 people had signed up to head west as word of the meeting and the Western Emigration Society spread, but in the meantime, there was something of a reality check delivered by a New York lawyer named Thomas Farnham, who had just returned from California. He was in Monterey in 1840 and had witnessed the illegal incarceration and deportation of a number of foreigners to a jail in Baja, Mexico, including mountain man Isaac Graham and some other Americans who had been making a nuisance of themselves. Bidwell later described them as "not generally a class calculated to gain much favor with the people."[24] Nevertheless, their arrest and detention was an illegal maneuver, over which Farnham was scandalized. He expressed these opinions in a manner that bordered on racist denunciation in a letter published

---

[24] Ibid.

widely on the Missouri frontier in the winter of 1840-41. At the same time, the local merchants, presumably fearing a serious loss of business with the departure of 500 customers, denounced the trek as "the most ... foolish wild goose chase that ever entered into the brain of man for five hundred people to pull up stakes ... and go away to a region that we knew nothing of."[25] The support for the Western Emigration Society evaporated as enthusiasm waned.

Bidwell traveled up and down the Missouri frontier all winter, trying unsuccessfully to find replacements for the dropouts. It was almost time to start for the Sapling Grove rendezvous and it was unclear if anyone other than he would show up there. At the last moment, Bidwell met a recent arrival from Illinois and persuaded him to join, and together they went to Sapling Grove on the outskirts of Weston. One wagon with four or five people appeared and together they proceeded to the rendezvous. When they arrived, there was one wagon there already, but over the next few days wagons trickled in until the party numbered around 60 men, women, and children. The group was short on cash but long on enthusiasm and eagerness. Bidwell noted, "I doubt whether there was one hundred dollars in the

---

[25] John Bidwell, in Nunis, *The Bidwell Bartleson Party*, Santa Cruz CA, Western Tanager Press, 1991, p. 103.

whole party, but all were enthusiastic and anxious to go."[26] Years later, one of the members of the party proudly stated, "This was the inception of the emigration across the plains. This party opened the road… [It] was the beginning."[27] For his part, Bidwell admitted, "Our ignorance of the route was complete. We knew that California lay west, and that was the extent of our knowledge."[28] In sum, they had no money, no real knowledge of the route, and no idea of how long it would take, or what they would need in the way of supplies. The only thing they had in abundance was indomitable optimism.

It was an odd collection of families, sporting adventurers, veteran and novice mountaineers, and missionaries. Though what they lacked in terms of practicalities, they made up for in luck. The first manifestation of that good fortune was when providence literally intervened, and word reached them that a party of Catholic missionaries was on their way from their headquarters in St. Louis to their mission in the Flathead nation in the Rocky Mountains of present-day Montana. Their guide was the mountain man, Thomas "Broken Hand" Fitzpatrick, who had trapped in the mountains for years before, attaining his grand old age of 42. The

---

[26] Ibid. p. 104.
[27] Ibid. p. 104.
[28] Ibid. p. 102.

head of the Catholic contingent was Fr. Pierre De Smet. Short and stocky, with sandy-colored hair and a positive and open demeanor, he possessed a hugely important asset for this kind of undertaking, a genial affability unshaken by the inevitable setbacks and disappointments of the trail. Under Fitzpatrick's direction, the combined party set out north-westerly over the prairie along the Kansas River towards the confluence with the Little Blue River and the Platte.

It was a day's ride west of Westport in the valley of the Kansas that Chiles and his all-male group of nine caught up with the main party, and the total group was ready to set out on 19 May 1841. The Chiles Mess was mounted on mules, Chiles's lifelong preference, and had one ox-drawn wagon in which they hauled their supplies.

The exact number of emigrants is uncertain, but most sources agree on a total of 69. Of these, almost three-quarters were men who could manage a rifle, many of them single, but others were heads of families scouting for a new life. Bancroft says there were 48 men and 15 women and children in the main party, with 14 members in the missionary group, which tallies with the figures in the Letters of Fr. De Smet. The group was dominated by single men, like Chiles. In this, the Bidwell-Bartleson expedition was the exception to the typical overland emigrant group that would follow in the years to come. Most of the latter were composed of families who had been reasonably successful at farming on or near the frontier. They would have farming tools, and a wagon and animals to pull it, as well as the necessary skills to drive it and repair it on the plains. At the same time, it is estimated that to contemplate this kind of venture with a fully-fitted wagon required $1,500. This would equate with more than $44,000 in savings today, based on the Consumer Price Index.[29] This sum would cover the costs of a wagon, oxen, and enough supplies to live for a year without any income or the ability to plant or harvest a crop. For many families it took careful planning over the course of three to five years to save enough for the trip west. This was in addition to the preparations for a camping trip lasting between four and six months, which would cross some very rugged terrain. On a largely unknown trail, a company of emigrants also had to meet any emergency and provide for all their needs, unable to rely on trading posts or any armed protection from the national government.

Getting to know each other at the rendezvous point, the emigrants were naturally nervous about the journey before them. Although Bidwell had been the chief organizer, he was only 22-

---

[29] Williamson, *Measuring Worth*.

years-old, and no particular hierarchy of command had been established. Into the leadership gap stepped the headstrong John Bartleson, who insisted on being elected captain and threatened to pull out of the enterprise if he were ignored. It was obvious that the 55-year-old "captain" Bartleson knew little more about plains travel than the next man, but he had seniority, was acquainted with most people in the party, and could claim to have directions to Marsh's rancho. The others let him have his way.

As recent historians have pointed out, for the emigrant setting out on the Great Plains, this was not completely *terra incognita*. Although most of the American public knew nothing specific of the lands west of the Mississippi-Missouri river system, most of the direction of travel was known to indigenous tribesmen and mountaineers. The mountain men had become adept at reading the signs to link up the segments of the time-worn ways to make a fairly continuous route across the continent. Despite any misgivings that these first emigrants might have had, in 1841 the west was not particularly wild in the sense that it was full of danger.

It was a huge grassy plain, a natural system on which roamed the equestrian Indian tribes of the Great Plains. Many groups, like the Pawnees and the Wichitas, practiced agriculture and used fire to promote the growth of the ground cover on which their life and economy depended. Other tribes, like the Blackfeet, Comanches, and Lakota Sioux, were largely migratory, following the herds of buffalo across the plains. Scattered stands of timber marked the great river valleys of the Arkansas, Kansas, Republican, Blue, Platte, Yellowstone, and Powder rivers, providing refuge and forage for the indigenous peoples. They functioned as small bands, congregating during the harsh winters. The blizzards of winter kept the size of their horse herds in check. During the summer, although the great bison herds grazed the prairie bare in spots, the grasses revived with the autumn rains.

The impact of this type of land usage by the native peoples of the Great Plains was relatively light, and with a succession of wet years from the mid-1820s through the 1840s there were bountiful grass crops and the promise that life would continue in its accustomed pattern. The migration started by the early pioneers of the California and Oregon trails in the early 1840s was about to change the landscape, more often for the worse, in every dimension.

CHAPTER 2

A Journey Without Maps 1841

And so the westering adventure began. At daybreak on Wednesday 19 May 1841, the party formed up into a single file of mixed carts and wagons. First were four Red River carts. At about six-feet long, two-and-a-half-feet wide, with three-foot high sides, these hand or animal propelled, two-wheeled vehicles formed the backbone of plains travel and commerce for much of the nineteenth century, and were a natural choice for the new trail. Following their lead were the small wagons of the missionaries, and then eight covered wagons drawn by mules and horses, and finally five wagons drawn by oxen. These were the typical farm wagons of the time, with a cargo capacity of about a ton, into which the owners had to cram all the food, bedding, utensils, tools, weapons and ammunition, and family treasures that they would need to cross the continent and start a new life. Some hard choices had been made before the day of departure.

It was a warm spring day and Bidwell notes that they made about 12 miles moving steadily across the sea of undulating predominantly green grassland, punctuated with the bright colors of spring flowers, before stopping for a rest. Here, they had their first encounter with the local Indians, with the appearance of several well-armed members of the Kansas tribe equipped to do battle with their enemy, the Pawnees who had attacked their village, massacring a large number of old men, women, and children while the young men were away hunting buffalo. Thanks doubtless to the experience of their guide Fitzpatrick, Bidwell records no panicky response to the Kansas, and the amiable meeting concluded peaceably. The travelers set out again, with the weather turning almost wintry in a heavy shower of rain and hail, but it soon enough improved again and continued tolerably pleasant as they crossed small streams that broke up the prairie with their accompanying stands of trees lining their banks. Not yet settled into a nightly defensive routine, they awoke the next day to find that many of their oxen had wandered off during the night, and it took several hours of searching to find them before they could make a start. The train continued across hilly prairie, making reasonable time, awaking Sunday morning to find that the oxen had disappeared again, which led to some vociferous complaints from the mule and horse owners that if they were forced to continually wait for oxen to be found, it would mean wintering in the hills that marked the western edge of the Great Plains rather than the rich valleys of California.

The main group moved off, leaving the owners of the errant oxen to search for their beasts, which they eventually found, catching up with their companions late in the afternoon. The next day the party arrived at the Big Blue River, one of the main tributaries of the Kansas, which was running high and heavy, though they managed to traverse it with no losses. The country and the weather continued to be favorable, though on 26 May they suffered their first wagon breakdown. Having already made about 15 miles for the day at that point, the whole group stopped and some of the hunters went off in search of fresh game.

Towards evening a lone stranger approached across the prairie. This was Joseph Williams, a Methodist minister who had arrived at Sapling Grove too late to join the party but had pursued them on his own, "depending wholly on Providence for protection and support," noted Bidwell in his diary.[30] Williams's simple belief in Providence served him well, giving him an optimistic approach to life that belied his 64 years, though his piety tended toward the sanctimonious when it came to judging his fellow travelers. He condemned most of them as wicked deists, lamenting their profanity and their breaking of the Sabbath with swearing and fishing. In their theological discussions, the wily Jesuit missionaries found him completely naïve.

---

[30] Bidwell, Diary Entry, May 26, 1841.

With the missionaries and their guide in the lead, and traveling at the pace of the slow-moving carts, they made about 10-15 miles a day, moving northwest over the prairie to the fork of the Platte River.

Life on the trail followed a typical routine. The emigrants would awake before dawn, yoke up the oxen or hitch up the horses, cook breakfast of bread and bacon; and get moving. At midday there was an hour break for lunch and at about six in the evening they set up camp. Generally, they made a hollow square of their wagons, leaving a space between each for tents and campfires. The arrangement provided a convenient corral to prevent loose livestock from wandering off. Campfires were lighted, and dinner was begun. Utensils were basic, an iron kettle suspended from a tripod over the fire, and a long-handled skillet used to fry whatever was available.

Meat and bread dominated the diet of the emigrants. Cooking bread over a campfire was something of a challenge—the result was usually burned on the outside and doughy on the inside. Even worse, keeping bugs and dirt out of the mix was nearly impossible. If they had been lucky during the day, the emigrants might have quail or buffalo with their bread, but most days—in other words day after day—they ate the bacon that they had brought with them. When they had wood for a fire they ate the bacon cooked; or uncooked when there was no wood or dried buffalo dung to burn. By nine p.m. they would be bedded down for the night. Some families had tents, but most in the party just slept on the ground. Pure exhaustion helped them get to sleep, but it is unlikely that they slept comfortably. Come five the next morning the whole process started again.

The end of May 1841 found the company still traveling along the wide but shallow Platte River, and though they always started at daybreak they began to find the heat oppressive, with variations in the topography governing their speed and the availability of forage for the animals. Their first encounter with anyone other than Indians was with a party of 18 fur trappers with six wagons of furs on their way from Fort Laramie, near the junction of the Laramie and Platte Rivers, to St. Louis. Bidwell noted that the much-scarred oxen and mules drawing the wagons were matched in their rough appearance by the hairy and ragged mountain men who drove them.

The first day of June dawned hot and oppressive and the party moved on early from an unpropitious camp site, welcoming an afternoon shower, followed by a heavy hailstorm that cooled the air. That evening, with the wagons drawn up, shutting out the vastness of the surrounding plains, there was a sense of domesticity. The Reverend Williams, overcoming his scruples about the absence of local law and a marriage license, married two of the younger members of the party—Zedidah Kelsey and Winifred Williams, son and daughter of two of the migrating families, no relation to the Reverend. It was probably the first Christian marriage to take place that far west on the Great Plains.

This would have been one of the few pauses in the progress of the Bidwell-Bartleson party, voluntarily halted on two occasions for couples to be married; the above mentioned one on 1 June and the other on 30 July. Musical accompaniment for the dancing after the ceremonies was provided by none other than Joseph Chiles, who played the violin he had bought in New Orleans on his way back from the Florida Wars of 1838. Within the circle of wagons, the firelight shone on the dancers, the melodic notes of the fiddle imparted a homey charm to the occasion in the middle of a vast and wild place. Those who danced or listened to Chiles's music that night were a long way from the settlements that they had left behind, but the hypnotic lulling repetition of the chords and the chorus of "The Arkansas Traveler" gave a sense of ease and security with its light-hearted lyrics.

Oh, 'twas down in the woods of the Arkansaw,
And the night was cloudy and the wind was raw,

And he didn't have a bed, and he didn't have a bite,

And if he hadn't fiddled, he'd a traveled all night.

But he came to a cabin, and an old gray man,

And says he, "Where am I going? Now tell me if you can.

Oh, we'll have a little music first and then some supper, too,

But before we have the supper we will play the music through.

You'll forget about your supper, you'll forget about your home,

You'll forget you ever started out in Arkansaw to roam.

It is likely that Chiles's repertoire included other frontier favorites such as "Betty Baker", "Cluck Old Hen", "Roaring River", and "The Money Musk", and that it marked what was probably a high point of harmony on the trail, before the privations and stresses of the journey began to take their inevitable toll on the assembled company.

A lot of that harmony had evaporated as early as the next morning in a tense meeting convened to deal with the complaints from some in the party that the missionaries were pressing ahead too fast for the ox-drawn wagons to keep pace. The God-fearing among the party also found the rough irreligiosity of Broken Hand Fitzpatrick scandalous, but they thought that they would be left to face unknown terrain and Indians without his counsel, and experience convinced the majority that they should do their utmost to keep up the pace as they continued up the wide valley of the Platte.

A few days later, seeing pronghorn antelope in abundance, one of the younger members of the party, Nicolas Dawson, was tempted to set off after them. Thus distracted, he blundered into a band of high-spirited Cheyenne Indians, who were "pleased to strip him of his mule, gun and pistol."[31] When they let him go he ran for the wagon train to raise the alarm. As he was describing the encounter, the Cheyenne band appeared and the settlers made a panicky defensive square with their wagons under the bemused eyes of the warriors.

These exemplars of one of the more prominent horse-and-warrior Plains cultures, demonstrated the shifting nature of life on the plains. In the eighteenth century, they were associated with the northern Plains of Minnesota, but other tribes, some equipped with guns acquired from French and British traders, pushed them south and west toward the Dakotas, where they came into conflict with the Lakota who in turn pushed them out of the Black Hills. With the introduction of horse culture on the plains, the Cheyenne became heavily reliant on the buffalo as a major food source. Early in the nineteenth century they formed an alliance with the

---

[31] Bidwell, Diary entry, June 4, 1841.

Arapaho on the central and southern plains which strengthened them and enabled the Cheyenne to expand their territory into the part of the plains that would be most heavily traveled by parties on their way west. Dominated by warrior societies, the males accumulated prestige and power by performing acts of bravery to show their abilities as protectors, providers, and leaders.

Once the raggedy square of the wagon train had formed up, Fitzpatrick ensured that no rash shooting commenced by confirming through their emissaries and plains sign-language that the Indians were perfectly friendly. That evening the mountain man guide organized a campfire where a negotiation took place over Dawson's confiscated equipment. After much discussion, with gifts of blankets and clothes, and the passing of several peace pipes, Dawson had recovered most of his gear, except for the pistol that he had thrown away in his terrified flight. The adventure ended peacefully, though it pursued Dawson for the rest of his life: he is known to history as Cheyenne Dawson.

The train started early the next morning, at least to put some distance between themselves and the Cheyenne party who did not share the settlers' view of private property and required constant vigilance. Across the river they could see a large herd of buffalo, and while they were looking at the beasts, a small flotilla of boats appeared and proceeded downriver. These boats carried trappers of John Jacob Astor's American Fur Company, the company that had monopolized the western fur trade since its founding in 1808. After an exchange of pleasantries between the two groups, and the departing of one of their number with the trappers, the emigrants returned to the trail. That afternoon, Bidwell recalled their experience of a sudden squall, which included a tornado that passed at a distance, followed by a hailstorm with hailstones the size of turkey eggs. While they were waiting out the storm, the Indians caught up with them and remained with them for the next two days. At this time, buffalo continued to dominate the emigrants' diet, though the white men tended to confine their eating to the choicest cuts, such as the tongue, and leave the remainder to rot on the plains. Bidwell was one of the first to be troubled by the waste of huge amounts of meat, a trend evidenced from the quantity of buffalo bones and mostly uneaten carcasses that littered the trail within a few years, making the Platte Valley, "nothing but a complete slaughter yard …". He noted, quite presciently as it turns out, "If they continue to decrease in the same ratio that they have for the past 15 or 20 years, they will ere long become totally extinct."[32]

---

[32] Bidwell, Diary entry, June 8, 1841.

They spent the day of 9 June fording the South Fork of the Platte. It was shallow enough that they did not have to float the wagons across, but its bottom was muddy and its width was estimated by Bidwell at two-thirds of a mile. The method of fording the river required elaborate encouragement of the oxen to keep them moving forward, outriders upstream with ropes attached to the wagons to keep them from tipping in the current, and a generous amount of cursing that scandalized the attendant clergy. For food that day, they killed a buffalo from a herd that came within 300 yards of the camp. Departure the next day was delayed by the now familiar need to track down the oxen which had either been led away by the Indians or mingled with a passing buffalo herd. During the entire distance of the day's travel, about 14 miles, they could see a continuous herd of buffalo grazing on the hills or drinking along the banks of the river.

The presence of the buffalo meant that food was not a problem, but the proximity of more warlike Indian tribes, the Lakota, Kiowa, and Comanche, who followed the great herds, meant that security was becoming an issue. Although nominal guards were posted at night, it was not until a "court-martial" was called to discipline watchmen found asleep at their posts that they began to take the need for night-time vigilance seriously. Their casual approach to watchfulness was sometimes replaced by panicky overreaction to the sight of small groups of Indians that in the minds of the observers quickly magnified into warlike hordes. The vast herds of buffalo along the river were still commonplace, and at times, instructed by Fizpatrick, members of the party were compelled to fire off guns in the night, or take up positions some distance from camp to turn the meandering herds before they overran the emigrants, potentially crushing people and wagons in the process.

No trip across the plains was spared its measure of tragedy, and for the Bidwell-Bartleson Party the first such one occurred on Sunday 13 June. In the preparation to set off in the morning, young George Shotwell carelessly reached for the barrel of his gun to pull it out of his wagon. The trigger caught on something and it went off, shooting him full in the chest. He died within the hour. Shotwell had been a popular member of the party, and of Chiles Mess. The others buried him with as much respect as they could, with the Rev. Williams preaching a funeral sermon to the somber company who formed a committee to administer his "estate."

In the meantime, the weather turned so unseasonably cold and rainy that they remained in camp for a full day. On the fifteenth, the train continued along the North Fork of the Platte, being the first settler party to see certain geographic features that would become landmarks for the many thousands who would follow. By this point they were regularly making 15-20 miles a day as Courthouse Rock, Chimney Rock, and Scott's Bluff came into and went out of view. On Sunday 20 June they were across what would become the Wyoming state border, making good time in the cool and windy weather. A fast 27 miles saw them within half a day's travel of Fort Laramie.

When they rolled into the fort, owned at the time by the American Fur Company, on 22 June, they were about 650 miles west of their Missouri starting point, with the Wyoming Black Hills [not to be confused with the Black Hills of South Dakota] on the western horizon. It had taken them 33 days to come this far, and though they were likely satisfied with their progress of about 20 miles a day, they also may have realized that they were barely more than a third of the way into their journey. They had moved at what proved to be a fast pace for the teams of oxen, requiring them to be in harness 8-10 hours a day, which was surely wearing, but the pace was forced by their guide Fitzpatrick, who insisted that all keep up the speed of the faster horses and mules. The emigrants held a meeting at one point to discuss whether they should drop behind, but decided that they had better stay with their guide, even at the risk of overtaxing their teams.

The party spent a few days at the fort, repairing the wagons, bargaining with the resident trappers, Lakotas and Cheyennes, and conducting an auction of the unfortunate George Shotwell's possessions. They departed the fort on 27 June and began winding their way through the Black Hills following the river and making reasonable time, finding water and forage almost every day. The buffalo remained abundant and they continued to eat their fill, and in spite of Bidwell's misgivings about the wastage, they ate mostly just the tongues and marrow bones, leaving the rest of the meat on the carcasses for the wolves and other prairie scavengers.

CHAPTER 3

From the Platte to the Bear

Still in the Black Hills, they forded the North Fork of the Platte on 1 July with considerable difficulty, losing one mule and having a wagon tip over in the fast-flowing stream. The weather turned hot and on 3 July they left the river whose course they had followed for almost five weeks. The Fourth of July found them still winding their way through the increasingly high hills, though still managing to make good daily distances. They felt confident enough to take time out to celebrate Independence Day, the fiddle music of Joe Chiles probably eased their minds as they found themselves in the middle of a landscape the likes of which they had never before seen. It was the start of a tradition in which the Fourth, said Edwin Bryant a few years later, "was celebrated with gunpowder, alcohol, and more spirit and zest than it is usually in the crowded cities of the States."[33]

The rounded loaf-shaped Independence Rock, rising to about 100 feet in isolation from the surrounding plain in the valley of the Sweetwater River, was named some years before by the

---

[33] Cited in Will Bagley, *So Rugged and Mountainous*, Norman, Oklahoma, 2010, p. 264.

mountain man and trapper William Sublette, for its first sighting on 4 July. His group of trappers had instituted the practice of inscribing their names on the sides of the rock, a rite of passage for travelers in the years to come. So eager were Chiles and the others to mark their passage on "The Great Register of the Wilderness" that they gave up the morning for the privilege of having everyone scratch or paint their name on the giant rock.

By this point they were passing tall and bare mountains and dried seasonal ponds thick with the white crystals of sodium sulphate. They recognized them as Glauber Salts, named for the German-Dutch chemist who discovered the substance in 1625. They collected some for future use, as it was much respected at the time as a laxative, and probably helpful given their steady diet of meat. The Wind River Mountains were now in sight, their snowy summits seen through the clouds obscuring the western horizon. Supplies of flour and bacon, with which they had optimistically started their journey, were now running low. Following the Sweetwater River, they began to dry and preserve some of the abundant buffalo meat that they would rely on farther down the trail, when the supply of bacon inevitably gave out. But it seems that they might have waited too long to start the curing process. Buffalo were scarce along the Sweetwater that year and although they preserved as much as they shot, they had a lot of mouths to feed.

They had sent two hunters in advance to the Green River to see if there were any trappers at the annual rendezvous, and to see how much game lay ahead. The hunters, John Gray and William Romaine, an "English adventurer" traveling with the missionary party, returned from the Green River after a week to report that there was no one at the rendezvous point and little game ahead. This lent some urgency to hunting and drying as much buffalo meat as possible, spurred on by waking on the morning of 14 July to a hard frost.

Also of concern to Joseph Chiles and other members of the party were trade goods and animals they had carried in the hopes of bartering them at the rendezvous. A collection was taken up to pay anyone who would go find the party of trappers, and on 15 July John Gray set off in search of them. The rest of the company moved slowly along the Sweetwater, camping opposite the Wind River Mountains, gazing through the haze of the July heat at their snowy summits. On 18 July, they left the Sweetwater, turning southwest in the process. They crossed the Great East-West Divide of the waters of the continent, another milestone in their journey.

More and more they were encountering terrain for which Americans raised in New England or the Mississippi Valley were psychologically unprepared. They were venturing into the arid west, and in an age with few outdoor photographs these first overland travelers were experiencing a landscape unlike anything they had ever seen or could even imagine. As one historian observed, western terrain was more alien to overlanders than the surface of Mars would be to their descendants in the 21st century. The English language lacked even a vocabulary to describe the scenery. Several diarists commented that there was no word equivalent to the Spanish cañon to denote "a narrow gorge or defile in a mountain where the sides are walls of rock, nearly or quite perpendicular, and of great height."[34]

On they went, traversing this strange dry country, with vegetation to be found only on the edges of the permanently flowing streams fed by the snows in the mountains above. They descended the Big Sandy Creek, a tributary of the Green River. Here they stopped upon finding some very welcome grass and were delighted to see the return of John Gray. Staggering on his last legs after many difficulties, he had succeeded in finding the party of about 20 trappers which included men who were

---

[34] Ibid., p. 78.

returning east to Fort Laramie and St. Louis from California. The day of 23 July was spent on the Green River trading with them. Dawson noted that they were a rough-looking bunch in their homemade leather clothes. At a distance they resembled native peoples, many of whose customs and attitudes they had taken on, including leaving all the camp work to their Indian wives.[35] Store-bought clothes and ammunition changed hands for dressed skins, buckskin clothing, moccasins, and rope. Reverend Williams found the spiritual state of the trappers as questionable as their appearance, but, as mentioned, he did not regard his own trail companions much more highly. He complained that on the Sabbath, "... we have nothing but swearing and fishing."[36]

The misgivings of the Reverend Williams aside, Joseph Chiles in particular was pleased with the encounter with the mountain men, as he managed to sell two yoke of oxen and one of his wagons which he deemed surplus to requirements. One of the other emigrants recalled years later that they were short of food, implying that Chiles had extra for sale, but it was at "trail prices" and her parents and six siblings could not afford it and had to do

---

[35] Nicholas 'Cheyenne' Dawson, *Narrative, in Camp*, San Francisco, 1933; also in Nunis, p. 148.

Williams, Joseph, *Narrative of a Tour from the State of Indiana to the Oregon Territory in the Years 1841-2*, Cincinnati, 1848, Reprinted, New York, 1921, intro by James C. Bell Jr.

without.[37] Years later, Bidwell recalled that Bartleson had some pure alcohol that he had brought for trading purposes with the trappers, who diluted it at the ratio of three or four to one, called it whiskey, and proceeded to get very drunk. The trappers who had been to California said flatly that it was impossible to get wagons across the mountains, chiming in with the view held by Fitzpatrick. Overall, they presented such a negative image of the territory they managed to dissuade several of the party to either turn back or elect to head for Oregon.

The emigrants took their leave of the trappers. Several members of the party, like Englishman William Romaine, who had joined them for the adventure, announced that he would now travel back to civilization. Romaine left with the trappers to continue their pursuit of buffalo as they headed east. Bidwell said that he heard later that they were set upon by Indians who killed several of them. Bidwell also noted several prices of trade goods in the middle of the Rocky Mountains that year. Blankets sold for $8-15 [$217-$407]; rifles between $30-60 [$814-$1630]. Gunpowder, at a dollar a cup [$27], sold for twice the price of flour. Dressed deerskins were valued at $3 and deerskin trousers at $10. Guns and horses were valued about equally, somewhere

---

[37] Cited in Will Bagley, p.98; Also reprinted in www.oregonpioneers.com/Williams.htm

between \$20 and \$100 depending, as ever, on the quality of the article and the need of the buyer.[38]

The party left the Green River, moving in a westerly direction and found a tributary on which they could camp. As before, except for narrow strips along the banks of rivers and streams, there was little vegetation that could be consumed by man or beast. They continued on this watercourse for four days and at the end of July were camped on a tributary of the Bear River, where a second trailside wedding took place. Fr. De Smet was called upon to marry the widow Gray to a one-eyed trapper named Phelan. He had joined the party about five weeks before at Ft. Laramie after having taken a shine to the widow when the emigrants passed through. Doubtless Joe Chiles's violin was called into service once again as the company wished the newlyweds well. The next morning all were back on the trail, camping that evening on another branch of the Green.

Bidwell notes that they had been supplementing their meat diet with serviceberries found on the hills, and currants collected down by the streams, both of which were maturing in the summer sun. And wherever the opportunity presented itself they caught large trout in the streams they crossed or camped alongside. They

---

[38] Bidwell, 'A Rendezvous on the Green River', cited in Gillis and Magliari, Spokane WA, Clark, 2004, p. 54.

saw the smoke of Indian campfires hanging over nearby valleys and were advised by Fitzgerald to keep a close watch on their horses lest the local Blackfeet take some of them. Crossing from the watershed of the Green to the watershed of the Bear River they were forced to backtrack laboriously down one defile and up another to find a practicable route for the wagons. Finally, they descended into the valley of the Bear, taking a day's respite from traveling to rest and take stock of their position. Nancy Kelsey, married at the age of 15 to Benjamin Kelsey, and soon to be famous as the only woman in the party to make it to California, noted her eighteenth birthday on the first of August.

Underway again, on 5 August they found the valley of the Bear easy going, making 43 miles in two days, enjoying the abundant and sweet wild currants along the river, and catching a large number of fish. The next day the narrowing river canyon forced them to ascend to the bluffs above the river in order to continue following it. Once they had achieved the elevation, the view afforded them the full grandeur of the country, with its high mountains to the west and the glittering Bear Lake on the southern horizon. Below them, the river that fed the lake meandered through its narrow valley. Bidwell, struck by the scenery of the country, pronounced it as grand.[39]

They continued to make good time, the days continuing fine and pleasant, and on 10 August reached Soda Springs, in present-day south-eastern Idaho, where they stopped to marvel at the number of warm gushing springs that had created mounded reddish mineral deposits. The particular appearance and attributes of the place struck the settlers, including an eerie hollow sound made by the wheels of the wagons as they passed over the area of the springs.

The combined emigrant group had come to a parting of the ways. That evening Fr. De Smet and three of his Indian guides set off for Ft. Hall, about 50 miles to the north-western route, to their mission destination among the Flathead Indians in the Snake River plain, about 50 miles further northwest of the fort. The rest of the company spent the night and traveled on together the following day before coming to a halt after about six miles. The contingent for Oregon were now to leave the Bear River and follow the lead of Fr. De Smet. The members of the larger party had shared many trials and tribulations together, but at about midday the two groups took their leave of each other. After so

---

[39] Bidwell, Diary entry, August 8, 1841.

many experiences it was a heartfelt farewell, though several of the California group accompanied the Oregon party on their way to Ft. Hall to see if they could engage a guide who knew the trail to California or at least to the head of the Mary's [Humboldt] River. One of the Jesuits, Fr. Mengarini, recalled, "Farewells were sad. Many prejudices had disappeared during the journey."[40] Predictably, cooperation in the face of adversity and daily familiarity had overcome the frontier Protestant distrust of their Papist traveling companions. Likewise, the Jesuits had come to appreciate the good qualities of their Baptist colleagues.

Feelings were especially keen in response to the strong admonitions of the mountain man Fitzpatrick on whose advice and counsel they had relied since early May. He was emphatic that the settlers should follow the better-known trail to Oregon by way of the Snake and Columbia Rivers, and the majority of the party, including the newlywed Phelans, decided to take that advice. When the two groups parted company, the directions they chose prefigured much of the early emigration to come. The more respectable, conservative, family-oriented emigrants headed with the clergymen north-westerly towards Oregon. The younger, male-dominated risk-takers turned their wagons toward the south

---

[40] Cited in Will Bagley, 2010, p. 100.

and west in the direction of California. A little over a hundred years later, Irene Paden expressed it thus, "Youth turned toward California. Turned also the hothead, the adventurer, the gay ne'er-do-well, the invincible optimist, the gambler."[41] Bidwell noted, "The two companies, after bidding each other a parting farewell, started and were soon out of sight."[42] They were now reliant on a sketchy map sent to Bartleson by Marsh, based on almost no knowledge whatsoever. Or, as Nancy Kelsey expressed it, they had, "... no roads and no pilot except the setting sun."[43]

---

[41] Irene Paden, *The Wake of the Prairie Schooner*, New York, 1945, p. 289.
[42] Bagley, 2010, p. 101
[43] Cited in Bagley, 2010, p. 106.

CHAPTER 4

No Pilot Except the Setting Sun

The resolute, or perhaps foolhardy, California party was now reduced to 34—all men, with the exception of Nancy Kelsey and her year-old child Ann, as part of the Benjamin Kelsey family. Chiles remembered years later that she explained her willingness to follow Kelsey's lead into the unknown, "Where my husband goes, I can go. I can better endure the hardships of the journey than the anxieties for an absent husband."[44] The men were mostly under 30-years-old and generally frontiersmen, raised on rough farms and accustomed since childhood to handling firearms. The oldest was Charlie Hopper who, at 41, was particularly respected for his hunting skills. John Bartleson remained the nominal leader, but this was not a group that was easily led. Benjamin Kelsey was often deferred to as a pathfinder. Kelsey's brother Andrew was described as a rough man who was often in trouble with the law. But as has been observed elsewhere, these Kentuckians were often the kind of people who had the frontier skills that would come in useful on a journey into unexplored

---

[44] Chiles, Col. Joseph B., 'A Visit to California in Early Times', MS Bancroft Library.

territory without maps or guides.[45] Nancy herself, married to Ben for three years at this point, was a good match for him. Chiles and other trail veterans tended, in later years, to sentimentalize her role somewhat, though her toughness was never questioned. The rest of the young group were resourceful and generally adventurous, as indicated by their later careers. This was not a party of mountain men with experience of the territory, nor was it a typical emigrant party in that, with the exceptions of Nancy and Ann Kelsey, it was all male. In spite of a lack of experience with the territory ahead, they were well-armed and had horses, mules, and oxen drawing their nine wagons.

The California contingent agreed to move slowly in their westerly direction until the messengers returned from Ft. Hall. After about 12 miles they established camp on the Bear River and Bidwell and James "Jimmy" John went off fishing. They found the day uncomfortably warm and looked longingly at the snowy peaks that surrounded them. They estimated that the snow was not more than four miles away, so, leaving their guns on the riverbank they set out to enjoy the experience of cool snow in August. They had seriously miscalculated the distance. What they took to be the snowy peak was in fact an intervening ridge, but having gone that

---

[45] Stewart, George R., *The California Trail*, 1962, p. 18 ff.

far, they dared each other to carry on in the direction of the snow, even as the sun began to drop behind the mountains.

Their misplaced youthful bravado (Bidwell was all of 22-years-old) forced them to spend the night on the mountain above the tree line. Signs of grizzly bears were everywhere, and their only defense was the knives that they carried. After a very cold and damp night on the mountain, they started up the last distance, filled a handkerchief with as much snow as they could carry and started back down, trying a different route from their ascent, which found them lost in a different way, down deep canyons barely penetrated by the sunlight, but well-frequented by grizzlies who they were fortunate to avoid.

They finally struggled back into a highly apprehensive camp at about midday. Fearing that they had fallen into the hands of unfriendly Indians, the others had mounted a guard all night and extinguished all their fires. When Bidwell and John eventually appeared and produced their much diminished ball of snow, Bidwell relates that they were greeted, "with a mixture of joy and reprehension."[46] Dawson remembered Bidwell triumphantly waving his handkerchief full of snow, and being greeted with the rejoinder, "Snow! [several expletives deleted]! We thought you

---

[46] Bidwell, Diary Entry, August 10, 1841.

were dead!"[47] For Dawson, and the rest of the party, their outrage at such foolhardiness was tempered only by the general relief felt by the company at not having lost two of its members. It had been a reckless venture, but Bidwell and John had escaped with only bruised and cut feet.

The company continued slowly the next day with the intention to stop and hunt in Cache Valley on the Bear. As the valley narrowed, they were forced to leave the river, but once on higher ground were rewarded by an abundance of choke cherries, whose ripeness in high summer rendered them sweet. A relative of the wild cherry, common across North America above the fortieth latitude, choke cherries were prized by the Indians across the continent as one of their most important fruit sources.

Still awaiting word from Ft. Hall, they carried on working their way across hills and ravines, moving southward with the direction of the Bear, not having found Cache Valley, stopping at small streams along the way to restock their water supplies in country that was becoming progressively drier. The choke berries continued to be plentiful, large and sweet. They saw distant smoke signals, which they assumed were being made by members of the peaceful Shoshone tribe to communicate the presence of

---

[47] Narrative of Nicholas 'Cheyenne' Dawson, cited in Nunis, p. 149.

strangers in their land. Now forced to leave the river again to search for a crossing of a deep salt creek tributary, they began to suffer from both the heat and a lack of water. It was beyond the middle of August and both these issues were becoming critical. They started early on the nineteenth, hoping to strike water before the sun was too high but found themselves crossing an immense, glittering, white salt plain in the searing sunlight.

There was an almost total lack of vegetation and they began to see mirages on the horizon, lines of trees that convinced them that water was nearby. Confused by a lack of landmarks, they backtracked eastward about five miles to camp under a mountain, by a pond of brackish water bordered by willows and salty grass. They remained in camp the next day, sending out two scouts to try to relocate the Bear River. These men returned with the news that they were within 10 miles of where the Bear emptied into the Great Salt Lake. The party set off in a north-westerly direction and intersected their trail from the previous week. They stuck a pole in the ground with a piece of paper attached so that the men returning from Ft. Hall would not repeat their error, and then proceeded to the Bear. The next morning, one of the scouts sent to Ft. Hall wandered into the camp, saying he was alone because he was unable to keep up with the others, and as a consequence he found the note left on the pole while the others were probably going the same rounds as the larger party. The others turned up that afternoon and communicated the gloomy news that no guide could be obtained at the fort. No one who knew the territory ahead from personal experience could be found.

There had been some hope that Joel Walker, brother of the better-known Joseph R. Walker, who was said to have crossed the Sierra, might be willing to help, but the former was in Oregon, and in fact had not made the journey they were facing. Bidwell, Bartleson, Chiles, and the rest were now not only on a journey without maps, but also without any reliable advice. They waited in their camp for others to locate and drive back some of the oxen that had wandered off. The group had reached a crisis point in a desolate country, a place markedly different from the hundreds of miles of streams and rivers they had followed.

The only advice that they had gleaned from Ft. Hall was what they had already heard from Broken Hand Fitzpatrick—head west without veering too far south into the endless salt plains or too far north where they would be trapped in steep canyons and could easily lose their bearings. With those generic cautions in mind, they set out in the direction of the setting sun, keeping the Great Salt Lake to their left. It was 23 August, the time of scorching days and cold nights. They plodded on over the salt plains for 20 miles, constantly on the lookout for water and finding none until midday the next day. Suffering a late start because their cattle had strayed in the night searching for water, they eventually came to some springs with potable, if salty, water. All around them lay the white glittering plains. They had not seen any rain since leaving the Platte at the beginning of July.

Chiles and the remainder of the party rested for a day and then set their course west again, traveling all day without encountering any water. After the heat of the day had passed, they sent two men in advance to search for water, but they returned just before dark with discouraging news of the dry country ahead, though they did say that they had encountered an Indian trail. Knowing that these trails almost always led to water sources, they determined to press on, continuing in the darkness, stopping at about 10 p.m., still with no sign of water, and having traveled about 30 miles.

When dawn came to their dismal camp they could make out a spot of green on the side of the nearby mountains. After traversing five more miles of plains, it was with joy and relief that they found a good spring and grass. They determined to use this location as a base, and to send scouts out to find the head of the Mary's River, so that the entire party would not have to run the risk of running out of water. Bartleson and Charlie Hopper volunteered to find a route through to the head of the river, and the rest of the company settled down to wait. As the company were going about their business, a Shoshone Indian wandered into their camp. He indicated that there were more Indians nearby who had horses they might be willing to sell. Several of the party including Bidwell went to find them.

The Shoshone, one of the tribes inhabiting this region, had made a life for themselves in the rugged country of the Great Basin between the Rockies and the Sierra Nevada. Traveling in small nomadic groups, their resourceful subsistence diet which relied in large part on the meagre animal population, was supplemented by roots. This earned them the derogatory name of "Snake" or "Digger" Indians by the whites who presented the Shoshone with possible targets for their habit of horse theft which they also practiced on their neighboring tribes, the Crow and Pocatello people. In these early encounters with white travelers, the Shoshone were generally cautious and helpful, though pressure in the coming decades brought them into conflict with white settlers with disastrous consequences for the Indians.

Along the trail, Bidwell and the others found another lone Indian in the process of skinning a deer, then farther along the rough trail, a little group of Indians overseen by their aged patriarch, estimated by Bidwell to be 90-years-old, who seemed to be subsisting on a few berries. After searching for a few more miles, they returned to camp without finding any horses. They were doubtless anxious to be going. The days were growing shorter and the nights colder, but their animals, having been driven hard without adequate food and water, needed rest, and they were unsure of which direction to take.

Before they had departed, the scouts, Hopper and Bartleson, estimated that they would be gone eight or nine days. As the others waited, several among them regularly went out hunting in the vicinity but finding no game after two days of searching, killed one of their oxen. Two more days went by and it was now September. A small group of Shoshones visited the camp and sold the party three horses and a few serviceberries. By this time, the grass around the campsite was largely gone and the emigrants decided to move on slowly in the direction taken by Hopper and Bartleson, traveling about six or seven miles a day. It was the end of the first week in September and although the days remained warm, the nights grew so cold as to freeze the water in their buckets. To the west lay a seemingly unbroken wall of mountains.

For the party of 1841, the pressure was on, and nerves were beginning to fray. Part of the company said that they should stay where they were and await the return of the scouts. Another faction wanted to press on, as the days were shortening quickly. The burden of uncertainty began to tell on the emigrants. Two of the wagons refused to remain with the majority and carried on down the trail. The next day the main party overtook the two wagons, the drivers of which had thought better of going on their own in unknown country, and fortunately Bartleson and Hopper now reappeared with the news that they had indeed found the Mary's River source about five days away. Re-energized, the party pressed on, traveling west about 15 miles and camping for the night without water. They traveled much of the next day before they arrived at a water source.

It was hard going, and tempers blazed on more than one occasion, though the one member of the party who managed to stay apart from the bickering was Nancy Kelsey. Like several of the others in the group, Chiles afterward remembered her "… cheerful nature and kind heart [that] brought many a ray of sunshine through the clouds that gathered round a company of so many weary travelers. She bore the fatigues of the journey with so much heroism, patience, and kindness that there still exists a warmth in every heart for the mother and her child …".[48] A less romantic and probably more realistic portrait of the lone woman in the group, coping with daily frustrations, was painted by Bidwell.

---

[48] Chiles, Col. Joseph B., 'A Visit to California in Early Times,' MS Bancroft Library.

"We had traveled all day and everybody was tired. It was hard work to get a fire built, but she managed to and was frying some bacon and tried to make some coffee… Just at that time the coffee upset and it went into the bacon and put out the fire. She threw up her hands and hollered out loud enough for the whole camp to hear: I wish to the Lord I had never got married."[49]

The last of the provisions they had put by were now gone. It was becoming clear that unless they found another source of food they were going to have to slaughter their oxen one by one. But this was only the first response to the exigencies of travel on this route, and the direction of how they would proceed was now clear. The first to accept the inevitable and abandon their wagon were the Kelseys. Killing their team of worn-out oxen and discarding whatever they couldn't pack on their horses, they left their family's wagon to its fate on the sands of the Great Basin. The group pressed on more than 50 waterless miles, moving south between the salt plains on the east and the mountain ridges on the west. On 15 September they passed through a gap in the ridge of mountains and came to a high plain. Confronting them in the

---

[49] John Bidwell Dictation from *General John Bidwell: An Autobiography*, p. 10, Dictation for HH Bancroft Collections, Bancroft Library, Univ. of California, cited in Gillis and Magliari, *John Bidwell and California*, Spokane WA, Clark, p. 37.

distance, like a row of broken teeth, were the peaks of the Ruby Mountains.

In the last six weeks, with their meanderings in search of the Bear River and a route across to the Mary's River, they had covered just 300 miles. The stress and worry about being lost in a trackless waste, between a great dry salt basin and impenetrable mountains, began to take its toll. There was no clear leadership, and different individuals responded to the challenges of the route in different ways. An atmosphere of mistrust grew, with notable friction between Bidwell and Bartleson. The former was too young to take the lead, and the latter was a combination of headstrong and inexperienced. The real leader who had emerged, more by setting an example than by insisting on recognition, was Benjamin Kelsey, and most of the party now looked to him for direction.

It was now the middle of September. The animals were staggering from lack of water, but near the end of the next day they found it, enough water in fact to prevent the wagons from making direct progress as their wheels sank into the muddy surface, forcing them to go around the accompanying marshes, taking even more time. This was enough for the rest of the party. By this point the wagons were almost empty and only slowed their progress. They resolved to follow the Kelsey family's lead, abandoning their wagons and loading whatever belongings they could on to the backs of their horses and oxen, keeping the latter in reserve until they needed to kill them for meat.

The packing was no easy feat. First there were decisions about whether they included things with which they were going to start a new life in California or just focused on speed and survival. Second, there were the practicalities of securing their goods on the animals, particularly on the backs of the oxen who were used to pulling loads and not carrying them. Although they had seen the technique used by the mountain men in packing goods on the backs of their horses, it was a knack that took much trial and error before they achieved stability and success, leaving a trail littered with belongings that had fallen from animals unused to carrying loads in this way.

They started down the trail, with different individuals having to stop as their badly secured belongings fell from their animals and had to be picked up and re-packed. At this point they were still using some of the remaining oxen as pack animals until they needed them for food, because game was becoming progressively scarcer, and their wagon train had metamorphosed into something else entirely. For one thing, they no longer traveled with wagons. It is difficult to overstate the significance of the act of leaving them in the Nevada desert. These hand-built vehicles that had taken them so far, were one of the last tangible links with the farming life they had left behind. They had become a badly lost group, trying to make their way to California as best they could. In terms of what was to become the California Trail, they were pioneering a route that no one afterward followed. Nonetheless, and in spite of some views to the contrary, they retain their significance as a group of settlers who were proving with every step westward that an overland crossing of the continent to California was possible. No matter the exact route, their role as the first overland party to California is unchallenged. Following an Indian trail they proceeded, the mountains on their right, until late into the evening, hoping to find water and a valley that would allow them to follow a more westerly direction. It was a vain hope and their troubles multiplied when it was noticed that two oxen, carrying baggage, had dropped behind and disappeared. The next morning when they still had not appeared, Bidwell volunteered to go after them and young Cheyenne Dawson offered to join him. Bartleson said that the rest of the company would progress slowly in search of water until the two young men could find the oxen and then catch up with them. Bidwell and Dawson tracked back for about 10 miles under a now scorching sun, finding nothing of their trail, and a discouraged Dawson made ready to leave Bidwell to rejoin the main party. There was nothing Bidwell could say to get Dawson to persist with the hunt for the missing oxen, but he continued on himself, eventually picking up their trail and following until just about nightfall, when he was delighted to find them. Given that it was almost dark, he was forced to pass the night without a fire or blankets, keeping one eye on the oxen and the other for the approach of any potentially unfriendly Indians. The next morning, as he headed back in the direction of the main party, he was met by three of the men who had been sent out to bring him water and food. All four of them made it back to camp. Having put in a good day's travel the day before, the whole party rested and observed the Sabbath.

They were now in the last week of September with no end of their journey in sight and with the weather, the nights in particular, turning cold. Beset by thirst and hunger, they still had not found the headwaters of the Mary's River, though they felt confident that they soon would. They sent out a couple of hunters the next day to try to find some antelope, and they reported back that they had seen several and managed to kill two. They found a group of hot springs at the base of the Ruby Mountains, where they boiled the meat that had just appeared. The chunks of antelope cooked through in about ten minutes and were pronounced "perfectly done" by Bidwell.

Predictably, disagreements continued to flare-up among the members of the party. On 22 September, they were approached at a gallop by a party of 80 or 90 Indians, well-armed with guns, bows and arrows, with one of them riding significantly ahead of the group. For Bidwell, this was a clear sign that they should send out one of their own to parley and determine the attitudes that the two sides would take. Bartleson disagreed, insisting that they should continue packing up normally and not show any fear and simply allow the Indians to satisfy their curiosity. The Indians, clearly a war party, quickly approached to the point that they almost surrounded the camp. Finally, Benjamin Kelsey demonstrated his leadership once again. Joined by Bidwell and a few of the others, he took matters into his own hands, brandishing his gun, and gesturing that they should approach no further. They were Shoshones, generally peaceful, but prone to "taking advantage"[50] where they could. In Bidwell's eyes, they had been encouraged by the emigrants not having followed the established protocol for parleying. An untoward incident was averted and the emigrants moved off with their pack animals, with the Indians, who remained hopeful of trading, following closely behind. This parade lasted for about four hours until the Indians tired of the

---

[50] Bidwell, *A Journey to California*, diary entry Sept. 22, cited in Nunis, p. 46.

pursuit and began to drift off. By nightfall there were only about ten warriors still trailing the party.

The next day as the emigrants scanned the horizon hoping to see an end to the valley in which they found themselves, or, better yet, signs of the headwaters of the Mary's River, they concluded that they had violated the advice from Ft. Hall and strayed too far south. They turned in the direction of the mountains to the north, where they were relieved to encounter a stream with grass along its banks and trout in its waters. As they descended the stream, which grew wider as they proceeded, they noted the desolate, bare hills away from the watercourses. The stream disappeared into a dry creek bed and its banks rose precipitately, though the party continued down the bed into another valley, all the while searching for a stream they could definitively recognize as the Mary's. They found themselves being drawn more north than west, raising fears that they were heading into a dangerous zone of disorienting canyons. The stream they were now following was taking them west by northwest and doubt began to magnify that this was not the river for which they were desperately searching. The stream had grown to the size they expected of the Mary's, but still it continued in a generally northerly direction, and their anxiety grew, only to be replaced by delight on 2 October, when the river changed course to the southwest.

The valley of the Mary's River, now the Humboldt in western Nevada, had excellent grass, and Bidwell recalled that it seemed to swarm with Indians, Shoshones who timidly withdrew to their huts when the travelers came near, gesturing to them to go on. They began to make up some distance as they followed the river in its meandering westward direction. But it was not fast enough for some in the party, which began to fracture along the lines of faster horses and mules versus slower oxen. Both groups were held together by the reality that their only source of meat was the oxen. With Bartleson and his faster group urging more speed, they made 55 miles in two days, though it was too fast a pace for the oxen. A small party of Indians visited the camp and one of them offered to act as a guide. One of the oxen was slaughtered and the meat divided. With these provisions, and having the tough hardy mules as mounts, Bartleson assumed that he could reach the mountains of California. He and his group pushed on, leaving Bidwell, Chiles, and the oxen herders to follow.

By the end of the week, Friday 8 October, they were encamped by a wide swamp with bad water and no fuel. Bidwell describes clouds of wild geese and ducks which rose from the water at the sound of the travelers' guns. Two more oxen, unable to carry on, were slaughtered for food. The following day they reached the swampy beginnings of what is now called the Humboldt Sink.

There they picked up the trail of Bartleson's breakaway group and crossed a plain that showed signs of being covered by shallow water in the rainy season. Beyond lay sand hills, where the going was difficult but from whose elevation they could see another lake, now called Walker Lake, and its accompanying swamp. They camped by the swamp, still desperate to keep heading generally west. They left the next morning, going southwest into the mountains, departing from the trail left by Bartleson. There was no way for them to have known that had they continued in this westerly direction, they would have stumbled upon Truckee Meadows, an oasis and the salvation of many an emigrant party in the years to come. But as the first travelers on the route they were without maps, experience, or directions, and they blindly continued southwest and came upon a stream with a reasonable volume and flow. Convinced that they were safely on the "San Waukeen", they prepared to follow it. Although what we now call the west fork of the Walker River was heading south, they were sure that it would soon turn west into the mountains.

By this time, the company had bartered with a group of Shoshones they encountered along the river, inducing them to not flee by means of a white flag. Once they were close enough to communicate in sign language, they managed to exchange a pair of Chiles's knives for what Dawson estimated to be "a gallon or two of pine nuts." These were shared out among the group as a handy and portable source of protein, which was doubtless why they were collected by the Indians.[51] They also took the opportunity to hire a guide who warned them after about four miles, with the size of the creek dwindling, that they would face a long day's travel to water after leaving the creek. The next day they continued to follow the watercourse, which grew ever smaller, by this point half the size at which they had first encountered it. During the morning, they caught sight of Bartleson and his group in the distance, but made no attempt to contact them.

It was now exactly halfway through October, and they advanced upstream to arrive at the base of the high Sierra. Gradually their journey had become what the historian George Stewart called a starvation march, setting a template for many an emigrant party that followed. They could see that there was nothing for it but to go westward, and no way to avoid scaling the mountains. Their Indian guides admitted that this was the limit of

---

[51] Nunis, p. 152.

their knowledge of the country, and that night they quietly stole away from the emigrants' encampment, having probably accomplished their true aim of taking the intruders far away from their tribe's lands.

James John, one of the original members of the Chiles Mess, wrote in his diary, "Our Indian pilot left us last night and left us in a bad condition here. We are nearly surrounded by high mountains on all sides. We see no prospect of getting over the mountains. They are very high and the top covered [with] snow and we have but 3 more cattle to live on and they are poor and consequently we have to live on small allowance or starve."[52] Four or five of the party volunteered to climb some of the peaks to see if there was a way through.

Just as they were about to set off, Bartleson and his men approached, having run out of food and enthusiasm for striking out on their own. The famished breakaways experienced a very muted reunion with the main party who nonetheless shared some of the butchered oxen that they had killed the day before. With only three oxen left, all in poor condition, they waited for the explorers to return from the peaks. When they did it was with the most dispiriting news. They could see no practical way to scale

---

[52] James John Diaries, quoted in Nunis, p. 176.

the mountains, which continued to increase in height as far as the eye could see. That evening they gathered together to discuss and vote on whether they should return to the lake they had seen a few days before and take a path leading to the northwest, or press ahead into the mountains. The vote was practically unanimous against turning back, thereby guaranteeing that they missed the safety and respite of Truckee Meadows, which later travelers found life-saving. Josiah Belden later summarized the situation when he later wrote to his sister:

> We were then in a most discouraging situation. We were in an unknown wilderness enclosed by mountains on every side rising to an immense height and covered in snow. To that there seemed to be no possibility of getting over them and when myself and another climbed to the top of one of them we could see nothing but mountains upon mountains as far as the eye could reach in the direction we wanted to go. We could not turn back as we knew we should starve before we could get back to where there was anything to eat for we were then just eating our last ox and there was no game to be found in the country.[53]

---

[53] Letter of Josiah Belden to his sister, Mrs. Eliza M. Bowers, Coe Collection, Yale Univ. Library, quoted in Nunis, p. 138 ff.

On 17 October, they set off into the mountains, reaching 8,000 feet in what is now Alpine County. The pregnant Nancy Kelsey was leading her horse and walking barefoot with the others, carrying her baby. The ground was covered in a light snow, but deep snow lay around them on the surrounding peaks. Their progress was heartbreakingly slow, given their general weakness from lack of food, but at last they could see the streams begin to flow west. In spite of their fears, they had traversed the crest of the Sierra about 12 miles north of Sonora Pass. West of the pass, they found themselves in the deeply cut canyon lands of the Stanislaus River, and their trail out of the mountains was hampered by steep cliffs and defiles, with pack animals laden with precious equipment lost over precipices. As they looked west, all they could see was mountains, and they began to think that their goal was unattainable. Charlie Hopper said to Bidwell, "If California lies beyond those mountains we shall never be able to reach it."[54] But what they were seeing from their high Sierra vantage point was the Coast Range, about 70 miles to the west, with the intervening valley, Marsh's "San Waukeen", obscured by autumn mists. Their eyes might well have caught sight of Mt Diablo, the closest landmark to Marsh's rancho, their ultimate

---

[54] Bidwell Diary, quoted in Nunis, p. 52.

goal for the last six months. The niceties of California geography and seasonal climate conditions were lost on them, and hunger and fatigue were constant companions. When it got to be too much for one of the pack horses, the emigrants would finish it off, butchering the animal on the spot. They were now heading generally downhill and encountering oaks, whose acorns could be ground into meal.

In many places it was too steep to ride and they had to proceed on foot, plunging into mountain valleys where they passed through ancient pine forests. Even their anxiety could not prevent them from marveling at the girth and height of the trees standing in these virgin groves. Near the peaks of the mountains, there was ice in the streams, permanently frozen from the winter before. That evening they were forced to kill another ox. A full day of effort had taken them just 12 miles closer to their hoped-for goal. The next morning, having ascended to a vantage point, Bidwell noted, "a frightful prospect opened before us, naked mountains whose summits still retained the snows perhaps of a thousand years … On the peaks, the winds roared and moaned, but in the deep valleys that surrounded them, profound silence seemed to reign."[55] As various members of the party spread out to

---

[55] Bidwell Diary, quoted in Nunis, p. 49.

seek the best way ahead, Nancy Kelsey found herself "… with my babe alone, and as I sat there on my horse and listened to the sighing and moaning of the winds through the pines, it seemed the loneliest spot in the world."[56] They wound around the peaks, avoiding the tallest, which they had feared to climb, then struck a small stream heading in a westerly direction by which they camped for the night. This day the party had made a distance of 15 miles.

The next day they began a rapid descent, with the small stream growing in size and widening out into a valley. In a short distance they estimated that they had dropped about a mile in elevation. The travelers stopped to measure a nearby pine tree, not the biggest, and found it to be more than 200 feet tall. They began to encounter small oak groves, which gave them hope that they were now on the Pacific slope, although now the going became even more challenging. The stream had swelled into the raging Stanislaus River, roaring down a canyon too steep to enter, though they could hear its deafening noise in the rocky gorge. They had come about 12 miles when they were brought to a halt at the edge of a cliff. After setting up camp they dispatched two volunteers, Bidwell and Jimmy John, to try to scout a route ahead.

---

[56] Kelsey, *Nancy Kelsey's Own Story*, Mattes Library, 4-5 cited in Bagley, p. 108.

Down below in the valley, the towering pines masked the way forward and covered the mountains they could see. They were struck by the roaring of the winds in the tree tops and the rushing of the river. Bidwell ironically noted that it would be a paradise for a hermit, but for the emigrants, fearful of the approaching winter, it only bred more anxiety.[57] They knew that the highly experienced mountain man, Joe Walker, had been lost in these mountains for more than three weeks before finding a way out. They were advancing along rocky shelves with outcrops that regularly threatened to dislodge the packs and the animals bearing them. This happened several times, constantly challenging the party to keep their spirits up as they stumbled on, leading their animals. It was a situation in which once again Nancy Kelsey provided inspiration to carry on. Dawson remembered years later, "... when I was struggling along trying to keep Monte [his horse] from going over, I looked back and saw Mrs Kelsey a little way behind me, with her child in her arms, barefooted, I think, and leading her horse, a sight I shall never forget."[58]

Volunteers from the party fanned out, desperately looking for a route that the rest could follow. They returned with depressing

---

[57] Bidwell, *A Journey to California*, 1841 entry Oct. 19, 1841, Nunis p. 49.
[58] Nunis, p. 154.

news. It was impossible to follow the route carved out by the river. One of the owners of a horse refused to accept this verdict, as did Captain Bartleson and his group. To general protestations, they set off down the stream, but they shortly found the going so difficult that they had to rest their animals for most of the day before they had enough strength to retrace their steps. The rest of the party, thirsty and hungry, turned north, eventually finding a source of grass and water. They killed and shared out the penultimate ox. The next day the going was better than they had feared. Bartleson's men returned, but Jimmy John was not with them. No search could be mounted—it was becoming a case of every man for himself.

They descended toward the river but found that they could not get closer to it than about a mile. When they called a halt, three Indians came into their camp, though they seemed unwilling or unable to indicate a clear route out of the mountains. It is likely that they were local Miwoks who lived in small groupings throughout the foothills up to the snow line. Theirs was a foraging economy, with a diet that relied on deer and other small animals supplemented by spring greens, roots, mushrooms, acorns, and pine nuts in their seasons. They lived in conical houses covered in bark and their little communities usually contained an assembly structure for communal activities that might be as much as fifty feet across. There were also sweat houses and structures for storing food. Their knowledge of their own territory was intensely detailed, but limited to that local knowledge, which would explain their inability to give advice to the desperate travelers.

It was the turn of the last remaining ox to fall under the knife, which promised a three-day supply of food. They would not eat again until they could kill something new, but they had seen hardly any game. This was a moment of reckoning. Having kept an upbeat quality to his diary, now Bidwell changed his tone, perhaps sensing failure and starvation, "Let this speak for our situation and future prospects."[59]

Like the rest of the party, he was not one to passively surrender to fate, and driven by hunger, he set off early in the morning, thinking he would go ahead of the group in the same direction it was heading, and when he managed to find some game, wait for them to catch up and share with them what he had been able to forage. Bidwell had not gone far before he encountered one of the Indians who had visited the previous evening, from whom he managed to buy some acorn meal at an unrecorded price. He continued above the river and met an Indian boy who took him to his house down in the river canyon, down a

---

[59] Stewart, *California Trail*, p. 27.

trail that Bidwell estimated to be about three-quarters of a mile perpendicular from where they had met. There was no food there and Bidwell pressed on following the river, scaling cliffs that towered above the stream. It took him four hours to return to high ground where he hoped to intersect the trail of the group. He searched until dark, finding no trace of their passage and finally lay down on the ground and slept.

The next morning he concluded that the group had gone north of the river, so he set off in an easterly direction to try, without success, to cross their trail. He turned south and came to the place where he had left them the morning before, having walked about 40 miles in an irregular square, and picked up their trail. They had descended with great difficulty to the river and followed it for about six miles. They then climbed on the south side, having hired an Indian guide who led them into a very difficult location, then, realizing his mistake, ran off rather than face the angry, famished, and anxious emigrants. Two other hunters, Ben Kelsey and Thomas Jones, had also left the main party with the same aim as Bidwell and had not returned. Bidwell noted that part of a horse that had given out the day before was saved for Kelsey and Jones as the group moved on. They went on about six miles, found it was impossible to continue, and retraced their steps to a place where they could make camp. Facing up to the fact that they were likely to lose all their horses and mules and have to proceed on foot with whatever they could carry on their backs, they began digging holes to hide what they could no longer hope to transport on their fast-diminishing number of animals. To dig a pit to conceal valuables, a cache, then cover it with earth, was a common practice. Their added touch was to build a fire on the spot to conceal the disturbed earth. But when they discovered that the Indians from the day before, including the guide who had run off, were watching them from a concealed position, the plan was abandoned.

The emigrants reloaded their possessions on the remaining animals and staggered on for about three miles, camping in a deep ravine. Anxious discussions ensued, with some convinced that they should kill all the remaining horses and mules, dry as much meat as they could carry, and try to work their way out of the mountains on foot. That night it began to rain and continued until the middle of the next day. The emigrants began to lighten their packs by throwing away their old clothes, fearing that the rain would create treacherously slippery footing worsened by heavy loads. Beset by fears of dying in the trackless wilderness, they began to see a cunning plot on the part of the guide to lead them into a cul-de-sac of narrow canyons and then finally overpower them.

In their extreme condition, this tortured logic made sense to several of the emigrants and one of them, Grove Cook, concealed himself when the others had packed up and moved on. He wanted to see if the guide who they blamed for their predicament appeared when the Indians who had been shadowing them foraged around the abandoned campsite. When the former guide appeared at the head of his little band, Cook shot him in the head while the others ran for their lives, according to the account of the laughing marksman. In the minds of the emigrants, the received wisdom was that, "… as he had undoubtedly led us into this place to perish, his crime merited death."[60]

In spite of the fact that the party had relied on the good will and help of the Indians whom they had encountered since the start of their journey, this tragedy marked the beginning of a devastating relationship. Founded largely on mutual incomprehension between the Native peoples of California and parties of settlers like this one, to be followed by gold seekers, this kind of clash would be replicated many thousands of times, usually to the detriment of the Native population of California. It declined due to enslavement, murder, and disease by an estimated 80 per cent between first contact with the Spanish in the 1760s,

---

[60] Bidwell diary, *A Journey to California*, quoted in Nunis, p. 51.

and the huge influx of white settlement, which flooded into California after the discovery of gold near present-day Sacramento in the 1850s.[61] The result was the near destruction of the native tribal cultures by the end of the century.

The emigrants staggered on about six miles down the canyon until they reached a vantage point from which they could look around them. The rain that they had experienced the night before had cloaked the higher reaches of the mountains that they had come through with a substantial layer of snow, extending down more than a half-mile from their summits. Chiles and the others continued to descend and climb steeply, often carefully balanced on cliff edges, but in spite of their care and the experience of their animals they lost several horses and mules who missed their footing and cartwheeled down the mountain sides, each lost animal representing a tragic double catastrophe to the party, in both the goods they carried and their usefulness as a potential source of food. Having fought their way six miles, the party stopped and ate what was left of the last ox and also butchered a mule to obtain enough meat for the whole group.

---

[61] Hurtado, Albert, *Indian Survival on the California Frontier*, New Haven, Yale Univ. Press, 1988, p. 1.; Clark, Chris, *Untold History, The Survival of California's Indians*, Link TV script, September 26, 2016, www.linktv.org.

The Indians, in spite of the fate of the guide, continued to shadow the emigrants, stealing a couple of horses in the night. The next day the party passed a few of the typical Miwok conical, bark-covered dwellings, though the inhabitants had absented themselves when they heard the approach of the emigrants. In one place, the bones of a horse were roasting on a fire, confirming the emigrants in their belief that they had found the guilty party. The mountains became progressively less rugged, but they still seemed to roll on forever. Charles Hopper's gloomy prediction to Bidwell about their inability to get beyond the distant mountains chimed in with that of the rest of the party. They were now mostly on foot, ragged, and weak from hunger. Often not bothering to cook their scant meat rations when the food was divided, they preferred to consume it raw wherever they stopped.

But in the end their worst fears were unrealized. On the last two days of October, to their great relief and delight, they found themselves traveling down the valley of the Stanislaus River. They saw the tracks of large herds of elk, and flights of wild fowl. When they finally reached the lower Stanislaus they saw thousands of antelope. On the first of November they stopped to hunt, bagging antelope and fowl. After a meal of antelope and duck, Bidwell wrote, "My breakfast this morning formed a striking contrast with that of yesterday which was the lights of a wolf."[62] For his part, Chiles recalled, "… every man wept that night as they feasted."[63]

Josiah Belden later wrote to his sister from Monterey, "We were much longer coming from the Rocky Mountains where I wrote you last, than we expected to be owing to our not knowing the way and in fact there were times when we scarcely expected to get here at all or anywhere else and almost made up our minds to starve to death in the mountains."[64]

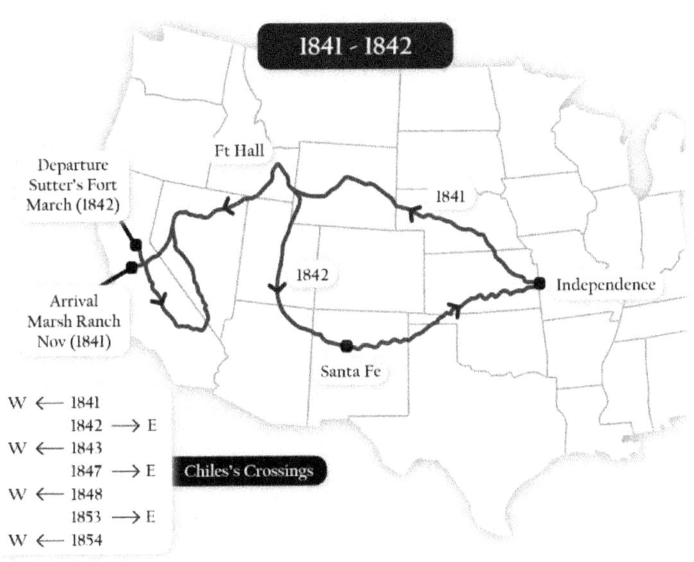

[62] Bidwell Diary, *A Journey to California*, quoted in Nunis, p. 52.
[63] Chiles, Col. Joseph B., *A Visit to California*, MS Bancroft Library, Berkeley CA.
[64] Nunis, p. 138.

CHAPTER 5

The California Chiles Found

Overnight Joe B. Chiles and his companions went from gagging down wolf guts to gorging on antelope steaks, and from hopeless desperation in the cold trackless mountains to an optimistic feeling that their journey was almost at an end. Dawson, who was almost forced to his knees from thirst and hunger, rejoiced with the others. "… and we decided to tarry, kill and eat … Bidwell says there were 13 deer killed and eaten, and as we remained there only two or three days, there must have been some tall eating."[65]

Bidwell, Chiles, and the others marveled at the warmth of the valley in the day, even if the land was dry and parched, with signs of damage from wild fires. Close to the river there was plenty of grass for the game to feed on, and "the land was as mellow and free from weeds as land could be made by plowing it twenty times in the U.S."[66] The first night in the valley of the Stanislaus River they satisfied their hunger with as much deer meat as they could eat, overcome with relief and delight as they did so. Wild grapes

---

[65] Narrative of Nicholas 'Cheyenne' Dawson, quoted in Nunis, p. 155.
[66] Bidwell, *A Journey to California*, p. 52.

still hung on their vines, sweet and thirst-quenching. After almost seven months on the trail, the first party of American settlers to cross the continent was in sight of their goal.

The next day the Bartleson group remained in camp to dress the game that they had killed the day before while the rest of the party set off downriver. As they followed the watercourse they were startled by the sudden appearance of Thomas Jones, one of the hunters who had been gone for just over a week. He explained that he had descended from the mountains looking for game a few days before the main party had done so and by the greatest stroke of good fortune had run into an Indian whose one word of English was, 'Marsh, Marsh.' The Indian had indeed been sent out by John Marsh, who had heard that a party of fellow Missourians was struggling through the mountains. The Indian had been told to give them supplies and guide them across the San Joaquin all the way to his rancho on the slopes of Mt Diablo. A most welcome item was farina meal for Nancy Kelsey, who a few days before had become too weak to travel until her husband shot a deer and brought her some meat to revive her.

The Indian took Jones to Marsh's house, about three day's march to the west. From there the two of them had brought provisions to the overland party, as well as mixed news. There had been no rain for 18 months, so there was a shortage of wheat and bread. On the other hand, beef was plentiful and Marsh was looking forward to welcoming them as soon as they could reach him.

They waited for Bartleson and his men to catch up and then all proceeded together to Marsh's rancho, crossing the San Joaquin River, the width of which they estimated at about 100 yards. The promised land of the San Joaquin valley looked like anything but a paradise to the new arrivals. The drought had left the land depressingly parched and sere, but Marsh cheered them up with a feast of a fat hog accompanied by some of his California brandy. Their welcome was warm, as their host happily showed off his surroundings and family, consisting of his common-law wife from one of the local tribes and several children, the latter of whom slept most nights out of doors unless it was raining, in which case they unrolled some skins on the dirt floor and slept inside.

After dinner, some of the travelers took up Marsh's offer to sleep under a roof after so many months under the stars. But Dawson and some of the others who did so found that between the fleas and the rushing for the outhouse by their companions, whose digestive systems could not cope with the fat pork that they had eaten so eagerly, they hardly slept. They had talked about the country and their plans long into the night. While delighted to have arrived reasonably healthy and safe in California, Marsh's rancho and the semi-indolent lifestyle he pursued failed to impress Chiles, Bidwell, and the others. They had come all the way to California to build new lives for themselves and their families. Marsh's small, three-room adobe brick house, with its dirt floors and furniture consisting solely of rough benches and a table, was unimpressive. Reaching California had been their goal for almost seven months, but now they set their minds on achieving other ambitions. What they had accomplished already in crossing the continent was not lost on their host. He noted in a letter to Commodore Thomas Ap Catesby Jones, Commander of the US Pacific Squadron:

> An event which will probably be regarded as of some importance in the future history of California, was the arrival in November last year of an exploring party from the United States. This consisted of 31 men and one woman and child from Independence a town on the western frontier of Missouri … If any proof were wanting of the unprecedented energy and enterprise of the people of our western frontier, I think this would be sufficient.[67]

---

[67] Letter from Marsh to Commodore Thomas Ap Catesby Jones, Nov. 24, 1842, cited in Nunis, p. 16.

Thus Marsh continued to play his role of inviter-in-chief to California. His own story, however, had its darker and lighter hues. Born in 1799, a native of Massachusetts, graduate of Harvard University, and inveterate optimist, he was an opportunist in a land that favored the chancer.[68] Marsh's route to California had taken him from the East Coast to the Illinois-Wisconsin border, which he fled under the cloud of a bad reputation for selling guns to the local Indian tribes. Heading south, his arrival in Independence, Missouri, where he opened a general store in the early 1830s, coincided with that of the Chiles clan, with whom he had some business relationships. By the mid-1830s, he was on the move again down the Santa Fe Trail. Some questionable business dealings in Santa Fe saw him heading for Los Angeles by 1836. On the strength of two years of on-the-job training with an army doctor on the Wisconsin frontier and his Harvard diploma, written in indecipherable Latin, he was accepted into Los Angeles society as a medical practitioner, dispensing medical advice and remedies in exchange for the local currency of cow hides. After a year he had amassed about $500

---

[68] Lyman, George D., *John Marsh Pioneer*, New York, Charles Scribner's Sons, 1930. This extensive biography, which reflects the time in which it was written by a San Francisco paediatrician, is the only complete life story of Marsh. A more contemporary assessment can be found in Cecilia Rasmussen, Los Angeles Times, February 05, 2006.

and headed north for the little town of Yerba Buena, on San Francisco Bay, buying a rancho, Los Meganos, (the sand dunes) near Mt Diablo in what is now Contra Costa County. With the help of the local Indians he built an adobe house and dispensary near a creek and began a new life as a *ranchero*, like his *Californio* neighbors.

An inveterate American booster, Marsh had written the letters that Chiles, Bidwell, and the others had found so compelling. But for all his enthusiasm for more settlement in California by Americans, Marsh's attitude toward his guests quickly changed, and he was distinctly gruff to them the morning after their arrival, complaining about what their eating and drinking had cost him. His ill humor was such that some in the party resolved to return to the San Joaquin Valley and spend the winter hunting the abundant wild game there rather than spend any more time with Marsh.

Those who remained, 14 in number, were advised by Marsh that their next task was to acquire Mexican passports, which would enable them to stay in California legally. In order to do so they set off for the pueblo of San Jose. Chiles, Dawson, Hopper, and Bartleson were among this group. Bidwell remained at Marsh's rancho to keep an eye on the party's possessions. The foursome passed two nights on the trail, one of them at the rancho of José Higuera, who staged a *fandango* (dance, or ball) on their behalf. This was their introduction to open-handed Hispanic California society, with its gracious living for the *rancheros* and their families, and their seemingly limitless landholdings. It was a life of leisure based on a cattle economy of tallow and hides that required little effort other than the yearly roundup. With music, dancing, and translated conversation about ranching life, Chiles and the others formed an increasingly positive impression of the place that they had struggled so hard to reach.

Setting out for San Jose the next morning, it was not long before they were overtaken by a troop of Mexican soldiers who refused to believe that they had come overland to California, and placed them under arrest, confining them to the local jail pending formal confirmations of their status. Several days later, the local military governor and commander of the North Frontier, General Mariano Vallejo, arrived with his troop on a tour of inspection.

Approximately the same age as Chiles, General Vallejo was the de facto government in this part of California.[69] His family history exemplifies the process of advancement and success in the New Spanish Province of Alta California. Mariano Vallejo was

---

[69] There are several books on the life of Vallejo. One of the best is Alan Rosenus, *General Vallejo and the Advent of the American*, Berkeley CA, Heyday Books, 1995.

the son of Ignacio Vallejo, a Spanish army sergeant, part of the military escort of Father Junípero Serra, who had traveled north from central Mexico City to the raw town of San Diego, where he founded the first mission in Alta California in 1774. Ignacio Vallejo accompanied Serra as the padre continued to travel up the California coast founding more missions in an attempt to Christianize the Indian peoples. The senior Vallejo was also present in 1776 at the founding of the San Francisco Presidio at the Golden Gate, and Mission Dolores on a hill above the Bay. Vallejo showed his leadership virtues and prospered, though it has to be noted that he never advanced beyond the rank of sergeant. Some say that this was because of "an excess of libido" in his pursuit of the local Indian women. It should be noted that many of his compatriots abused their "right of conquest", over the Indian women they encountered. Presumably, if Vallejo's career was derailed because of philandering, he must have been excessive even by the permissive standards of the day.[70] Vallejo's ardor was presumably cooled after his marriage and the birth of 13 children. In the insular world of Hispanic California, he did his best to see that his sons and daughters took up positions of responsibility, continuing the advancement of the family.

---

[70] Alan Rosenus, *General Vallejo and the Advent of the Americans*, pp. 4-5.

By the time Mariano Vallejo and Joseph Chiles met, the former had already, in less than ten years, risen from being secretary to the governor of Alta California, Luis Antonio Argüello while still a teenager, to military command of the Northern Frontier in less than a decade. He was now charged with colonizing the wide-open spaces of Northern California.

Having learned English in his early twenties while working as a clerk for an English trader, Vallejo could interview the detainees directly. When he ascertained that they had traveled from Missouri at the invitation of John Marsh, a letter was dispatched to Marsh, commanding him to come to Mission San Jose to stand bond for the men and give a guarantee of good behavior.

As military governor, Vallejo's responsibility was to secure this northern frontier of Mexico from the incursions of foreign powers. The anxiety of the Mexican government, based in far-off Mexico City, was realistic. By this time the Russians were well established at Fort Ross, about 100 miles north of San Francisco, and the area also was receiving unwelcome attention from the British and the French, who perceived its attractions and the colonial authorities' weak hold over their distant province. Intelligent and widely read, Vallejo may already have concluded that, ultimately, some nation other than Mexico was likely to control the province of California. It was his preference for Americans, as opposed to other foreign nationals, that motivated him to leniency in the face of this group of illegal immigrants. He singled out the redheaded man who stood several inches taller than his companions and soon discovered that Chiles and Charlie Hopper were Missouri friends of George Yount, whose land grant in the Napa Valley had been approved by Vallejo himself in 1836. Furthermore, Chiles and Hopper intended to visit Yount once they were free to travel.[71]

Vallejo and Yount, living less than a day's ride apart, were well acquainted and admired each other's enterprise. It was encouraging to Vallejo that some of these travelers knew someone in California other than the reclusive Marsh. Vallejo figured that if emigrants from the United States were of the same caliber of Chiles and his companions, and had connections with respected locals like Yount, then they should be released to travel around California. In leaving the new arrivals free to explore the territory, Vallejo was showing his practical side. The presence of the Russians at Fort Ross, had highlighted the need for the Mexican government to attract skilled settlers to northern California in

---

[71] Rosenus p. 38-39 erroneously says that Chiles had met Vallejo on an earlier trip; other details cite Ellen Lamont Wood, *George Yount*, San Francisco, The Grabhorn Press, 1941, P.69.

order to create a bulwark against other foreign powers who might try to gain a foothold in the area. And because the Hispanic settlers had largely alienated and abused the local Indian populations, there was a real need for people with specific skills, especially in building enterprises like water-powered mills.

In the meantime, as Marsh traveled to San Jose in response to the summons of Vallejo, he was vexed by the notion that he should have to post bond to ensure the good conduct of the emigrants. This led him to hatch a plan to see that his guests would end up footing the bill for the bond to guarantee their own good behavior. Vallejo duly issued the passports to the group in San Jose, and then gave Marsh enough passports for those remaining at the rancho. The passports had cost Marsh nothing, but when he returned to his rancho he sold them to his guests for $5 a piece [$147 in 2013 equivalent], or for whatever they had of any value amongst their meager belongings, compensating himself with the sum of about $180, or about $5,000 in 2013 dollars, for his not so gracious hospitality. These expensive passports were actually individual letters from Vallejo. They identified the bearer as "having presented a certificate of good conduct, seeking to obtain residence in this country, who should be allowed to travel freely in the jurisdiction and to be accorded by the local authorities passports for places to stay."[72] The documents were to serve as a provisional letter of security until a permanent one could be issued. It proved to be a lesson learned by the emigrants that they could expect no more help from Marsh, and they returned to the San Joaquin valley to hunt and trap, gradually making their way to the recently established fort of the Swiss-born adventurer John Sutter at the confluence of the Sacramento and American Rivers. Their experience with Marsh was over, but it lived long in the collective memory as Bidwell, who outlived Marsh by several decades, re-told the episode in various writings down the years, branding Marsh "one of the most selfish of all mortals."[73]

By early the following year the dust had settled a bit and Marsh was on better terms with most of the immigrant party of 1841. The historical importance of their crossing and his role in it were now much on his mind. He wrote a letter to his parents in Massachusetts the following year, carried east by Chiles and a group of eight others, which read in part:

---

[72] Translation of Bidwell's original passport, Courtesy of California State Library, cited in Nunis, p.26. Other details of the stay at Marsh's and the occurrences at San Jose from Bidwell, *Echoes of the Past About California*, Milo Milton quaife, ed.

[73] Bidwell, 'Life in California Before the Gold Discovery', Century Magazine 41, (December 1890) p. 163, cited in Gillis and Magliari, 2004. P. 81.

A company of about thirty of my old neighbors in Missouri arrived here the first of November last, and some of them are about returning and are the bearers of this… From all the numerous letters I have received from the United States I am satisfied that an immense emigration will soon swarm to this country … the Anglo-Saxon race of men who inhabit the United States are destined very shortly to occupy this delightful country … It is an object I much desire and have long labored for, to have this country inhabited by Americans. It will now soon be realized.[74]

By the time Bidwell and others arrived at Sutter's Fort at the end of November, the political landscape of California had changed significantly. The Russians had made a strategic decision to pull back from their overextended presence on the Pacific Coast and entered into negotiations with Sutter for the purchase of Fort Ross and all its furnishings. Sutter was greatly in need of men to help bring the fixtures and equipment, including two small cannon he had bought from the Russians to his fort. He offered generous wages to any man who would help him. Bidwell accepted Sutter's offer but Chiles, along with Robert Rickman and Charlie Hopper, declined since they had plans to see more of

---

[74] Lyman, *John Marsh, Pioneer*, p. 249.

the province and visit George Yount. It was Sutter's suggestion that the three men pay a visit to Monterey, the provincial capital, and stop in to see the mill near there owned by Isaac Graham, former mountain man and trapper. He sent them with a letter of introduction for Chiles and his companions to the American Consul, Thomas Larkin, in which he noted their respectability as men of property and means and their intention to settle in California.

The California the three men were entering was underpopulated and wild in many places, even along the coast, but that did not stop it from being socially stratified and riven by conflicts that stemmed from race and class. These issues had begun to express themselves in contention between political factions that sometimes developed into armed conflict. It was also a time of great social change. No sooner had the last gasp of Spanish expansionism expressed itself in the chain of missions and pueblos along the western edge of the territory, then Mexico earned its independence from Spain in a victorious struggle ending in 1821. For all its good intentions, the mission system, with its combination of cross and sword, had adversely changed the face of indigenous California by gathering a large number of the coastal Indian groups into the missions. There they provided the forced labor to build the infrastructure of Hispanic society, and at the same time contracted deadly diseases for which they and the other Native peoples of California had no natural resistance. As the diseases spread from mission to mission, they decimated the indigenous population.

The effects of the victory of the Mexicans, their government seated in far-away Mexico City, over their Spanish colonial masters were gradually felt on the northern frontier. By decree of central government in 1833, the missions were turned into parish churches with minimal land holdings. Their Indian charges were nominally given small plots, and the great land holdings of the missions often found their way into the ownership of the governing faction. In the words of one historian, this vast transfer of land ownership had a huge impact, "… transforming the poverty-stricken frontier garrison state, headed by a military elite, to a proud, pastoral civilization and prosperous economy …".[75]

Chiles, Rickman, and Hopper took the road from the San Joaquin Valley to Monterey via Mission San Juan Batista and the Salinas Valley. They were much taken with the beauty of the countryside. Monterey, the provincial capital, impressed them with its streets lined by adobe brick buildings, but they were less taken with the general unhurried air of the local population. In this

---

[75] Miller, Robert Ryal, *Juan Alvarado Governor of California*, Norman OK, Univ. of Oklahoma Press, 1998, p. x.

admiration for the countryside and the disparagement of the *Californio* lifestyle, they were falling into line with many other commentators who felt that the local Hispanic *Californios* were not worthy of the magnificent land they occupied. Among others subscribing to a self-serving condemnation of the local population as "lazy, uncouth and filthy" was Richard Henry Dana in his widely admired memoir of sailing from Boston to California and back 1834-36, *Two Years Before the Mast* (1840). In Dana's eyes, the *Californios* were "idle, thriftless people and can make nothing for themselves."[76] His account was widely read and was one of many stories of life in California that helped shape the attitudes of Americans moving westward. It laid the groundwork for many an American land grab in California in the 1850s, actions ultimately backed up by the Land Commission and judiciary.

It is unlikely that the 1841 emigrants had already formed any kind of coherent racist argument that underlay their actions. What is more probable is that they were struck by the richness of the country and, aside from the coastal plains, its under-utilization. For Chiles, Rickman, and Hopper, they were a long way from the Protestant work ethic of the American frontier, but they saw this as confirming California as their land of opportunity.

---

[76] RH Dana, *Two Years Before the Mast*, New York, D. Appleton & Co, 1899, p.81. Originally published 1840.

When the three reached Monterey, Larkin welcomed them to dinner at his adobe home and supplied them with an interpreter to help smooth their path when they explained their aim of acquiring land in California. The first step, Larkin told them, was to obtain Mexican citizenship, which did not particularly faze Chiles, who was becoming more and more enthusiastic at the prospect of applying his Missouri farming background and ability to some of the rich California land that he had seen.

But first there was more of California to explore. Chiles reluctantly said goodbye to the Larkin family and Rickman who would meet him at Sutter's Fort for the return journey in three-months' time. Chiles and Hopper rode around Monterey Bay toward the Santa Cruz mountains to call on Isaac Graham, who, after his central role in the "Graham Affair" described below, had just established a distillery and sawmill at Rancho Zayante, in the mountains near present-day Felton. Chiles's friendship with Billy Baldridge back in Missouri had launched the idea in his mind that building and operating a water-powered sawmill in California would be a good business opportunity.

Graham, whose reputation as a mountain man, fur trader, explorer, and troublemaker preceded him, had enjoyed a checkered past, starting with his departure from Missouri in 1830 with a party of mountain men. After many a scrape and adventure across the Great Plains, Rockies, and Sierra, by 1836 he was ensconced in Monterey, where that year he got involved in the struggles among the arcane political factions that dominated the life of the Mexican province. Graham led a group of foreigners who backed Juan Bautista Alvarado, propelling the latter into the governorship.

A close relative of Vallejo, Alvarado had, like his slightly older relation, risen to prominence in California society.[77] Bull-necked, with a fondness for drink, and an unwillingness to let an insult go unanswered, he had risen to become California's youngest governor and the only one in this tumultuous period to serve his full six-year term. The missions were being secularized and this gave him the power to distribute the extensive mission lands to *Californios* deemed to be worthy recipients. Initially these were to be retired soldiers who needed land to support their families after years of service, but the concept quickly broadened to those who the government, or the governor, judged worthy as settlers who would help the progress of the semi-autonomous province.

Alvarado took office on a wave of dissatisfaction with secularization plans and the appointees of the central Mexican

---

[77] For a full discussion of the life of Alvarado, see Miller, Robert Ryal, *Juan Alvarado Governor of California*, Norman OK, Univ. of Oklahoma Press, 1998

government. These individuals potentially would have sidelined the *Californio* elites in the distribution of the large mission land holdings. With the help of Graham, and the two or three dozen foreign "sharpshooters" of dubious character he had gathered around him, Alvarado pursued a military campaign. Like most of the military actions in this period, it was more shadow boxing and rhetoric than actual blood and thunder. By November 1838, Alvarado was confirmed in his role as the governor of all of California.

This should have been a satisfactory end, but after they were stood down from their role of "Household Guard" Isaac Graham and his friends felt that their contribution to Alvarado's success was not being sufficiently recognized or respected. Given their rough nature, this dissatisfaction often took the form of low-level verbal harassment in the streets of Monterey, petty vagrancy, and public order offenses. These were, however, the sorts of insults that Alvarado found hard to tolerate. "I was insulted at every turn by the drunken followers of Graham; and when walking in my garden, they would come to its wall and call upon me in terms of the greatest familiarity, 'Ho Bautista, come here I want to speak to you'…". [78]

---

[78] Alvarado, "Historia" vol. 5, pp. 3-4, cited in Miller, *Juan Alvarado*, p. 80.

When one of the foreigners who had married a local woman went to Alvarado with a story that Graham and his followers were plotting to take over the government in Monterey, Alvarado was alarmed. The story might have been dismissed as drunken ranting, but it was common knowledge that Graham and his cohort were dissatisfied and that, only recently, a similar rough-and-ready group led by Sam Houston had recently carried out a similar seizure of power in the former Mexican province of Texas.

Alvarado moved swiftly to issue orders for the arrest of all foreigners illegally in the province, except in those cases in which the individuals had married locally or were well known and had respectable occupations. With the help of Vallejo, who arrested the non-*Californios* in his northern district, almost one-hundred foreigners were jailed in Monterey, though more than half of them were quickly released for lack of evidence. On the advice of a judge who held that because the remaining men had entered the country without a passport they could be deported legally, the forty-five of them, half American and half British, were shackled and shipped off to the western Mexican mainland to stand trial in Tepic. There the British vice-counsel, Eustace Barron, and an American lawyer and journalist called Thomas Farnham, weighed in on their behalf. Known by the name of the prisoners' ring leader as the Graham Affair, it became an international cause celebre, in part thanks to Farnham placing his version of the story, rife with anti-Hispanic stereotyping, in the *New York Times*.[79] The verdict of the Monterey judge was reversed and Graham and his companions were eventually returned to Monterey and recompensed by the government for their trouble. Nonetheless, as we have seen, Farnham's published letter almost destroyed Bidwell's Western Emigration Society plans, as the lawyer's highly prejudicial account of Mexican justice caused most of the enthusiasm for the Far West to evaporate between 1840 and 1841.

So, it was with a certain amount of care that Chiles and Hopper would have approached the recently released Graham and his newly purchased establishment, though as a fellow Kentuckian, Chiles would have been confident that he had the measure of his man. In the event, they received a cordial reception, with a typical Mexican-California meal featuring "Good beef, plenty of beans and red peppers, good coffee and nice milk," [80] Chiles recalled years later.[81] Not much of a drinker, Chiles didn't mention the main incentive that motivated the ragtag group that hung around Graham's distillery, "... drinking raw whiskey, swapping stories, amusing themselves with horse races

---

[79] Miller, *Juan Alvarado* pp. 82-83.
[80] Chiles, 'A Visit to California,' MS Bancroft Library, Berkeley.
[81] Giffen, p. 25.

and shooting matches …". [82] Instead, Chiles was much impressed with Graham's milling operation, the only one in that part of California, which brought timber out of the Santa Cruz mountains for shipment from the coast. With the expertise of Billy Baldridge, master millwright, Chiles was certain that he could make a similar success elsewhere in the region.

After a few days assessing Graham's setup and enjoying his hospitality, Chiles and Hopper set out over the Santa Cruz Mountains for San Jose pueblo to visit the man who had acted as their interpreter when they first arrived and had been jailed due to the misunderstanding about passports. The interpreter, Thomas Bowen, and his partner William Gulnac, were happily distilling whiskey and tried to convince Chiles that this was the business of the future and the area in which he might prosper, but there was much more of California to see before Chiles and Hopper could make a decision.

It was already early February, and Chiles and Hopper knew that they had many a mile to cover before they could achieve their aim of calling on General Vallejo and George Yount, and still arrive in time for the spring rendezvous at Sutter's Fort with the

---

[82] Kevin Starr, *Americans and the California Dream*, New York, Oxford Univ. Press, 1973, p. 13.

others who were returning to the United States.[83] They proceeded with a certain amount of haste up the old road that connected the missions, El Camino Real, through the Santa Clara Valley and up the San Francisco peninsula, where they were again impressed with the fertility of the soil. Chiles and Hopper would have seen how it could be made to flourish from the gardens of Mission Santa Clara and the tree-lined *Alameda,* which connected the Mission with the Pueblo of San Jose.

The two explorers experienced a vivid contrast a day or two later, when they came in sight of the largely abandoned Mission Dolores surrounded by sand dunes. In the eight years since the missions had been dissolved by the Mexican government, which revoked the clergymen's rights to their supporting land holdings, and to the labor of the dependent Indians, they had fallen on hard times. Missions like Dolores, with its hinterland sold off to one of the officers from the San Francisco Presidio, now had no resident priest and just a few resident Indians. Most of the Indians had been removed inland to Missions San Rafael and Sonoma some years before, where the warmer climate was considered healthier.

---

[83] The returnees in 1842 were John Bartleson, Joseph Chiles, George Henshaw, Charlie Hopper, John McDowell, Nelson McMahan, Andrew G. Patton, Robert Rickman, James Springer and Ambrose Walton. Chiles, Hopper and Springer returned to live in California at a later date. Noted in Nunis, p. 256.

With no reason to linger at the mission, Chiles and Hopper followed the well-worn trail over the dunes to the little settlement on Yerba Buena cove. The six-year-old hamlet that would become the city of San Francisco consisted of a small number of unimpressive rough structures. One of these was the store established by Jacob Leese, on what later became Montgomery Street. Leese, a brother-in-law of Vallejo, acted as a middleman between the local ranchers around the bay and the so-called Yankee ships that called on California ports to trade for hides and tallow to take back to their home ports in Boston and others on the East Coast. Shortly before the arrival of Chiles, ownership of Leese's store had been transferred to the Hudson Bay Company and Leese and his wife, the sister of General Vallejo, moved to Sonoma. Nearby, on the water's edge, was a combination washhouse and slaughterhouse, and farther up the hills were two or three houses and a self-described hotel and tavern run by a Swiss *émigré*. It was here that Chiles and Hopper met John Davis, the owner of the little schooner *Susana*, moored down at the waterfront. They made arrangements with him to transport them across the bay to Sonoma.

By the afternoon of the next day Chiles and Hopper were making their way on the hour-long walk from Sonoma Creek to the pueblo itself. They walked along the broad roadway, laid out seven years before by Mariano Vallejo as an approach to the pueblo, where the headquarters of the Northern Frontier of the state of Mexico was located.

Commandant General Vallejo, whose meteoric rise has been previously discussed, had gotten a head start in his career when barely into his teens by having been selected as a protégé of Governor Pablo de Sola in 1818. Vallejo had learned commercial skills and languages at the hands of English merchant and rancher William Hartnell a few years later. When Sola returned to Mexico in 1822, the ambitious teenaged Vallejo became personal secretary to his successor, Luis Arguello, the same year that Mexico seized its independence from Spain.

Freed from Spanish mercantile regulations, foreign ships could now trade legally along the coast and the soldiers of various *presidios* were now able to receive grants of land to which the missions no longer had title. Two years later, Vallejo enrolled in the Monterey company as a cadet. In his early twenties, he put down an Indian uprising, one of several local Indian wars noted for their ferocity. In 1833, his career took off when the governor, Jose Figuero, authorized him to establish a military post at Sonoma on the site of the northernmost mission, San Francisco de Solano. To help Vallejo, Figuero gave him title to a grant known as Rancho Petaluma, which was soon enlarged to include 66,000 acres—all the country between the Petaluma River and Sonoma Creek. With the Sonoma Mission secularized, Vallejo was appointed administrator of its cattle, sheep, and other agricultural assets, and charged with dividing them between the Sonoma pueblo and the local Indians. From the mid-1830s until the Gold Rush, Vallejo held sway in Sonoma. He was noted for his fair-mindedness and his sense of humor—but at the same time he rode the countryside with a military escort, unafraid to dole out punishments for infractions of the law.[84]

Vallejo had been at the side of his nephew, Juan Alvarado, in the 1836 military campaign to ensure his governorship, and he had helped in the rounding up of foreigners in the Graham Affair in 1840. He had earlier introduced Alvarado as the leader of the territory to Chief Solano and his Suisun tribe when they met in the company of about 1,000 warriors. The Suisun Chief instructed his people to look kindly on the two *Californios* as people who had worked for their liberty from the mission system. Cooperation, one might say co-option of the local tribes, was all part of the Vallejo strategy to create a prosperous northern California. This did not indicate any antipathy to settlers from other countries. Vallejo merely wished for the kind of settlers who would

---

[84] Rosenus, pp. 8-16.

contribute to his vision of California as a prosperous, well-governed entity. In Chiles and Hopper, he could see the kind of people who fitted his requirements.

In the distance, the two men could see the four-story tower that topped the General's home. They admired the oak-dotted hills surrounding the town, which gave a protective air to the landscape. The road led to the generous plaza dominated by the mission with its church and outbuildings, the military barracks, and the much-admired house of Vallejo from which he could survey the surrounding countryside. His Rancho Petaluma, comprising almost 67,000 acres, was one of the largest ranchos in Alta California. Notwithstanding Richard Henry Dana's views on *Californio* indolence, Vallejo's rancho employed hundreds if not thousands of Coast Miwok, Southern Patwin, Southern Porao, and Wappo language speakers, and produced livestock, agricultural products, and manufactured goods for both its own needs and for trade. Vallejo's operation produced wheat for British ships in San Francisco Bay and the nearby Russian colony, and manufactured blankets, shoes, candles, and other goods for trade beyond the rancho's own needs. In contrast with most of his peers, it is said that Vallejo treated his employees kindly, paid them in silver, and did not interfere with traditional religious observances.[85]

The patron of the rancho himself was awaiting the arrival of Chiles and Hopper, and sought to erase the memory of their previous meeting in the San Jose jail with generous amounts food and drink. Given some of the rough, dirt-floor accommodation that they had experienced in California, Vallejo's home was a striking contrast, with its cleanliness and comfort that spoke of the general's wealth and civility. For Americans in the province, Vallejo's baronial estate was an example of how, with good connections and a willingness to take on huge expanses of land on the edge of "civilization" and develop its mixed use, one could capitalize on the latent riches of California. That he was said to be fifty years ahead of his time and to favor American annexation of the province was widely believed among the newly arrived American contingent.

The General saw himself as a progressive, transformative, and transitional figure who would help usher in the new age of modern liberal values. He was familiar with the formative documents of the founding of the American republic, and felt that

---

[85] *Lost Laborers in Colonial California: Native Americans and the Archaeology of Rancho Petaluma*, Stephen W. Silliman. Tucson: University of Arizona Press, 2004, p. 3 ff.

the example of the United States was the one for California to follow, and that California should join the Union when the circumstances were right. That translated into giving a cordial welcome to would-be settlers like Chiles who could make a measurable contribution to California's embryonic economy and society.[86]

After some pleasantries, Chiles got right to the point. Having noticed that California was extremely short of skilled "mechanics" he proposed to return to the United States and recruit millwrights who could construct and operate a sawmill to be located somewhere in the locality. Vallejo felt sure that this would aid the development of Alta California (which comprised the present-day state of California) by providing lumber for construction. Amused by the haste and directness of his American visitor, the General was well disposed to Chiles and to his ideas. "I liked his appearance," he said later, "and granted his request and we shook hands ... [with Chiles] promising to bring the mill next year."[87]

In return, Vallejo would grant Chiles some land of his choosing, though one of the stipulations was that he convert to Catholicism. For Chiles, a lifelong frontier Baptist for whom

---

[86] Rosenus, pp. 40-43.
[87] Bancroft, *History of California*, Vol IV, cited in Giffen, 1969, p. 29.

Catholicism was strange, foreign, and un-American, this was a big ask, but presumably he went ahead with his fingers crossed behind his back, as there is no record of him actually practicing his new religion—and he got the land grant when he returned the next year. The inclusion of Chiles, and immigrants like him, was a good fit with Vallejo's views on the creation of California as a developing, inclusive place. Some years later, in his memoirs, he summarized his attitude at the time:

> The arrival of so many people from the outside world was highly satisfying ... to see numerous parties of industrious individuals come and settle among us permanently. Although they were not possessed of wealth, due to the goodly share of enlightenment, they could give a powerful stimulus to our agriculture which, unfortunately, was still in a state of inactivity, owing to the lack of strong and intelligent workers ...[88]

While Vallejo's attitude toward newcomers was doubtless gratifying to Chiles and his ilk, it betrays a viewpoint held by Vallejo as a man of his times who largely dismissed the indigenous population in the plans for the development of the

---

[88] M.Vallejo, 'Historical and Personal Memoirs,' vol 3, p. 384, cited in Rosenus, *General Vallejo*, p.41.

region. The *Californios* might freely admit that in their performance of unskilled and semi-skilled labor, the local Indians had played a central role in the development of the region thus far, but the concept of the native population as unpaid, unskilled labor kept to the margins was widely held. Vallejo himself had grown up with Indian servants in the house, and used the unpaid northern California Indians in the agricultural activities of his rancho. They were crucial in his harvesting of grain and wine making, but their labor was predictably grudging and they were often ready to follow charismatic leaders like Chief Marin in northern California or Estanislao near Monterey and rise up when they felt they had been pushed too far. There were notable uprisings and clashes involving troops, priests, and the local Indians throughout the 1820s, engendering a good deal of respect for the military skills of the indigenous population.

Vallejo's amalgam of good and bad motives played a major role in the subjugation of the indigenous people, and usually ensured that his aims were paramount in his dealings with local Suisun and Miwok, but at the same time, he tried to resolve conflicts by treaty rather than war and was a close personal friend of Suisun Chief Solano and Miwok Chief Camilo Ynita.[89]

---

[89] Rosenus, Alan, *Vallejo*, p. xiii.

The relationship between the *Californios* and the natives was a complex one and Vallejo was no exception, combining aspects of exploitation, respect, and *noblesse oblige*. There was mutual respect between Vallejo and Chief Marin of the coast Miwok, and Vallejo had gone on record in 1833 to voice his indignation about physical abuse of Indians at San Rafael mission. "These poor Indians are being abused with the most dire results ... The treatment would horrify the most feral man."[90] In his history of California, Vallejo commented, "the missions acquired great wealth, but the unhappy neophytes got little benefit of it."[91]

The Americans, in general, did not suffer from these pangs of conscience, pressing the Indians into unpaid labor whenever they got the chance, and treating them roughly when the Indians did not cooperate. But this still lay in the future. In the meantime, the thinly scattered white settlers like Vallejo's neighbor, George Yount, largely got along with neighboring tribes.

The next day Yount, Californian and former Missouri neighbor of Chiles, arrived at Sonoma to conduct Chiles and Hopper to his ranch in the Napa Valley. No stranger to the Vallejo household, the General and Yount had known each other since the

---

[90] Letter May 5, 1833, Santa Barbara Mission Archives, 3414, cited in Goerke, Betty, *Chief Marin, Leader Rebel, and Legend*, Berkeley, Heyday Books, 2007, p.130.
[91] Vallejo, *History of California*, Vol. 2,1875, p. 108-09, Cited in Goerke, p. 138.

early 1830s, when Vallejo employed Yount as a carpenter. It was through the influence of Vallejo that Yount had received his Rancho Caymus land grant, covering the area of present-day Yountville, Oakville, and Rutherford, becoming the first Anglo-European settler in the Napa Valley. Yount had arrived in California from Missouri in 1831 via the Santa Fe Trail, having left his wife and three children with a vague promise to return. They had not heard from him in seventeen years, during which time he had trapped in the southern Rockies, hunted otter on the islands off southern California, finally pitching up in Sonoma in 1834. Three years later he was on Rancho Caymus, building an eighteen-foot square log blockhouse to a design more common to the forested frontier of Kentucky than to California, with an upper story that overhung the lower, enabling defenders to fire down upon their attackers. Given the generally un-warlike nature of the California Indians of that area, and the excellent relations that Yount enjoyed with the local Caymus tribe, the defensive capabilities of the fort were never tested. When Chiles and Hopper arrived, Yount had just completed a more appropriate adobe brick house close to the Napa River, about a mile north of the center of today's Yountville, and about 200 yards west of the site of the mill that Yount would build on the river itself.

Chiles, whose experience with Indians had included the ferocious Seminole fighters of the Florida campaign, and the proud and aggressive Indians of the plains, found the local Caymus less impressive physically, though he appreciated their friendliness and later lived in close proximity to them in the Chiles Valley, using their labor as and when needed, and naming his ranch Catacula, the Indian name for the valley. Chiles was said to be noteworthy in his interest in the Native Americans that crossed his path. In subsequent travels between Missouri and California, he often went out of his way to meet and communicate with any Indians he encountered. He was said to often ride at the rear of the wagon train to engage with any Indians who were following, squatting on the ground with them, communicating in sign-language, perhaps initiating them into the mysteries of rolling a cigarette.[92]

Chiles and Hopper took advantage of their time with Yount to explore thoroughly the Napa Valley and its environs. They enjoyed the hot springs that are now a popular tourist feature of the town of Calistoga. The two Missourians hunted deer and mountain lion in the hills, and one day, drawn along an Indian trail through a narrow canyon, they came upon a hidden valley,

---

[92] Giffen, 1969, p. 30.

lush with winter grass that extended up to the foot of the encircling hills. Chiles said afterward that he knew this was the place he had been looking for. The hills provided protection, the valley bottom had the potential for good farming, as well as rich grazing for cattle and horses. There was a lively stream which could power a sawmill and the distant trees on the mountains looked like a good source of building timber. This was the place that he could claim as his own, that could draw him back to California, where he could make his dreams of a farm and a mill come to life.

After a few more days of hunting and exploring, Chiles and Hopper became anxious to make their way in the direction of Sutter's Fort on the Sacramento River. The hospitable Yount had his Indians make up a mixture of powdered elk meat packed into skins, which could be combined with water, wheat, and dried peppers to make a nourishing soup, a perfect early day trail mix that would keep them well fed to Sutter's fort and beyond. Their host had a request to make of Chiles and Hopper. Yount, having heard Chiles's excited description of the valley he would like to claim on his return to California, asked if Chiles would, when he returned to Missouri, call on the wife and two daughters that had not heard from him in seventeen years, and take as a peace offering two mules. And if they were willing, could Chiles arrange for them to travel out to California when he returned. This Chiles and Hopper promised to do, and taking their leave, they headed northeast towards Sutter's Fort by way of the rancho of John Wolfskill on Putah Creek. There they were caught by a winter storm and forced to shelter with Wolfskill for several days along with a large party of trappers.

When the storm cleared they headed on their way, though the going was heavy as the abundant rainfall had turned the Sacramento Valley into a sea of mud. At the crossing of the surging Sacramento River they fired their guns to attract the attention of some of Sutter's Indian hands who operated a primitive hollow log ferry to effect the crossing. This was done, though with the height of the water and the drag of Yount's mules being towed behind, along with their own, the crossing was precarious.

Why did this group of returnees set out for Missouri so soon after finishing such an arduous journey? For some, like Bartleson and Rickman, it was enough that they had satisfied their curiosity about California. For others, like the strategic Chiles and Hopper, they liked what they had seen, they were confident that they could make the crossing again, and they wanted to get back east to make plans to bring out their families. On arrival at Sutter's Fort, they were able to organize their plans for the return journey. The news of their plans spread. A messenger from Bidwell arrived from Fort Ross, where he was working for Sutter, with a letter that he hoped they would take for him. Included in it was an abridged version of his journal of the crossing the previous year, which he asked to be delivered to the newspaper in Independence, Missouri, to encourage more settlers to make the trip to California. It would be the first published account of their overland journey, firing the starting gun for one of the biggest land migrations in the history of the United States.

CHAPTER 6

The Return to Missouri and Planning the Next Crossing 1842

The group that assembled for the return to Missouri in 1842 was about one-quarter the number that had entered California the year before. Some, like Bartleson, had since decided that California was not for them. But for those like Chiles, they were making the return journey in order to persuade friends and relatives to return with them to California and settle there permanently. Far from being discouraged by how close they had come to complete disaster in 1841, these individuals were busy making plans to launch another effort to find a better overland route to California in the 1843 migrating season. In any event they were, of course, a much more experienced group than that which had gathered at Sapling Grove the year before. They had a much better general sense of the geography, specifically of the ranges of mountains that ran from north to south. In addition, they had practical knowledge about how to ford rivers, how and what to pack, and the most useful types of wagons. They knew how best to arrange a camp at night, allowing for animals to graze yet not be run off by Indians, and how to find water and grass in the desert. They had learned how to calculate the timing of their crossing, and that local Indians were generally not very useful as guides, whereas the service of an experienced "pilot", like the mountain man Fitzpatrick, was invaluable.

At Sutter's Fort, the early spring rain continued relentlessly, but rather than wait for it to end and risk missing the rendezvous on the San Joaquin with the others who had spent the winter hunting along the river, they set out, making their first stop at Marsh's rancho by Mt Diablo. Here they were entrusted with another packet of letters, from Marsh to his parents. With the letters in their saddlebags wrapped in oilskin, they set out for the rendezvous. Waiting for them on the San Joaquin River were the veterans of the previous year's crossing, John Bartleson, Henry Brolaski, John McDowell, Andrew Patton, Robert Rickman, James Springer, and Ambrose Walton.[93] With the rivers in spate, the going was slow as they lost time having to build rafts for each river crossing on their route.

Their progress was further hindered as Hopper was struck down by an illness that his companions judged to be typhoid fever. His condition worsened to the point where he could no

---

[93] Bancroft, Sacramento Transcript, May 21, 1850, cited in Nunis, p. 267. According to Bancroft, Ambrose's brother, Major Walton, started to return east in 1842 as well, but Bancroft notes that according to some statements, he was drowned in the Sacramento River.

longer sit on his horse and a tense standoff ensued. Anxious because of the time that they were losing, some of the men wanted to leave him on his own to either recover or die. His close friends, like Chiles, were having none of that and rigged up a litter between two mules in which to transport their friend and managed to make some progress. But when one of the mules bolted, Hopper was almost thrown from the litter and, in fear of it happening again, he remounted. Summoning up all the strength of his rugged constitution, he was able to hang on to his saddle for short stages, which gradually lengthened as his strength returned and he made his recovery.

Not much is known about their exact route back to Missouri. Having doubtless discussed it with Yount, who had come to California by way of the Santa Fe Trail and the Old Spanish Trail, Chiles and Hopper aimed to avoid repeating their difficult crossing of the Sierra by skirting its southern edge. They headed for Walker Pass, first charted by Joseph Reddeford Walker in 1834, which crosses the southern Sierra east of today's Bakersfield, but it would appear that rather than heading northeast out of the southern Central Valley, they went slightly southeast, skirting the approaches to Tejon Pass. In the process they came within about seventy miles of the little pueblo of Los Angeles. From here they turned east, in all likelihood passing to the north of the Mojave Desert until they could see they were east of the Sierra, and east of Walker Pass in a depression known today as Indian Valley.

From here they swung north along the east side of the Sierra. It was a dry, rugged route. In a much-repeated story, they ran out of water and after two thirsty days, with some misgivings they followed a dream vision of Charlie Hopper's toward a patch of green in the distance. This turned out to mark a small spring which provided the desperately needed water, enabling them to carry on.[94] When they reached the familiar Mary's River they followed it north and east to Fort Hall, retracing their trail from the previous summer. They had covered 1,500 miles and were still only about one-third of the way to Missouri. Their route now took them to Soda Springs and eastward to the Green River, where they met some trappers with bad news about Sioux war parties ranging across their intended route. Rather than take their chances with Sioux warriors, they decided to turn south toward Santa Fe and pick up the Santa Fe Trail back to Missouri. Charlie Hopper volunteered to be the guide, recalling later that, "I told them I did not want to have any grumbling or fault finding if we got into tight places ... We continued our journey and met with nothing

---

[94] Charles Hopper, Narrative, MS Bancroft Library. Cited in Giffen, p. 33.

worth mentioning until we got to the Spanish village of Abiquiu."[95]

They were camped near that village, about 50 miles north of Santa Fe, when they received a summons from the local Apache chief. After some discussion, they decided that Chiles, Hopper, and Rickman would go to the Indian camp to parley for permission to cross the tribe's territory. Once there they were quickly hemmed in by a crowd demanding presents. As Chiles dismounted from his mule the gathering pressed in, making any movement difficult. His six-foot four-inch stature and his red hair made him stand out from the assemblage that surrounded him, but he and his companions were completely outnumbered. Keeping outwardly calm, Chiles and Hopper attempted to gauge their next step. Hopper was convinced that they should beat a retreat, but the difficulty was that the bridle of Chiles's mule was being held by one of the Indians and he was completely surrounded by the throng. A subterfuge occurred to Hopper as he called out to Chiles to lend him some tobacco. Understanding what he meant, Chiles pulled his braided plug from his pocket and proceeded to cut off a number of pieces, closely watched by the Indians. When he had a handful, he threw the pieces in the air. The Indians scrambled for

---

[95] Ibid., p. 33.

them, and in the confusion Hopper, Chiles, and Rickman were able to beat a hasty retreat. Back in their own camp, they quickly packed up and moved on, putting as much distance between themselves and the Apaches as they could.

They soon reached the city of Santa Fe, and picked up the Santa Fe Trail, following it without incident to Missouri, skirting the northern edge of Mexican territory, crossing the Canadian, Cimarron, and Arkansas rivers, traversing the width of Kansas territory and arriving in Independence in early September.

The return had taken more than six months, covered almost four-thousand miles, and traversed the present-day states of California, Nevada, Utah, Idaho, Wyoming, Colorado, New Mexico, Kansas, and Missouri, but none of the fast-moving adventurers who made the journey had much to say about it except the occasional aside in a memoir. The historical importance of their return at the end of summer 1842 was to spread the word, principally through the diary of Bidwell and the letters of Marsh, that it was possible for settlers to go overland to California. For some in the party, this was enough. Others, principally Chiles, saw his experience as a springboard from which to launch another crossing to further cement his fortune on the West Coast.

This was, however, business for the following year. On reaching Independence, Chiles was happily re-united with his children at the house of his eldest brother, Joel, and would have instinctively wanted to take them with him on his return to California. But the oldest of the four was only ten-years-old, and the youngest five. With no one to share childcare responsibility on the trail, no fixed abode in California, and a very green memory of the hardships of the way west, he convinced himself and his brother that they would have to wait until he had a more permanent arrangement of his life in California.

Chiles's next call in town was to carry out his commission from his friend George Yount. The transplanted Missourian had not seen his wife Eliza since he set out on the Santa Fe Trail 16 years before. The two-mule peace offering via Chiles was for his new son-in-law Bartlett Vines, in the hopes of finding forgiveness that would allow him to see the children he had abandoned when they were aged seven, five, and one. Two prime mules were a fine peace offering that could have been worth about $200 [$5,900 in present value] but circumstances had moved on in Yount's absence. After four years of waiting, his wife had divorced him and married local man, Joseph Wright, who showed no inclination to wander. She listened with icy calm to Chiles's description of his journey, and his encounter with her ex-husband and the former's situation in the Napa Valley. Joseph Wright graciously offered Eliza the freedom to be re-united with the man who had probably been considered legally dead, but she emphatically declined. Such was not the case with the elder of her two daughters, Frances. Now 21-years-old, married with two children, she and her husband, William Bartlett Vines, were very interested in accompanying Chiles when he next went west. The youngest of Yount's children, Elizabeth, 16, who had been an infant when her father left, was also entranced by Chiles's descriptions of the trail and life in California, and she also asked for the opportunity to accompany the Vines family on the trek west. The eldest of Yount's children, Robert, now 23, had the strongest memory of his father, and held as much of a grudge against him as did his mother. He had no desire to see the man who had left his family on their own. Both mother and son died without ever seeing Yount again, but his two daughters excitedly began making plans to join Chiles the next spring when he would once again be heading west. And although Robert Yount refused to see his father, some years later his daughter went west and married the pioneer winemaker for whom the town of Rutherford in the Napa Valley is named.

As the year 1842 slipped into 1843, Chiles found himself something of a celebrity after the publication in the local newspaper of Bidwell's account of the crossing of the plains. The journal-letter was introduced by the editor who noted that although Bidwell had many friends and a good measure of success in Missouri, "... because of the many inducements held forth to enterprising young men to go to California, caused him to adopt the motto 'westward ho', shoulder his rifle and join one of the California companies which leave the rendezvous near Independence annually." [96] The effect of the journal-letter on emigration was decisive, particularly with, as Cheyenne Dawson put it, "adventurous youths … who wanted nothing but to see and experience." [97] The letter proved to be the same sort of spur as the letters of John Marsh two years before, only this time there would be someone leading the party who had actually made the journey. It seems likely that the ultimate success of the previous expedition, rather than the hardships experienced along the way, was featured more heavily in Chiles's verbal accounts to the adventurous spirits in town.

In addition, there was the continuing hangover of the economic depression that had settled on the western frontier following the Panic of 1837. Lack of a commercial outlet for frontier produce was hampering recovery, and the arrival of

---

[96] Nunis, p. 27.
[97] Nicholas Dawson, Narrative … cited in Nunis, P. 146.

experienced pioneers like Chiles from California and Marcus Whitman from Oregon, both of whom had made an overland crossing both ways, boosted confidence in heading west as a way out of the economic malaise.

It is clear that in returning from California to undertake another trip across, Chiles was ambitious. Certainly his aims included fortune, as well as a desire for a new, bigger life. There was also perhaps the desire for a bit of fame as the actual finder of a usable California Trail, as opposed to the desperate scramble across the Sierra that he himself had experienced. He knew from his time in California that manufactured goods and the wherewithal to use water power to process local produce, either grain or wood, would be more than welcome and could command high prices. We do know that his wagons were at least partly loaded with goods that would make a quick profit in California. He also had direct experience selling to trappers on his previous crossing, and had an entrepreneurial inclination.

It was in this frame of mind that he turned to his old friend William "Billy" Baldridge. They had known each other since the arrival of the Chiles family in Missouri in 1830. Billy had become an apprentice millwright when he was seventeen and was now highly skilled in every part of the milling business, having built mills all over Kansas and Missouri. Baldridge had been in the grip of California fever since 1830, when he talked to a trapper named Mills who had been to California and described it in glowing terms. It had, as mentioned, been his plan to make the 1841 crossing with his friend Chiles, but business interests had intervened and he was committed to a deal to set up some mills locally in Independence. A man of substance, single and an experienced millwright, Baldridge was the perfect choice to help Chiles fulfil his promise to Vallejo that he would return to California with the hardware necessary to equip a sawmill. It had been this prospect of a mill in that part of the country that moved Vallejo to offer Chiles his hidden valley.

Baldridge could source and assemble the nuts and bolts, the iron wheels and gears, for both sawmills and flour mills. Between them, they decided that California represented a great opportunity for pioneers who could build and use mills, and, having seen Isaac Graham's operation in the Santa Cruz Mountains, Chiles felt certain that he and Baldridge could duplicate Graham's success. They made preparations to pack all the necessary sawmill irons, including three saws.

Chiles and Baldridge were building a nucleus of an overland party that would draw in others. Included in this group were the two daughters of George Yount, Frances, the elder with husband and two children, and Elizabeth, the younger with a healthy appetite for adventure. Another family to join was that of Julius Martin. He was about thirty-years-old, and westerly moving was, so it seems, his established habit. He had lived in North Carolina, Alabama, Mississippi and Missouri, and in that sense was the embodiment of the frontiersman. With his wife and three girls, he was ready to head to the Far West. In addition to being skilled in survival and frontier farming, he could display his University of North Carolina education by quoting Latin and Greek poetry.[98]

This nucleus of Chiles, Baldridge, the Vines, and the Martins attracted a dozen of the more typical westering types; single young men in the adventurous mold of John Bidwell and Cheyenne Dawson.

Based on his experience, Chiles now faced the choice of the means of transportation. In 1841, this had been whatever an emigrant showed up with at the rendezvous, horseback, cart, or wagon. The three had shown their differing capabilities over the years of travel on the plains and mountains. Horse or mule pack trains, with each animal loaded with a small amount of cargo, were favored by trappers because of the speed and versatility. There was also the possibility of using Red River carts, which had proved their value on the Santa Fe Trail, and for the missionaries

---

[98] Stewart, *The California Trail*, p. 37.

on the northern plains. Two-wheeled, and pulled by two or three mules in tandem, Red River carts could carry a reasonable amount of cargo and were highly maneuverable.

In the course of his travel to and from California, Chiles had seen both of the two methods of transport employed, and now he rejected them equally. A pack train could move quickly, but was ill-adapted for women and children. And in case of illness, like the fever that had almost killed his friend Charlie Hopper on the return from California, a pack train was impossible. Even having seen the Red River carts leaving his ox-drawn wagon in the dust on the previous trip, he remained unconvinced that they were superior to the traditional farm wagon, adapted for life on the plains.

Chiles's choice of wagons might have been mere traditionalism, but there was also practicality and availability to consider. Flatbed farm wagons were more common than carts on western farms, and they were easily adaptable to carry women and children. With the addition of curved bows which served as the framework for a canvas covering, they could be easily made weatherproof, and would be more maneuverable and lighter for the crossing of deserts and mountains than the big freight wagons that were starting to ply the trade routes on the plains, like the Santa Fe Trail. For those who wanted to go to California in 1843 and profit from Chiles's experience, the choice was the traditional farm wagon, available and ordinary, with canvas covers. On this trip, in his particular case, with the cargo of mill equipment, he had special heavy-duty wheels, with extra-large hubs, spokes, and axles. His wagon was to be pulled by mules, which, though more expensive than oxen, were faster and proven over all terrains. As the Missouri spring came on, the party made ready to depart.

CHAPTER 7

Chiles's Year—1843

At the beginning of May, the party of 30 men and six women was in place at Fitzhugh's Mill, a few miles west of Independence. They settled down to wait while the grass, delayed by a late growing season, developed enough for the animals to graze out on the prairie. After almost three weeks they, "left the frontiers in high spirits for a seven month trip through pathless country to a little known home in the west." [99] On 31 May they shared a camp at Elm Grove with John C. Fremont, soon to be internationally acclaimed as "The Great Pathfinder", explorer of the west, self-publicist, and controversial would-be politician. In his journal, Fremont noted, "several emigrant wagons constituting a party which was proceeding to Upper California, under the direction of Mr. J. B. Childs" (sic). [100] He commented on their relatively large amount of goods, furniture, and farming utensils, "containing among other things machinery for a mill."[101] This would appear to be the first endeavor to haul freight across the plains in order to

---

[99] Charles Hopper, Narrative, MS Bancroft Library.

[100] Fremont, J.C. Lieutenant, A Report on the Exploration of the Country, Lying Between the Missouri River and the Rocky Mountains, on the Line of the Kansas and Platte Rivers, Senate doc. 243, Washington 1843.

[101] Ibid.

take advantage of the huge premium that could be charged for manufactured goods in California. Whether the goods were to be transported for sale at a large profit in California, or they were part of the possessions of the three families traveling with the party is unexplained, though to some historians it is seen as evidence that Chiles increased the amount of goods on the wagons at the expense of a sufficient amount of food. It was an ambitious gamble to rely on hunting to supply their daily sustenance, and it almost had dire ramifications.

Fremont had assembled a party of 21 men, nearly all of French origin. Fremont himself was fluent in French, which enabled him to speak with the French mountaineers who formed the largest non-Native population in the Far West. Through these men he could communicate with almost everyone else, for they also spoke Spanish and a host of Indian languages.[102] The Chiles party and Fremont's explorers traveled together for several days. According to his son Will, Chiles and one of his companions acted as hunters for both groups, as the combined party dined on turkey and deer. But when Fremont appropriated the choicer hindquarters of the deer for himself, leaving only the forequarters for the emigrants, Chiles abruptly terminated the arrangement at

---

[102] Bagley, Will, *So Rugged and Mountainous*, p. 188.

this show of arrogance.[103] They might have fallen out over who would do the hunting and enjoy the best cuts of meat, but Chiles was delighted to encounter Kit Carson and Broken Hand Fitzpatrick in Fremont's group, and together Chiles and Fitzpatrick were able to share stories of what had happened since they parted company on the Bear River almost two years before.

Their progress was slowed by the wetness of the season, which complicated the crossing of creeks and rivers, but before long they overtook the fleet of Oregon-bound wagons that made up the Great Emigration of 1843. For the next few weeks they followed at the rear of the would-be Oregonians, enjoying the safety of numbers, though moving at a slower pace than they did on their first trip west, and slower than Chiles would have liked.

We are indebted to Jesse Applegate, Missouri emigrant and leader of one of the wagon trains of that year to Oregon, for a description of a day in the life of this large company.[104] Applegate's party was composed not only of about 75 wagons, but also a large herd of cattle being driven west by their owners. While they were traveling through country where they feared

---

[103] Ibid.

[104] Will Bagley, *So Rugged and Mountainous*, Norman Oklahoma, Univ. of Oklahoma Press, 2010, pp. 193-195.

Indian attack, the party, which for the time being included Chiles's company, maintained a military-like discipline.

Applegate, in his memoir, "A Day With the Cow Column" takes us through a twenty-four-hour period on the plains, from the pre-dawn rifle shots of the sentinels that signaled the time to arise. While the families organized themselves, packing up and making a breakfast fire, the herders headed out of the circle of wagons to gather in the herd of cattle that might have spread out across the plains during the night, perhaps as far as two miles. "In about an hour," Applegate says, "five thousand animals are close up to the encampment, and the teamsters are busy selecting their teams and driving them inside the corral to be yoked."[105]

The "corral" was composed of the circled wagons linked together by their tongues and ox chains forming a defensive perimeter. Between six and seven o'clock, breakfast of bread, pork, and coffee was eaten, the tents struck, and the wagons made ready for the day's march. It was decided in rotation which group or platoon would take the lead, so that when the bugle blew at seven, every wagon was in its allotted place in the column. The

---

[105] Applegate, Jesse, A Day With the Cow Column, 1843, *The Quarterly of the Oregon Historical Society* Vol. 1, No. 4 (Dec., 1900) pp. 371-383.

penalty for tardiness was traveling all day at the rear of the column in a cloud of dust.

In Applegate's evocative memoir, the pilot of the column stood ready to give the signal to move out. A group of mounted young men gathered off to one side, ready to go on a hunt for buffalo. At the bugle signal, the wagon train moved out, led by the pilot and another group of horsemen to make sure that the column formed up properly and maintained its shape, which might have been several wagons abreast. The lead group was responsible for choosing the exact route along the bank of the Platte that the column would follow, identifying the crossing point of every tributary, doing whatever was needed to make it passable. They stayed in visual communication with the lead teamster of the column to make sure that he followed their route. Some wagon drivers were riding on their jolting wagons, others were marching alongside their oxen. Some of the women and older children were walking alongside the wagons as well. There was also a band of horses, tended by a group of older boys. The straggling herd of cattle brought up the rear, in the charge of whip-cracking drivers. The pilot measured the distance they traveled and moved ahead to find a place where they could have their mid-day rest. Here the wagons were drawn up four abreast and the oxen of the would-be Oregonians were un-yoked. On some days there was business to be conducted as well at this mid-day break. Perhaps this could be a meeting of the presiding council of "elders." On one particular day in Applegate's memoir, they met to decide on the legal rights and wrongs of a case involving a wagon owner and a young man whom he had hired to provide help in exchange for bed and board. The council heard testimony from various witnesses and made a final decision from which there was no appeal. It was all done quickly because the mid-day stop was brief.

An hour passes and the bugle sounds to signal the resumption of the journey. The whole column re-forms and moves out at the same pace, but, it is far less animated than the morning march; a drowsiness has fallen apparently on man and beast; teamsters drop asleep on their perches … the words of command are now addressed to the … oxen in the soft tenor of women or the piping treble of children, while the snores of the teamsters make a droning accompaniment.[106]

As the day lengthened, the company began looking out for the place the pilot found and measured out for making the wagon circle for the night. When the first wagon reached him, the others

---

[106] Ibid., p. 379.

fell in behind as he guided the lead wagon around the circle he had marked out. Each wagon stopped in position, dropped its team and made ready to lock itself to the wagon in front. Within ten minutes the final wagon arrived to make up the circle and the corral was formed. Soon everyone was busy making evening campfires from buffalo chips that they had collected along the march. With the evening meal taken care of, the evening watch was set by the company who had the responsibility for that night. They were divided into watches, to guard the camp and the herd in the hours of darkness, beginning at eight and finishing at four in the morning, when the day, with its familiar routine, began all over again.

But, Applegate tells us, there was also the possibility for a few tunes on the violin and a few dances by the younger members of the party. The council might meet in the evening to consider any new matters for their jurisdiction as the camp settled into repose.

On that particular evening in the cow column, the pilot was called at about ten with the news from the night watch that there was a party of horsemen approaching. Rather than rouse the camp to come to some kind of military readiness, it had been agreed that the pilot would make the determination about whether it was necessary to wake everyone. In this case, it was the returning hunters who were approaching and the pilot returned to his tent and the camp slumbered on until the dawn. Clearly, much had been learned in terms of trail organization since Chiles had crossed the plains two years earlier.

For all of their organization, progress was slow. After thirty-four days, the combined group had only reached the crossing of the South Fork of the Platte, almost a week later than in 1841. On the bank of the river, they lost several more days waiting for the water level to recede to the point where they felt it would be safe to cross. They were now concerned about losing so much time and determined to make boats that would ferry their goods across the swollen river. A member of the Oregon-bound party described the method of making hide-covered boats.

> ... we procured ... a sufficient number of green buffalo hides, and having sewed them over the wagon beds as tight as we could, with the flesh side out, and then turned them up in the sun to dry; and when they became thoroughly dry, we covered them with tallow and ashes, in order to render them more impervious to the water. The boats being completed, we proceeded to cross the goods of the company. Each boat was manned by six men. Some waded or swam along side; while others pulled by a long rope which was attached forward. The River here was about a

mile wide. In this way the goods were ferried over, and the empty wagons were drawn across by the teams a short distance below, where the River was wider and shallower. The crossing was effected in six days, and without any any serious accident. We passed here the fourth day of July.[107]

Once across, Chiles's group picked up the pace, bypassing some of the Oregon-bound wagons. In the shifting pattern of this year's emigration, eighteen of the Oregon-bound group elected to join the Chiles party and head for California. For some, the decision was apparently induced by meeting up with former neighbors from Missouri. For others, the presence of, "some very handsome young ladies ... accomplished and intelligent..." was influential.[108] Initially, the decision was a less dramatic choice, as the two groups continued to travel within sight of each other, and the apparently formal associations adopted at the beginning of the trail became more fluid as the emigrants acquired more confidence in their westering ability.

They continued up the Platte, though finding game scarce. On 9 July they were in sight of Chimney Rock, making close to

---

[107] Johnson and Winter, *Route Across the Rocky Mountains*, ed. Angela Fircus, West Lafayette Indiana, Notabell Books, 2000, p. 56.
[108] Journal of Pierson B. Reading, written during his journey from Westport, Missouri, to Monterey California in 1843, Society of California Pioneers, Vol. 7, No. 3, San Francisco, 1930.

twenty miles most days, as they approached Fort Laramie and the outliers of the Rocky Mountains. By mid-month they were at the American Fur Company's fort. Within the sheltering confines of its tall thick walls, they could let their hair down and enjoy a couple of social occasions. It is likely that Chiles's fiddle was pressed into service once again for dances on two successive nights. The social aspects of life at the fort met their expectations, but the more important prospect of buying needed supplies proved to be a disappointment. The Oregon-bound emigrants who had preceded them had bought what little there was, and the fort was waiting for a re-supply train to bring needed goods down from the Missouri River, about 250 miles away. After a brief pause the Chiles group set off once again, as much in search of game as continuing with their journey.

It was a warm clear Sunday in mid-July when they passed out of the gates of the fort, having been joined by young Pierson Reading from New Jersey who had left his Oregon-bound party and taken up with the hopeful Californians. Reading had been assiduously keeping a diary of his first experiences in the west, and in his first days with the Chiles party he noted their entry into the Wyoming Black Hills, with their high stone bluffs and mountain sheep, which he proclaimed as delicious, when some in the group finally succeeded in killing one. Other game remained scarce until the second day out from the fort when they managed to kill four more sheep and an antelope. Seemingly, the choice of trade goods and mill irons over food to fill the wagons was already becoming an issue, but for the time being, although they had been disappointed at the lack of supplies at Fort Laramie, they were managing to stay fed with what they killed from day to day. They were now on a gradual upward gradient approaching the Rocky Mountains.

A couple of days later they left the Platte and were camped on Squaw Butte Creek when two mountain men appeared, a lucky chance that would affect Chiles's thinking about the route and key decisions in the days to come. One of the men was Joseph Walker, an old friend of Chiles's from Missouri. At six feet, four inches and well over two hundred pounds, Walker, in his hand-crafted deerskin leggings, shirt, and hat was an imposing individual whose trail craft and leadership abilities had been honed by almost 20 years of frontier life, ten of them in the far western deserts and mountains. In the 1830s, leading a group of trappers, Walker forced a crossing of the Sierra with great difficulty into California. He knew the territory of the Great Basin as well as any white man and had pioneered the route around the southern end of the Sierra. Given their common Missouri roots, he and Chiles hit it off well, and Chiles concluded that the party should hire Walker as their guide for the next stage of the journey. He was one of the very few white men, along with Jim Bridger and Broken Hand Fitzpatrick, who had broad experience of the territory ahead.

Walker knew the geography, and he had fine hunting skills and familiarity with the local Indians. There was just one gap in his knowledge. That was handling a wagon train, as his previous trips into and across the mountains had been with small groups riding horses. A wagon train was another proposition, but here is where Chiles had the relevant knowledge, and the more recent experience of crossing to California. Clearly they discussed various options for traversing the geography ahead. Chiles might have been intending to follow the same route as had the Bidwell-Bartleson party of 1841, though he would doubtless have been mindful that they had been forced to abandon their wagons east of the Sierra. Perhaps he was thinking of picking up the route that he had followed returning east in 1842 south to Walker's Pass. It is likely that there was no set plan agreed between the two men. They would leave their options open and let circumstances on the ground dictate their route. One thing that was concluded was the fee. Walker would act as guide for a fee of $300 [about $68,000 in current values].

The trail headed west, rising toward the mountains, and through the clear atmosphere they saw their peaks covered with July snow. They were still following the Platte at this point, in tandem with another company of Oregon emigrants, making a good rate of nearly twenty miles a day. On 27 July they encountered the Sweetwater River at Independence Rock, a little more than two weeks behind the schedule of two years before. Setting off up the Sweetwater, they camped in a valley surrounded by mountains with good grass for the livestock. Chiles decided to stay there a few days while they sent out hunters in the hopes of replenishing their food stocks with buffalo meat that they would dry for consumption further down the trail.

Pierson Reading, the diarist, was relieved to get a few days' rest from the trail, as he was ill with the type of vague malady that was often identified as prairie fever. It is a comment on the state of trailside medicine that his first recourse was to attempt to bleed himself, at which he admitted failure. Reading's condition continued to worsen, and Marcus Whitman, the doctor and missionary who was leader of the Oregon party, was called. He administered some medicine and bled the patient, cutting, "an orifice in my arm large enough for a beaver to make his ingress."[109] The next day, in spite of the significant wound in his arm and loss of blood, Reading announced that he was feeling better, surely a triumph of mind over matter.

On 1 August they moved on again, having killed several buffalo and dried the meat. This was done by the women who cut thin strips from the large sections of buffalo brought in by the hunters. These were attached to ropes slung under the wagon beds to dry in the air as the wagons continued on their way. One of the women in the train remarked that after three days the meat was cured and ready to be packed away.[110]

They continued to make reasonable progress following the Sweetwater, keeping to their average of twenty miles a day. A week later they had traced the river almost to its source, and crossing another ridge they reached the great divide. Behind them were the rivers draining into the North Fork of the Platte, the Missouri and the Mississippi. Ahead were the tributaries of the Green River, feeding into the Colorado as it ultimately made its way through the slick rock country and the Grand Canyon to the Gulf of California.

---

[109] Reading Diary, Entry for July 30, 1843, *Quarterly of the Society of California Pioneers*, Vol. 7, No. 3, 1930.

[110] Owens-Adair, Mrs. Bethenia, Some of her Experiences, Portland, Mann and Beach, 1906, p.145.

There was a brief pause on 9 August for the trailside burial of a man from Kentucky, who died of "congestion of the brain," likely to have been a stroke. After a prayer and covering the shallow grave with large stones to prevent it being excavated by wolves, they continued on their way. The next day they were at the Green River. Although it was 100 yards wide and between 3 and 8 feet deep, such was the level of trail craft experience that Reading notes they took the river in their stride, crossing it without incident.

Four days later they camped by the newly established Fort Bridger. The fort was symbolic of the new realities of the west. After more than 20 years in the mountains, Jim Bridger, despite his fame as a mountain man, realized that the days of trapping were over and that the emigrant trains offered a steadier and more lucrative source of income than the declining prices offered for furs. With his business partner Luis Vasquez he settled down, selling supplies and buying worn-out oxen from emigrants. The traders would let the animals recuperate on the rich local grass and then sell them on to the next year's crop of emigrants traveling through. Anticipating an annual influx of emigrants, Bridger was establishing his own variant of frontier arbitrage.

Ft. Bridger's pleasant well-watered valley, with good grass and good hunting, was the destination at which Chiles thought the party would replenish its supplies. He had not, however, anticipated that the Sioux and the Cheyenne would come raiding that year, frightening off the local buffalo. Chiles and the company arrived at the Fort on 14 August, intending to stay for ten to fifteen days to "make meat," but after conferring with Bridger they moved on the next day. They would have to go farther along the trail, or perhaps off it, to find enough buffalo to feed the entire party in the days and weeks ahead. Now the decision to favor trade goods over food in the wagons was starting to take on ominous overtones. How much food to carry was always a calculated risk and Chiles's bet on acquiring it along the way did not appear to be paying off. They decided to leave the established trail to see if they could find some buffalo, and within two days they reached the Bear River. The company was now in relatively virgin territory, but still there were no buffalo to be found. And even when the hunters in the party struck out on their own, all they could get were some deer, antelope and elk, with the occasional bear.

The supply problem was still unresolved. The hunting party continued north along the valley of the Bear River and after a few days regained the main trail, passing Soda Springs. Here, they did not turn south as Chiles had done two years before, but continued northwest toward Fort Hall. This fort, established by Nathaniel

Wyeth of the Boston-based Pacific Trading Company for the purpose trading furs with the Indians, had stood there since the 1830s. It was now under the ownership of the Hudson's Bay Company, commanded by Captain Richard Grant. The main part of the party reached Fort Hall on 12 September. On this day two years before, Chiles had been west of the Great Salt Lake.

There was little that could be bought from Captain Grant that year at Fort Hall. Although Reading found him kind almost to a fault, Grant had to think of getting his own people through the winter. He had a few cattle grazing nearby, but refused to sell any of them at any price. Whatever sugar, flour, and dried meat he did sell, was predictably priced to meet the demand. In today's money, a pound of sugar was $24, a cup of flour was $8, and a pound of dried meat the same. To put this into perspective, two years earlier, the sum total of cash in the possession of the 69-member Bidwell-Bartleson party when they began their trek was $100 [$2,750].

As negotiations between Grant, Chiles, and Walker proceeded, there was a visit from a party of about 50 Snake Indians. Reading found them "very civil" as they enjoyed a communal session with the pipe. It was when one of the elder Indian women failed in her attempt to interest the young diarist in trading a "young and quite pretty squaw" for one of the party's horses that the mood was soured. The old woman departed, raining down a hail of curses on the heads of Reading and his companions.

The food situation remained at an impasse. The Oregon-bound train needed sufficient food to allow them to cross 800 miles before they reached a settlement that could offer them relief. Equally, Walker refused to lead Chiles's California emigrants unless they had an adequate supply of food. On 16 September, the two wagon trains departed. With the Oregonians and the Chiles-Walker groups safely on their way with the women and children, Col. Julius Martin, one of the would-be Californians, along with one of the Oregon-bound leaders, returned to the fort, resolved to compel Grant to sell them some more food. They enlisted the support of a small party of Fremont's explorers camped by the fort, who promised to help persuade Grant if it came to shooting. Led by Martin, they strong-armed Grant into submission, and the latter parted with several of the cattle that he had been reserving to get the fort through the winter. It is easy to understand the food anxiety of the emigrants, but the use of armed threats to obtain it from someone who would likely need it as much was a thoroughly unpleasant episode; the result of not ensuring an adequate supply of food to complete the journey. It conclusively colored Grant's views of Americans who passed Ft. Hall thereafter. In the following years, he was very careful in his dealings with them, being, "too well acquainted with the disposition and nature of these animals," to challenge them.[111]

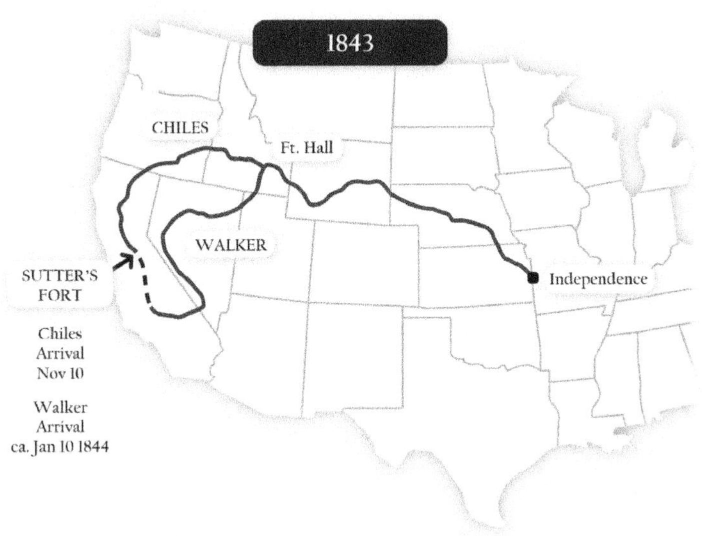

In the end, the four cattle wrested from the fort pacified Walker and Martin, who were ready to set out. But the tense negotiation had sparked some innovative thinking, and Walker and Chiles agreed to a dramatic change of plan. They would split the party, with Walker leading the wagons with some of the men, and all of the women and children, over the route followed by

---

[111] Cited in Bagley, p. 126.

Chiles two years previously. They would go as far west as the Sierra, then south to the pass at the southern end of the mountains, which Walker had pioneered in the 1830s. In the meantime, Chiles would take a dozen young men on horseback who could travel fast and live off the land. They would attempt to skirt the northern end of the Sierra, make their way to Sutter's Fort, re-supply, and then head back across the mountains with supplies to meet Walker's group as they emerged from the desert east of the Sierra. The plan was daring and optimistic in equal measure, leaving much to chance, but it showed a growing knowledge of the major outlines of the mountain wall that lay to the west. The horseback group, each with a pack mule and ten days' provisions, was to be led by Joe Chiles. He was gambling that their provisions would last them until they had covered the 300 miles following the Snake River to Fort Boise, which was operated by the Hudson's Bay Company on what is now the Idaho-Oregon border.

Pierson Reading was part of the Chiles horseback group. In his diary he recalled a cold, wet start to the journey from Fort Hall, with snow storms and high winds. Within a week they were already short of food and were relieved to meet a party of 200 Indians with dried salmon to trade. The weather continued cold, with high winds, though they managed to find other small groups of Indians who bartered fresh salmon, which was much preferred by the whites. Reading described the local tribes as miserable and largely unclothed, but the civilization he described was one which was well-adapted to its circumstances in a generally inhospitable country, with well-organized strategies for maximizing their most plentiful food source, the salmon, which swarmed seasonally in great numbers. One strategy in particular involved using wooden stakes to create an artificial narrows for the fish to pass through. The Natives then stood above and speared their food as it passed through the "gate." For the Chiles party, living entirely on fish was a mark of primitive culture, but from a dietary point of view it was certainly healthier than the westerners' preference for a regime that largely consisted of bread, fat pork, and beef.

On the first of October they reached Fort Boise, with its imposing, fourteen-foot high, three-foot thick adobe brick walls, enclosing approximately the area of two football fields. Presided over by French-Canadian Francis Payette of the Hudson's Bay Company, the fort conducted a lively trade with the local Indians for fish, which in turn it supplied to other Company forts in the region. The Chiles group passed that day and the next at the fort, making preparations to head southwest, and questioning Payette and his employees about the terrain that lay ahead. Unfortunately, no one there was able to tell them much about the whole route, having only explored the first part of it. They were able to confirm that it was high and rugged and populated by Indians who vigorously protected their territory, having killed a number of trappers over the previous years.

In terms of provisions, the story was much the same as at Ft. Hall. Payette and his men barely had enough to get themselves through the winter, let alone supply a party of thirteen with enough to get them to the "California Valley" where they could expect to find game. Yet in an act of typical generosity, Payette gave them enough provisions for one meal a day per man and a map of as much of the territory as he knew. Their hope was to reach California in 30 or 35 days. They had no way of knowing, but they were perhaps 350 or 400 miles from the point where they could reasonably expect to re-supply themselves, and perhaps 500 miles from Sutter's Fort.

They set off down the Malheur River on a south-westerly course. It was heavy going, winding through rocky, mountainous country. Following Payette's directions, they were making about 20 miles a day, encountering a few Indians as they went, one of whom spent the night in their camp and left early in the morning with one of their rifles. The next day, they found their camp the center of attention of a large number of Indians, which caused them to be on their guard, having been told by Payette about the fate of several white hunters in the area. They hired "an old Indian prophet" to act as guide and left early the next morning to try and distance themselves from the Indians who had begun to be troublesome and threatening.

The weather remained clear and cold as they set up camp on 12 October. They rested their animals, leaving at dawn the next day, finding the going almost impassibly cut with deep chasms, making only 14 miles. They were now short of water, though the weather had become warmer and the sky clear. After 30 hours without water, the following day they found a lake, but were disappointed to discover that it was too salty to be potable, and surrounded by poisonous grass. But at the west end of the lake they were relieved to find a spring of good cold water, where they camped. After another day's travel, they stopped at mid-day to rest their animals and managed to shoot a few ducks to augment their nearly exhausted provisions. On 16 October Reading noted, "We have been living for the past three days on a pint of weak soup for each man twice a day, not knowing the distance we may have to travel before finding game. Leaves us in a most unpleasant uncertainty."[112] They were now moving slowly, having

---

[112] Reading diary, Society of California Pioneers, Vol 7, No. 3, 1930.

been forced to dismount and lead their exhausted and starving horses and mules.

Chiles and his men camped in a gathering storm of mixed rain and snow, having enough flour and grease for one more meal. They moved on early the next day, and early in the afternoon found themselves in a small valley where they were relieved to see some antelope prints. Calling a halt, the best hunters in the group set off to see what they could find. Shortly thereafter, an echoing rifle shot announced the killing of a small antelope buck which they immediately butchered and lashed to their packs, determined to push on and find a good camp site where they could enjoy their first real meal in five days. This they did, not leaving much for another meal. As the sky darkened, it began to snow, but they built a big fire and made themselves as comfortable as they could.

They awoke the next morning, the nineteenth, and delayed their start in order to dry out their packs, which had been standing in the rain and snow all the previous night. There followed a good day's travel, topped off by their arrival at a mountain lake where they killed a buck and settled down for the night. The next day they made good time, traveling for another 30 miles along the lake, though their departure the following morning was delayed so that they could re-shoe their mules, whose feet had been heavily worn by the sharp rocks over which they were passing.

The route continued mountainous, crossed by many streams. Through the trees they glimpsed Indians who avoided contact, in spite of the efforts of Chiles's party to communicate with them. The white men mused on how the Indians managed to live in the area, as in the winter season it seemed to be largely devoid of game. The explorers themselves had gone two days without food. Over the next two days, discouragement spread from one man to the other as they looked ahead from vantage points and saw nothing but ranges of high mountains in front of them. The two days without food stretched to four. On 22 October they saw in the distance a high cone-shaped mountain covered in snow which would later be called Mount Shasta. They passed several Indian villages, hastily abandoned on their approach. When Chiles's men camped that night, they were the object of a sudden Indian attack, whose arrows were quickly overcome by the rifles of the white men. They left that camp early the next morning, moving slowly through a small prairie so that their horses could feed on the grass. The group began another climb following a creek and were encouraged when they reached the summit to be looking down on foothills to the south and west, rather than another mountain range.

It was the end of the day and the end of the month when the Chiles party made camp, weak from starvation with a handful of antelope grease for supper. They had let their horses loose to graze overnight and in the morning found that the Indians had killed three mules and a horse, which was infuriating, but at the same time gave them a source of food with which to carry on. The next morning was taken up with re-packing the remaining mules and burning the now-unusable packs and saddles. They were descending slowly through table land, when traversing a high hill, they could see below the beginnings of the great Sacramento Valley. "... and never were a set of poor worn out travelers more gratified than we were, after so much toil and travel, to have the Eldorado in view."[113] It was the first of November, the grass was green, and they could hear birds singing. After their passage through the mountainous country to the north, they felt that they had walked from winter into spring. With the weather soft and balmy, even the horsemeat for their evening meal tasted good.

They broke camp the next morning and headed southwest, and were only two miles down the trail when the sound of rifle fire signaled that two of their hunters had managed to bring down two deer. The whole party halted on the spot, threw away the

---

[113] Pierson Diary, entry October 31, 1843, Society of California Pioneers, 1930.

horse meat that they had been husbanding, and made a big meal of the newly killed venison. They made 16 miles that day, killing two large grizzly bears along the way, for no explicable reason other than to say they had done so. It is worth noting that at the time, grizzlies were so common in the area that in his diary Reading mentions seeing dozens of them as the group proceeded south. They set off the next morning on the left bank of a main stream, camping at about sunset on a small tributary creek. During the day, they had seen many Indians who were markedly friendlier than those they had previously encountered. Reading notes that they were timid on their initial approach, but brought some acorn meal cakes with them as a sign of friendship, and joined the party for several miles. This was the kind of situation that Chiles in particular enjoyed. He was notable among the emigrants for his attempts to communicate with the local natives. The weather closed in with rain and clouds as they continued along the stream, winding up the side of a high ridge from where they descended into the Sacramento Valley proper. Reading exulted, "The climate is most delightful, the grass and trees are as green and fresh as in the latitude of Philadelphia in the month of May!"[114]

---

[114] Ibid. entry Nov. 3, 1843, p. 191.

The men in the company were struck by the beauty and the richness of the valley as they moved slowly southward to accommodate their well-worn horses. The friendliness of the Indians, described by Reading as "Nature's children," offering presents of acorn flour cakes, was welcome, as they were entirely out of provisions. In the distance they could see the buttes that marked the confluence of another major river (the Feather River) with the Sacramento. Hopeful of reaching Sutter's Fort within a few miles, they pressed on toward the Feather River, on whose south bank they found one of Sutter's outlying settlements. They were made welcome and dined sumptuously on bread, coffee, and beef at the first white farm settlement that they had seen in six months.

Hearing of their arrival, John Bidwell hastened over from one of the other ranches to greet them and renew his acquaintance with Chiles, his old friend and trail companion. On the morning of 9 November, they repeated the repast of the previous evening and continued southward, camping by another ranch where they were treated to the luxury of some salt by the German proprietor. They made camp on a fine evening, having been assured that Sutter's main establishment was but a few miles down the road. Early the next afternoon, they were in sight of the fort at New Helvetia on the banks of the Sacramento River. In front of its imposing four-hundred-foot-long adobe brick walls, which stood three-feet thick and fifteen-feet high, with several cannons prominently on display, they were personally welcomed by Sutter, who congratulated them on their safe arrival.

In outflanking the northern edge of the towering Sierra, Chiles and his company had done what they set out to do, exploring a region largely unknown to white men, and achieved their goal of California by a new route, sections of which would be used by later emigrants. In spite of the rough terrain, semi-starvation, and harsh winter weather, they had averaged about 20 miles a day from Fort Hall, for a total of almost 1,100 miles to shake the hand of Sutter on the Sacramento. On the other hand, they had woefully underestimated the total distance. Their part in the grand plan to send relief supplies directly eastward to intercept the other part of the company led by Joe Walker was not successful. One of Chiles's contingent, experienced frontiersman Sam Hensley, was meant to cross the mountains and find Walker, but the news of snow levels at the higher elevations prevented him from making the attempt. Chiles and his company had simply arrived too late and the still largely unknown high Sierra passes were blocked. Chiles and three others prepared a relief party to head south and meet Walker at the southern end of the Sierra, which was their contingency plan if the central crossing failed.

As for the well-tailored man with the military bearing who greeted them, the long and colorful career of Johann Sutter spanned most of the nineteenth century. A native of Switzerland, in 1834 at the age of 31 Sutter was facing prosecution for debt when he fled his country, a wife to whom he had been married for ten years, and five children. This would be a recurring theme that would define Sutter's early life. He had a habit of living beyond his means, trading on his impeccable manners and bearing, running up unsustainable debts, and slipping away ahead of his dumfounded creditors. Like many in similar circumstances at that time, he headed west, embarking from Le Havre for New York.[115]

From New York, he found his way to Missouri. There he tried his hand at trading on the Santa Fe Trail. When that failed, he dodged his incurred debts and joined a company of fur traders along the Oregon Trail to Fort Vancouver. From there he sailed to Hawaii, and then to California, each time ingratiating himself with the leading citizens of the place. He arrived in Monterey in 1839, armed with letters of introduction from officials in Hawaii and Yerba Buena. In Monterey, Governor Alvarado viewed Sutter's plans for a large colony in the central valley as a timely

---

[115] Albert Hurtado, *John Sutter*, Norman OK, Univ. of Oklahoma Press, 2006, pp.7-15; Richard Dillon, *Fool's Gold*, Sanger CA, The Write Thought Inc., 1967, pp.36.

buttress against the intentions of the Russians, British, and Americans. Sutter was given Mexican citizenship and awarded a grant of 11 leagues—about 44 square miles. His establishment began to grow and prosper, with the help of local Indians who contributed their labor to raise the 18-foot adobe brick walls, but Sutter's manner and his flexible relationship with credit left his *Californio* neighbors, specifically Vallejo, with a mixture of bemusement and annoyance. Nevertheless, the Swiss continued to make progress with his combination of bluff, bluster, and occasional force, coming to a working relationship with his large pliable Indian workforce and fending off other Indians who had more warlike intentions. Sutter managed to steer clear of involvement in the Graham Affair, and he entertained a stream of visitors to his expanding headquarters.

In 1841, when Chiles and Bidwell arrived in California, Sutter had just bought out the Russian interest in Fort Ross on the northern California coast. The next year, when Chiles and some of the others from the party of 1841 went back to Missouri, Sutter employed Bidwell to act as a clerk, helping him remove usable goods from the coast to the Sacramento settlement, now named New Helvetia. Sutter's further career, his participation in the political infighting of 1845, his contract with James Marshall to build a sawmill on the American River, where gold was discovered in 1848, and his subsequent loss of most of his hard-won holdings in the aftermath of the Gold Rush, are well documented elsewhere. But for Joseph Chiles and his grateful companions, Sutter represented civilization and the chance to recoup before starting south to find Joseph Walker, whom they hoped was now past the southern spur of the Sierra.

* * *

What of Walker and his company of wagons, women, and children who had separated from the Chiles horseback party almost two months before? The group of twenty-five included sixteen men, two married women, two unmarried girls, and five children. Walker had been well paid to ensure their safe passage to California. The men in the party were energetic, willing, and largely experienced frontiersmen, including Chiles's great friend, Billy Baldridge, with his wagon load of mill irons. One of the others had ridden east with Chiles in 1842, and the remainder hailed from different parts of the frontier, from Texas and the Great Plains.

Walker calculated that he could get through to Sutter's Fort in sixty days, using a yet-to-be discovered pass through the mountains, or by reverting to a pack train for the most arduous part of the journey. They followed the Oregon Trail for about three days west of Fort Hall then turned south. This was another of the great western adventures on which no one kept a diary, so the exact route can only be surmised, though much of it is known because it later became a heavily-traveled section of the California Trail. The first part was likely to have been a trappers' trail that Walker had blazed or followed in 1834. Chiles had followed it eastward in 1842, and it involved crossing three divides in what are now called the Sawtooth Mountains. In this, Walker was playing it safe and following a known course. He eventually reached the Raft River, on what is now the Idaho-Nevada border. The party then headed south to reach the headwaters of the Mary's River, which would soon be renamed by Fremont as the Humboldt. Following this river, during the last week in October, he would have reached the point at which it disappeared into the sands of the Nevada Desert. Walker hoped to see Hensley already at the sink with a pack train of provisions and news of a quick route through the mountains to Sutter's Fort. In fact, Hensley, Chiles, and the rest of that company were still fighting their way through the mountains well to the northeast of Sutter and would not arrive there for another three weeks. Walker's company settled down to wait, with their eyes trained on the western horizon for rising dust which would signal the arrival of approaching horsemen and a pack train. In the meantime, the animals rested and built up their strength on the grasses near the sink.

After several days of anxious waiting, the central weakness in the strategy of division of the whole party was apparent. There was no way that they could communicate if either part of the party encountered disaster or delay. There was the contingency plan that allowed for the two companies to act independently, and in the absence of Hensley it became clear that was what they would have to do. They had used up 45 of the 60 days' worth of provisions which Walker had allowed for, so it is likely that short rations started at this point. He began to follow the trail that he remembered from 1834 and which another of the emigrants who had traveled east with Chiles also knew. Given the lateness of the season they would proceed directly south, skirting the eastern Sierra, and cross the mountains at Walker's Pass, which was unlikely to be blocked by snow even in midwinter. Ironically, they were only about 250 miles from Sutter's Fort, but it was much too late in the year to consider anything but the less risky, if circuitous, southern course. And although it was a reasonably safe route over the mountains, Walker's Pass required traversing more than 300 miles, including several stretches of waterless desert, and a good deal of rough country which wagons had never traversed.

They worked their way down the desert south of the sink. Their well-rested teams managed to make progress even in the soft ground, and they knew from experience how far the distance was across the desert. Their first destination was the river flowing eastward, which Fremont would later name after his scout Kit Carson. Forty miles to the south they came to another river. This one would later be named for Walker himself. Following this river south, they came to a lake that they circumnavigated on its eastern side because it was easier going for the wagons.

Carrying on in a southerly direction, they encountered rough country, showing signs of recent volcanic and seismic activity, a land newly born. Hot springs and hard black basaltic rocks marked the way. With scorching days and freezing nights, long stretches without water meant that grass for the animals was poor or non-existent. The company was on reduced rations and the animals suffered for lack of feed. The local Indians made their presence felt, ambushing one of the emigrants as he was standing watch at night. He took an arrow in the chest before seeing off the attackers. His companions managed to remove the shaft, but the head remained lodged in his chest muscle, giving him great pain and keeping the party jittery.

Two-thirds of the way through November, they were now following a southward-trending valley flanked by high mountains on the east side, and even higher peaks on the west. The glittering snows of the high Sierra reflected the winter sun, but Walker was undeterred and he pressed on toward his pass following the stream that flowed the length of the valley. In spite of Walker's confidence, the moment for a hard decision was approaching. The teams hauling the wagons were rapidly failing, and the food allotted for the trail was fast disappearing. The members of the company were facing starvation if they could not speed up the pace. Something had to give. At the end of the month, when the little river they had been following ended in a large brackish lake, they took the decision to leave the wagons. Though there was little or no food left to be carried, it was particularly hard for Billy Baldridge, whose future and that of Joe Chiles was tied up with the mill machinery he was carrying in his wagon. He did the best he could, burying it in the hopes of returning to claim it the next year. Some of the wood from the wagons was fashioned into pack saddles and the rest went into a good bonfire to warm the weary travelers in the freezing night air. They were near what was later called Owen's Lake and their situation was serious, but compared to the desperation of the party that had included Chiles in 1841 they were better off, knowing that they were just a few days from a usable pass over the mountains into the great Central Valley of California. They were short of food and had the responsibility of women and children, but they had a reliable guide who had their confidence. The women could ride some of the remaining mounts, carrying the children or stowing the smallest of them in saddle bags.

As Walker knew, a few more days brought them to the pass on 3 December. They were about fifty miles northeast of what would become Bakersfield and crossed through six inches of snow at about mid-day, having slaughtered one mule for food. It hadn't been comfortable, and they had been hungry. They had to leave their wagons, but they were all alive and in reasonably good spirits. Proceeding into the Central Valley, Walker kept the mountains to his right for several days, reaching the area of modern-day Visalia where he hoped to meet Chiles. With food extremely low and no relief party in sight, he took the decision to turn due west across the valley toward the Coast Range.

Walker had experienced a warm welcome and good hunting in that area about ten years before, and this is likely to have influenced his choice, but it was a risky decision. The lower Central Valley was largely uninhabited and it had been a drought year. Having survived all the desert conditions east of the Sierra and made the crossing successfully, the company was still without food, in the same circumstances as on the other side of the mountains. In the meantime, Chiles and his small relief party were searching the southern Central Valley up to Walker's Pass but failed to find Walker's trail and eventually returned to Sutter's Fort. The Walker company struggled across the desiccated valley and on Christmas Day made camp in the Coast Range on a tributary of the Salinas River. It had been the site of Walker's camp ten years before, and as he remembered, there was plentiful game, deer, wild turkey, fat young wild horses, good water, and warm winter sunshine in which they could recuperate from their ordeal.

On New Year's Day, they left the mountains and reached Alisal, the rancho owned by the *Californio* Feliciano Soberanes, not far from Mission Soledad and not much more than half a day's march from Monterey. It was here that they made their final camp before the company broke up into groups that went their separate ways, to San Jose pueblo in the Santa Clara Valley or Sutter's Fort. Billy Baldridge, Elizabeth Yount, and the Bartlett-Vines family went to San Jose and obtained their Mexican passports. From there they continued on to Sutter's Fort and were reunited with Chiles, to the great relief of all concerned.

This ended the westward saga of 1843. They had trod a fine line between triumph and disaster, and there is divided judgement on Chiles's heroism and leadership qualities, characteristics which he shared with many of his fellow trailblazers. In the words of one historian:

> Those who admire reckless optimism, sanguine energy and making decisions on the wing will always admire Chiles; those who do not will consider him a man who made his mark on the history of the western trails by sheer ubiquitous perseverance.[116]

Another historian summed up Chiles's efforts thus far in his career:

> For good or bad, '43 must be counted as Chiles' year … Chiles showed himself outstanding in courage, enterprise, energy, and breadth of vision. He suffered, however, from over-optimism. […] He wrecked a good possibility of success by loading his wagons with ironwork and other goods and expecting to get through by killing buffalo.[117]

The journey did not end at Sutter's Fort. Accepting the kind invitation by the Swiss to use his schooner *Sacramento,* which was heading for the Napa River to load lime, Chiles and Baldridge, along with George Yount's children, headed for the

---

[116] Frank McLynn, *Wagons West*, London, Jonathan Cape, 2002, p. 176.
[117] Stewart, *The California Trail*, Berkeley, UC Press, 1962, p. 51.

Napa Valley. Chiles was anxious to fulfil his promise to his friend to see the Yount family reunited. This was soon accomplished to the immense gratitude of his friend, with Yount and his children becoming reacquainted after 15 years apart.

His duty discharged, Chiles was anxious to show Baldridge the valley he had set his heart on. He wanted to be sure that it was as fertile and protected as he remembered, the place where he could ranch and build the mill that they had planned, even though the loss of the mill hardware in the desert was a setback yet to be overcome. They followed the eastward trail along the stream out of the Napa Valley through the narrow canyon until it emerged into the protected hidden valley which was the perfect site for a water-powered mill. As they looked over the land, Chiles could see that its fertility and beauty were as he remembered. Enjoying it through Baldridge's eyes would have enhanced Chiles's appreciation of the site, and he was more determined than ever to make it his own. The tall, rangy Chiles and the shorter, stocky, and powerfully-built Baldridge were a good combination, ready for the hard work ahead that would make their dreams a reality.

CHAPTER 8

Rancho Catacula Gained, Mexican California Lost, the Family Reunited

The first step on Chiles's and Baldridge's path toward achieving commercial success in California was on horseback over the hills to Sonoma to meet with Mariano Vallejo. The two men were apologetic to the general about having to abandon the saws and mill hardware east of the mountains, but Vallejo had another idea. The need for sawn timber was less pressing in a California society accustomed to building with sun-dried clay bricks, and they agreed with Vallejo that a grist mill for grinding wheat and corn rather than a sawmill, would be more useful in the existing circumstances. It could also be constructed from local materials, without the necessity to import any hardware.

There remained various formalities, such as becoming a Mexican citizen, to address. By September, Chiles had his certificate of citizenship signed by the governor and the next month he presented his petition for the ownership of his desired land in the valley, which he called 'Catacula' from the local Indian name of the place. The request for the 8,700 acres [almost two leagues] was delivered to the local *alcalde*, Jacob Leese, an early-American settler and Vallejo's brother-in-law, on a piece of paper for which Chiles had to pay $10. This was seemingly the only expense incurred in the transaction.[118] The *alcalde* verified that the valley was 'vacant', though it is not at all likely that the Indians who ranged through the area had been consulted. Having taken these preliminary steps, Chiles was now free to apply to the governor for a grant of the land. In the formulaic language of official documents, and dated 9 November 1844, it began:

> Most Excellent Sir: Joseph B. Chiles, Mexican by naturalization, respectfully appears before your Excellency and says that having a considerable number of black cattle, horses and mules, and no proper place to put them upon, he applies to Your Excellency to do him the service to grant him two square leagues in the place called Catacula which according to the tenor of the annexed document given by the Justice of Sonoma is found to be entirely vacant.[119]

Baldridge drew up a map to accompany the petition, and he and Chiles set out for Monterey to see Governor Micheltorena. Chiles was granted Rancho Catacula in November 1844, subject to the approval of the Departmental Assembly, which would be meeting in the following year, a formality that would return to

---

[118] Originally published in 'History of Napa and Lake Counties' California, Slocum, Bowen & Co., 1881, Transcribed by Geneologytrails.com/napa.
[119] Cited by Giffen, p. 50.

cause him serious problems in the future, when it became apparent that the Departmental Assembly never had time to ratify the grant. The sub-surface instability of California politics was about to erupt into a series of conflicts that would fracture the civic society of California, drawing in Sutter and the American population as the *Californio* factions sought to bolster their strength to confront each other. The febrile atmosphere continued bubbling away, and meanwhile events in Texas that would lead to war between Mexico and the United States were coming to a head.

In the meantime, Chiles got on with creating a homestead. He hauled in timber to build a cabin, and later the mill. He planted corn and wheat. The mill stones were cut in slabs from the mountains east of the Berryessa Valley and hauled down to the Catacula. We have to assume that the local Wappo Indians played a significant role in all this activity. By 1845 the water from the creek feeding Catacula was filling the millpond, which in turn provided the water to turn the mill wheel. It was considered the most up-to-date facility of its kind in California and continued in operation until the 1880s. Meanwhile, the walls of an adobe house were rising, brick by brick.

Chiles Mill (early 20th century), about 20 years after it stopped working. Courtesy of Marc and Nancy Douglas.
The Adobe House - Chiles adobe (early 20th century) courtesy of the Society of California Pioneers.

All this activity in his sheltered and remote valley left Chiles without time for involvement in the political and military factionalism then sweeping across that part of California. When invited to join a military company organized by Sutter to help the cause of newly appointed governor Manuel Micheltorena in 1844, Chiles refused, in spite of the fact that many of his companions with whom he had crossed the plains in 1841 and 1843 had joined the revolt in anticipation of a Texas-style repudiation of Mexican rule. After two armed confrontations near Los Angeles, with artillery duels in which the only casualties were two horses, Micheltorena was ultimately sent packing by the *Californios* under Juan Alvarado and Jose Castro. He was the last governor sent by the central Mexican government.[120] After a period of house arrest in Los Angeles, Sutter was allowed to return to his Fort. At Baldridge's urging, he and Chiles did attend a public meeting in Sonoma in mid-1845 to discuss the possibility of California achieving independence from Mexico. They spent the night at the home of Jacob Leese, Vallejo's brother-in-law, who argued at length for the establishment of an independent California, adding the inducement that the plans called for all the

---

[120] Robert Ryal Miller, *Juan Alvarado*, Norman OK, University of Oklahoma Press, 1998, pp.97-110

Indians to be parceled out to the ranch owners as slaves.[121] Seemingly, this was not enough to tempt Chiles, because when the meeting broke up without conclusion, he returned to the simple life of his ranch.

In the centers of power, Monterey and Los Angeles, the populace was much concerned whether it was Micheltorena or his successor, Pio Pico, formerly leader of the provincial assembly, who was governor, and whether or not Sutter joined with various Americans to challenge the powers that be. These causes mattered little to the man who was consumed by his vision of building a self-supporting homestead. We can but speculate as to his motives, but based on what we do know of his character, the politics of the wider world, and the conflicting ambitions of would-be politicians, we might conclude that Chiles had little desire to get involved in armed skirmishes. He had seen enough of war in Florida, and he had no desire to re-live that experience. Essentially, Chiles was content with how things were turning out for him in California. He was well integrated into the small society of that part of the world, and Vallejo and a number of other *Californios* had been hospitable and helpful to him over the years. This attitude aligned him with the 'gradualist' faction,

---

[121] Giffen, p. 54.

composed mostly of Americans who had become naturalized Mexican citizens. They were in favor of California becoming part of the United States but felt that it would be best to accomplish this aim gradually, without risking bloodshed.

But events would soon outrun the aims of the gradualists. In December 1845, John C. Fremont turned up at Sutter's Fort at the head of a column of 64 well-armed men. Officially on a topographical mission, he proceeded in the direction of Monterey, posturing defiantly in the vicinity of the capital of the Mexican province. In the spring, Fremont's actions encouraged the discontented non-Hispanic population of Alta California to dream of staging an armed uprising like the one the Anglo settlers had perpetrated in Texas ten years earlier. Since the uprising, Texas had won its independence from Mexico and at the end of 1845 would be annexed by the United States, sparking off war between the United States and Mexico. Fremont's camp at the Sutter Buttes, to the north of Sutter's Fort, became a focal point for these rambunctious elements under the leadership of Ezekiel Merritt. The so-called Bear Flag revolt, named for the banner under which they marched, began with the capture of a small squad of Mexican soldiers and their 200 horses near the Buttes. The horses were handed over to Fremont and the Bear Flaggers set off for Sonoma, where they believed the *Californios* were plotting to revoke their privileges. Fremont was playing a cagey game of quietly encouraging the insurgents, without overtly straying into engaging in warlike behavior with a peaceful neighbor, an offense that would lead directly to court-martial.

Word had percolated into the Catacula in early June that there would be a Fremont-inspired capture of Sonoma and General Mariano Vallejo. Chiles and Baldridge were uneasy. Many of the proponents of aggressive action were hard and largely rootless men like Ben Kelsey. On the Catacula they did not see how a revolt against their friends and neighbors like Vallejo would help settlers like themselves.[122] A few days later, the Bear Flag banner, to show strength and unyielding resistance, was crudely designed by the cousin of Mary Todd Lincoln using ink, linseed oil, and red paint. It was then stitched together by Nancy Kelsey, and decorated with some blobs of paint meant to represent a grizzly bear. Confused local *Californios* took it to be a pig.[123]

Nonetheless, under its colors the insurgents from the Napa region marched on Sonoma, surprising Vallejo and his handful of

---

[122] William Baldridge, *Days of '46*, MS Bancroft Library, Univ. of California, Berkeley, p.32; Giffen, p. 58.

[123] H.H. Bancroft, *History of California*, Vol. 5, 146-148; Bidwell, 102, cited in Rosenus, p. 139.

troops, who were packed off by Fremont to Sutter's Fort to be locked up. Fremont was soon recruiting volunteers for taking the "war" to southern California.

Ultimately overcome by curiosity, in early July, Chiles and Baldridge rode over to Sonoma to see what was happening. Vallejo had already been captured and packed off to Sutter's Fort, where he would be held until the beginning of August, when he was paroled on the condition that he swore to "never take up arms against the United States of North America ... or leave his own district without permission upon penalty of death."[124]

The rich irony of all this was that Vallejo had long been an admirer of the United States and had made a speech to the governor and junta (ruling body) in Monterey just two months earlier, in which he posed the questions:

> Why should we shrink from incorporating ourselves with the happiest and freest nation in the world, destined soon to be the most wealthy and powerful? Why should we go abroad for protection when this great nation is our adjoining neighbor? When we join our fortunes to hers, we

---

[124] M.G. Vallejo, *Release from Fort Sutter*, Special Collections, Stanford University, cited in Rosenus, General Vallejo, p. 166.

shall not become subjects, but fellow citizens possessing all the rights of the people of the United States.[125]

Vallejo had been taken away to Sutter's Fort two days before Chiles and Baldridge arrived in Sonoma, but on the scene were old friends and companions like Benjamin Kelsey and Bartlett Vines, awaiting the arrival of Fremont and the Fourth of July celebrations. Lots of patriotic rhetoric was aired, but when the reading of the Declaration of Independence and the subsequent carousing was over, Chiles and Baldridge returned to the Catacula to mind their own business, although Baldridge later joined Fremont's Bear Flaggers for the brief time that they were actively engaged in the fighting in the southern part of California. The American flag was now flying over the capital in Monterey after the intervention of Commodore John D. Sloat of the US Navy, but the prudent Chiles issued orders that no one was to leave his property after nightfall.[126]

Chiles maintained a delicate balancing act that kept him out of the posturing and flag-waving that accompanied the Bear Flag revolt He did not join those flocking to Fremont's call, in spite of the fact that the two men were friendly, and Chiles had played

---

[125] History of Solano and Napa Counties California 1912, www.wikiquote.org

[126] Giffen., p. 58.

host to Fremont's earlier exploring party at the Catacula in 1844.[127] On that occasion, Fremont delivered a banker's draft for $600 to Chiles, drawn on his US government account, in part payment for horses and supplies furnished him by Sutter. Sutter used this draft to repay an old debt owed to Chiles when they had had dealings in Missouri.[128] Clearly, Chiles's allegiances and relationships were complex. When he became aware of Vallejo's incarceration dragging on, he and several others went to Sonoma to see that Vallejo's property was being protected and ensure the safety of Vallejo's family. Their intentions were good, but they were too late to prevent the loss of 1,000 cattle and 600 horses.[129]

Those who enthusiastically joined Fremont were later characterized by Bidwell as a mixed bag, including settlers, hunters, good men, "and … some as rough specimens of humanity as it would be possible to find anywhere."[130] Vallejo, despite his patience and generosity with the Americans, ultimately would have agreed. He later noted that when the *Californios* saw parties

[127] Fremont [1845] 1988: p. 270,255-256; cited in Thomas Howard, *Sierra Crossing*, Berkeley, UC Press, 1998, p. 32.

[128] Larkin Papers, 1: 159, Sutter to Thomas Larkin, cited in Hurtado, *John Sutter*, Norman Oklahoma, Univ. of Oklahoma Press, 2006, p.128.

[129] M.G. Vallejo, Historical and Personal Memoirs, Vol. 2, p. 31; Vol. 3, 387-88; cited in Rosenus, *Vallejo*, p. 167; Dale Walker, *Bear Flag Rising*, London: St. Martins Press, 1999, p.127.

[130] Bidwell, "Fremont in the Conquest of California", 1891, p. 520; Cited in Gillis and Magliari, *John Bidwell and California*, Spokane 2002, p101-02.

of men riding over their plains and forests under the Bear Flag, exhibiting an animal that was an emblem of "rapine and force", they thought that they were dealing with robbers and took the steps they thought most effective for the protection of their lives and property. In Vallejo's view, this misapprehension of the Bear Flagger's intentions led to the fighting on the northern frontier. In hindsight, this would be a fair appraisal, given what had followed early that summer.[131]

Responding to orders from the new ranking naval officer, Commodore Robert F. Stockton, Fremont marched his troops and the Bear Flag insurgents as the "California Batallion" to Monterey. There they were ordered to board ship and sail southward to San Diego, from where Fremont and Stockton's combined forces marched north and triumphantly entered the pueblo of Los Angeles in mid-August. Stockton sailed on to Santa Barbara and Monterey while Fremont marched his men north up the Sacramento Valley. Both men thought that the revolt was over, but not long after they left Los Angeles with Major Archibald Gillespie in charge, he was facing an uprising by the

---

[131] Mariano Guadalupe Vallejo, translated by Earl R. Hewitt, *Historical and Personal Memoirs Relating to Alta California* [*Recuerdos Historicos y Personales Tocante a la Alta California (1875)*], Vol. 5: 1845–48, 87–90, 93–98, 101–103, 106–107.

local *Californios*. Outnumbered and defeated, he pulled back to San Pedro on the coast. Stockton asked Fremont to hurry back to Los Angeles by land while he sailed south. As Fremont and Stockton converged on the pueblo, the figure of Brig. Gen. Stephen W. Kearny, US regular army, was approaching San Diego from the east with a small force of dragoons. Encountering a larger force of *Californios* at San Pascual, he suffered a humiliating defeat. Eventually joining forces with Stockton, the two commands marched north together from San Diego. The convergence with Fremont's forces pitched three headstrong leaders into a test of wills that would represent the fight for power between the Army and the Navy.

As the political fate of California hung in the balance throughout 1846, it was already being overtaken by events. More than 2,000 people completed the journey pioneered by Chiles and the others, tipping the balance of the California population in favor of the United States. The last of the wagon trains, the famous Donner party, was trapped for the winter in the high Sierra, with disastrous consequences. There were various relief efforts launched that winter, including riders who spread out through the settlements seeking donations. A stop by one of the relief organizations at the Catacula yielded a horse, a mule and two wagon covers that could serve as tents. One source says that these were donations freely given. Another says that Chiles sold these items to the relief party.[132] It seems unlikely that someone who had experienced the hardships of the trail would take such an uncaring attitude, but it remains a possibility. Chiles was not overly prosperous and horses and mules were very valuable and not let go of lightly.

Earlier that year, down at Sutter's Fort in the fall, Chiles had been waiting for new arrivals who might contribute their labor for the completion of his new adobe house at the going rate of a dollar a day. Several of the new arrivals accepted, and moved into the adobe on its completion, bringing a family atmosphere to what had been a male-dominated world. Quilting bees and fiddle-led musical entertainment were a big feature of the months of bad weather. Here, Chiles's ready wit and musical ability ensured his popularity. Although he won the warm admiration of newcomers and old California hands, a misunderstanding over some cattle hides caused a falling out with George Yount. It led to harsh words, a lawsuit for slander, and the loss of the friendship that had

---

[132] Lin Weber, *Old Napa Valley*, St. Helena CA, Ventures Publishing, 1998, p. 103; This author cites Dale Morgan, ed. *Overland in 1846: Diaries and Letters of the California Trail*, Vol. 1, Talisman Press, Georgetown CA, 1963, p. 342. [Diary says that Chiles sold these items to Reed et. al.]

lasted for years and spanned the distance from Missouri to California.

One old friend lost, but new friendships found, in the Jones and Allen families, who had come to help finish the adobe in exchange for a place to live until they could get established in the new country. Mary Jones, aged 21 years, described their arrival and first few weeks at the Catacula:

> ... we got to Chiles' home in the morning ... and that was the tenth of November 1846, just six months from the time we left the Missouri River. That night we stretched our tent as usual and went to bed but not to sleep. For Chiles' Indians [he kept a lot of them to do his rodeo work] began, soon after we lay down, to howl and cry. Then the wind blew our tent down and we had very little sleep that night. After it quit raining our men went to the mountain near by and got out timber to cover the adobe for it was only walls without a roof. They covered the house and all moved in. We occupied the first room at the north end of the house. We had a fireplace where I cooked and I had a cupboard in the wall where I kept my few dishes and we were comfortable. Old Mrs. Allen ... and Andrew Allen had the two rooms next to us and Sam Brown and his wife and baby lived with Mr. Chiles in the wooden part of the

building where we often met of an evening and listened to his and Mr. Bradley's music for they were both fine violinists and often had spelling matches, would choose sides and spell. Mr Chiles and Mr. Bradley were both redheaded and always full of fun and had something amusing to tell us.… We lived at Chiles' ranch until the next June, and left there about the 15th of June 1847 and went to San Jose.[133]

The reference to Chiles using local Wappo Indians for "rodeo work" raises the point of his relationship with the Natives of that part of Napa County. The evidence about work on the Catacula is unclear, but given the widespread abuses of the freedom of the aboriginal population and the system of debt peonage and indentured servitude that grew up from the time of the establishment of the missions, it is unlikely, that Chiles did not participate in the prevailing system to some extent.[134] The fact that he had taken to maintaining a presence at Sutter's Fort during

---

[133] Personal Diary of Mary A. Jones, Bancroft Library.

[134] Debt peonage was widespread, and most of the big *rancheros*, notably John Sutter, John Marsh, Mariano Vallejo and his various relatives, participated in its abuses. The subject of unfree labor in California at this time is discussed in depth in Albert Hurtado, *Indian Survival on the California Frontier,* New Haven, Yale University Press, 1988; Richard Steven Street, *Beasts of the Field*, Palo Alto, Stanford University Press, 2004, and Michael Magliari, 'Free Soil, Unfree Labor: Cave Johnson Couts and the Binding of Indian Workers in California, 1850-1867', *Pacific Historical Review*, Vol. 73 No. 3, 2004, among others.

the "emigration season" speaks to the chronic shortage of labor that many early settlers pressed the local tribes to fill. At the same time, Chiles was willing to hire workers at the prevailing wage, so it could well be that there were relatively few local Indians to be exploited, as many of them had been displaced into the local mission where they were decimated by diseases against which they had no immunity. Locally, the Wappo population had significantly shrunk as a result of a smallpox epidemic spread by an employee of Vallejo in 1837. Additionally, for Indians who had survived the Mission Era, there was often a sad outcome. Andrew Kelsey, brother of Benjamin Kelsey, trail companion from 1841, was notorious for his abuse of Pomo Indian labor at his ranch on the southern shore of nearby Clear Lake, where he and his partner Charles Stone "…maintained their home with Indian slave labor," molesting the females of the tribe and using extreme physical punishments for minor infractions of their rules.[135] So cruel was their regime that the Indians rose up in December 1849, killing Kelsey and Stone.[136]

In the Chiles Valley, come the start of 1847, with the adobe brick house finally roofed, its cosy rooms filled with friends, its

---

[135] *History of Napa and Lake Counties*, San Francisco, Slocum and Bowen and Co., 1881, p. 56.

[136] Bancroft, *History of California*, 4:698; cited in Street, p. 114.

warming fireplaces at each end of the building, and the new mill up the creek turning the millstones to grind the wheat from the fields, Chiles decided on another return to Independence, this time to bring out his children. As spring moved toward summer, he left the Catacula in the hands of Billy Baldridge, and rode over to Sutter's Fort to see if there was a party heading east. There he found Commodore Robert Stockton gathering a small force to return to the United States in mid-June.

At the beginning of the year, in January 1847, with the signing of the Treaty of Cahuenga, hostilities between the Mexican government and the combined forces of the Americans ceased, ending the conflict in this theater of the Mexican War. The Treaty, which ceded control of Upper California to the United States, was signed by John C. Fremont, acting in his self-appointed capacity as, "Military Commander of the Territory of California." In doing so, the naïve Fremont launched himself into a prickly power struggle between the two branches of the military, represented by Commodore Robert F. Stockton and General Stephen W. Kearny, both of whom outranked him. Confusion reigned about where actual power lay. Mariano Vallejo, acting for the defeated Mexicans, received three letters in a week, each purporting to be from the "Governor and Commander-in-Chief of California." Commodore Stockton, in spite of his initial irritation at Fremont's presumption, within a few days decided to return east and named him California's governor. This infuriated the stiff-necked Kearny, ranking regular Army officer, just recently appointed General. Fremont, with Stockton's backing, refused to recognize Kearny's authority and continued to style himself "Military Commander of the Territory of California," setting up headquarters on the plaza in Los Angeles.[137] There was nothing Kearny could do because Fremont's California Batallion held the balance of power at the time, making the latter untouchable. Kearny took himself off to Monterey, commandeering Consul Thomas O. Larkin's house as his headquarters. Fremont continued to hold sway in Los Angeles, where the *Californio* population warmed to the Lt. Colonel as he adopted elements of their colorful dress, but rumors of his personal corruption and immorality began to gain currency, particularly among Americans in that part of the state. For three months, Fremont continued to ignore direct orders from Kearny. But when the Bear Flaggers dispersed at the restoration of peace, and Kearny had reinforcements sent from the east to back him up, he prevailed and ordered Fremont to accompany him eastward to Fort Leavenworth to answer charges

---

[137] Andrew Rolle, *John C. Fremont, Character as Destiny,* Norman, Univ. of Oklahoma Press, 1991, pp. 90-92.

of insubordination and mutiny.[138] Fremont agreed to do so, trusting in the influence of his powerful father-in-law, Thomas Hart Benton, to see him triumph. They departed from their camp at Sutter's Fort near the end of July 1847, heading over the Sierra via the increasingly well-established California Trail, arriving at the Kansas fort near the beginning of the fall.

Up in northern California during this tumultuous period, Chiles never showed much interest in the skirmishing politics of the new territory. In this, he was typical of his type of frontiersman who sought open space and generally asked to be left alone. Chiles held his neighbor Mariano Vallejo in high regard, but kept to his policy of non-involvement throughout that tumultuous year of 1846. Now it was more than six months since the fighting had ended and, with the departure of Kearny and Fremont, life was returning to normal. Chiles still wanted to get back to Missouri to see his children, with the intention of bringing them west to share the new home he had made.

Commodore Stockton, the ranking officer still in California at this point, was encamped near Sutter's Fort, preparing for his return to the States. He reportedly liked to do things in a grand style, and he had a government budget of $5,000 for his trip. In

---

[138] Ibid., p. 96.

today's dollars, this would amount to $146,000.[139] The commodore insisted that all the civilians accompanying him be paid $2 per day, (twice the going rate), in exchange for which they would accept military discipline. In today's dollars, this would have amounted to a payoff of more than $7,000 for about four months' work, a nice nest egg with which Chiles could re-equip himself for the next trip west. Never one to miss an opportunity to profit from necessity, he was happy to accompany Stockton as a "guide." Joining him were several other early travelers to California, including Peter Lassen, mountain man Caleb Greenwood, and perhaps two of Greenwood's sons.

Rather than take the California Trail, Stockton chose a route that took the group south from Sutter's Fort down the Central Valley, skirting the southern end of the Sierra and picking up the Old Spanish Trail, the well-traveled trade route between Santa Fe and southern California. The trail, pioneered in the late 1820s, had been named and partly mapped by Fremont's second expedition in 1845. Originally following a route that would later become famous as Route 66, in the 1840s the Old Spanish Trail had begun to take a northern loop in an effort to avoid the fierce southern mountain and desert tribes. As a very well-equipped and armed

---

[139] Giffen, p. 66

party, Stockton's column would have felt relatively confident of withstanding Indian attacks, but they nonetheless recorded a number of skirmishes with the Indians of the region north and west of Santa Fe.

The Commodore stuck to his orders to not engage in hostilities with the indigenous population, in spite of various provocations. He won Chiles's approval for quick thinking when they were led into a potential ambush by their Indian guide. Sensing a trick, Stockton told the guide to call in his chiefs. Once about 20 of them appeared, the Commodore surrounded them with his marines and hired guides like Chiles and read them the riot act. He explained that they were just returning from a great war in the west in which there had been much combat and he feared that in the face of the slightest provocation his men would open fire. Leaving a few moments for the meaning of his words to sink in, he then presented the chiefs with the gift of a horse and demanded that they hold a feast out in the open plain. The chiefs were then herded some distance from Stockton's party and turned loose while the Commodore and his group made a discreet escape.[140]

---

[140] Ibid. 66-67.

Despite Stockton's evident pomposity, it was this resourceful response to apparent danger that captured Chiles's admiration. If it had come to a real confrontation, Stockton's outnumbered party may have fared badly. The peaceful resolution of this particular incident was typical of Chiles's career crossing the continent. His inclination to seek a peaceful solution held him in good stead in almost every situation in which a hasty response might well have brought tragedy. Stockton's party continued on its way in a state of readiness, still shadowed by Indians, probably Apaches, who showered their tents with arrows on several occasions, one such arrow hitting the Commodore in the leg one morning as he sat eating breakfast.

This nagging resistance from the indigenous population notwithstanding, the party made reasonable progress along the Old Spanish Trail, reaching Santa Fe in late September and soon thereafter following the well-worn Santa Fe Trail toward the western frontier of Missouri. The company's destination was Fort Leavenworth, Kansas, where Fremont had been officially arrested and readied for transportation to Washington DC, for court-martial. Chiles, his duty discharged on arrival at Leavenworth, made the short trip from there over to Independence, arriving in early November. He was once again reunited with his three daughters and his son at the home of his brother Joel and wife

Azubah. Now ranging in age from 16 down to 11, Joe-Jim, Frances, Lizzie, and Mary were old enough for him to propose taking them west, a notion that they greeted with enthusiasm. In the meantime, it was winter and months would pass before he began organizing a new westward journey. In the meanwhile, seemingly encouraged by Stockton, who felt that character witnesses like Chiles would help Fremont's plea for exoneration, he took the decision to go to Washington and attend the court-martial.

Fremont's trial began on 2 November. This was just about the same time as Chiles made it back to Missouri, where word had been left that he might be called as a character witness. At the court-martial in the Washington Armory, Kearny charged Fremont with mutiny, disobeying the commands of superiors, conduct prejudicial to military discipline, and insubordination. Fremont could only hope that the influence of his father-in-law would prevail with President Polk. Benton was convinced that Fremont was being prosecuted because he was not regular army, owing his rank of Lt. Colonel to his command of a "scientific exploration party", and he vowed to fight for him to the end. Friends and acquaintances like Chiles also came forward to testify as to Fremont's character.

Chiles and Fremont had known each other since 1843. The two men had met in California and on a number of occasions on the trail west. Although Chiles had little interest in the Bear Flag Rebellion, one source indicates that Fremont sought Chiles's opinion before embarking at the head of the Bear Flag insurgents in 1846. Given that he was a popular figure whose reports about the west had been widely circulated, and that his father-in-law was a politician of national importance, the affair was widely covered in the national press. It was also reported in the trial's official proceedings that "Joseph B. Childs (sic) now (15 December) at Mrs. Peyton's boarding house, in this city, be summoned for the defense."[141]

In the event, the presiding Judge Advocate took the view that Chiles's testimony would not be pertinent to the case and refused to have him sworn in. The proceedings dragged on past Christmas and into the New Year. Chiles was probably long gone from the capital by the time the court found Fremont guilty of mutiny, disobedience to a superior officer, and military misconduct. For political reasons, the decision suited President Polk. It gave him the possibility of upholding the court's decision while recognizing Fremont's services to western exploration. He used his

---

[141] Senate Document No. 33, 30th Congress, 1st Session, cited in Giffen, p. 68.

presidential powers to commute the sentence and to cancel Fremont's discharge from the army. Rejecting Polk's conciliatory gesture, Fremont resigned from the army and returned to California to become the prosperous owner of a large estate near Mariposa that comprised several gold mines. He became extremely wealthy, and in the next two decades "The Great Pathfinder" was seldom out of the public eye, his orbit taking him far from the California of Joe Chiles. Before his life ended, John C. Fremont led further expeditions in search of an all-weather route for a transcontinental railroad, became the talisman of the gathering anti-slavery sentiment in the United States, and ran as the first presidential candidate of the new Republican Party in 1856, later briefly commanding the Army of the West in the Civil War.

CHAPTER 9

The Chiles Family, "The Plains Across", 1848

Leaving Fremont to his fate, Chiles returned to Independence to stay with his brother's family and his four children for the rest of the winter. By springtime he was ready to return once again to California, and at last take his children with him. With his reputation as a highly experienced pilot, he soon assembled a party of more than 100 men, women, and children. Shortly after starting in early May, as one of the last parties to set off that season, they were joined by an additional 12 men with pack mules and 18 wagons. The overland immigration wave was somewhat meager in 1848. The Mexican War and delays in concluding a peace treaty combined with the publicizing of the tragic fate of the Donner Party in 1846 kept many indecisive would-be pioneers off the plains that year. Chiles's party was one of the last of the few to set out that spring.

They started rolling in mid-May along the well-marked trail by the Blue River. Many of the daily details of this crossing were noted in the journal of one of the members of the party, Richard May. Chiles's easy-going style as leader stood in contrast to many of the captains of other trains who from the outset tried to enforce military-like discipline, which seldom lasted very far down the trail. By this time, the demand for guides who could find the trail had sharply declined. It was now well-known and even signposted, at least as far as South Pass and Ft. Hall, though inexperienced emigrants still were often happy to pay for the knowledgeable trailcraft of the likes of Joe Chiles.

May was impressed by Chiles's willingness to hold up the train so that he and his family could catch up, and when they met some ten miles west of Independence, "we had the joy and pleasure of arriving at Capt. Child's (sic) who very kindly had us take supper with him."[142] May's appreciation of the landscape was similar to that of many emigrants who had left the heavily wooded areas of Missouri, Kentucky, and other states:

> The landscape on the Blue River is delightful, the lowlands being as level as a bowling green and as rich as could be wished. The high prairie is undulating and in every way calculated for agricultural purposes ... The prairie all the way to this point is handsomely decorated

---

[142] Richard May, 'A Sketch of a Migrating Family to California in 1848', Fairfield WA, Ye Galleon Press, 1991, p. 5.

with wild flowers which would give a botanist employment and diversion. [143]

May and others in the group found much to admire, despite the rainy weather and the inevitable boredom during the long days on the trail. In addition, they were making good time: a start of 300 miles in the first two weeks was respectable; and on the second of June they were camped by the Platte River. It was with great excitement that May met his first Indian, a Pawnee reduced by circumstances to begging food from the passing wagon trains. Wanting to maintain good relations with the local tribes, Chiles and company fed him and saw him on his way. For May, in spite of this pleasant encounter, there was a lingering mistrust, one probably brought on by expectations of bloodthirsty savages. With the widely experienced Chiles in command, there was little likelihood that relations with the Indians would be anything but benign. Later in the week Chiles killed their first buffalo and shared the meat out among the company. It was a much-appreciated experience, the first of many buffalo that they encountered and ate at this phase of the journey.

Richard May's journal records the details of trail life on this particular trek west, including how, with the approach of evening

---

[143] Ibid, p. 7

each day, Chiles would ride ahead to find a suitable campsite with water and grass, turning his horse sideways as a welcome signal that they could soon catch up and circle the wagons, forming a corral to contain the livestock. The Lakota, or Sioux, were much in evidence, so circling the wagons in camp was considered a necessary precaution to keep their cattle and oxen safe from Indian raids. There was also the necessity of using buffalo chips or wood cut from trees growing on the islands in the river to make their campfires. What little wood that could be gleaned from along the banks of the river had long since disappeared into the campfires of the earlier trains. The days passed without particular incidents, apart from pleasant ones like a dance organized by the younger members of the party, with music likely to have been provided by their guide and his violin. There was plenty to eat as buffalo, elk, and deer were found in reasonable numbers, and the hunters were led by Chiles who brought in several game animals at a time to be divided among the wagons.

In the early stages of the crossing, Chiles's company was 112 strong, including 37 men, but by the time it arrived at the forks of the Platte the train had grown to 47 wagons, and nearly 80 men. This was a formidable force. They passed the guideposts of Chimney Rock and Scotts Bluff, and by late June they were at Fort Laramie, 640 miles west of Independence on the upper reaches of the North Platte, where they caught up with the last of the preceding wagons. The man in charge of the post, James Bordeau (Burdien, according to May), provided "an entertainment" and several young ladies and gentlemen from the train "partook of his generosity", May noted approvingly.[144] Others were less amused, complaining that, to the shame of all concerned, some of the young emigrant ladies were present when some of the gentlemen got infamously drunk.

The Glorious Fourth was celebrated with a buffalo hunt which yielded 12 buffaloes. The rest of the day was spent in drying the meat for later use. This was done by spreading strips of meat on low wooden platforms with a small fire underneath. In three or four hours the meat was sufficiently dried to be packed away and consumed in the days and weeks to come.

By now they were in the Laramie Mountains, and across the great divide at South Pass by the middle of July. On the nineteenth, on the Big Sandy, a day was given over to trading with a mountain man named Kinkaid who had cattle, buffalo hides, and other dressed skins to barter for coffee, bacon, and flour at mountain prices. From experience, Chiles knew that there was a dry 40-mile stretch from the Big Sandy to the Green River

---

[144] Ibid, Diary entry, June 23-24, 1848, Galleon Press edition, 1991, p. 15-16.

so they took to the trail at three in the afternoon and traveled all night and part of the next day, arriving on the Green in mid-afternoon. May was much taken by the effect that life in the mountains had on the health of those who lived there. Like other commentators, he ascribed much to the beneficial properties of the mountain air and water. May noted that he himself had lost 49 pounds since the start of the journey.

Near the end of July, on a fork of the Green River, the train encountered Chiles's old friend and colleague Joseph Walker, with his sons and their entourage of various wives and children. The two groups traveled together for a few days and Walker showed them a pass that eased their journey through that section of mountains, later called the Greenwood Cutoff. Ever the entrepreneur, Chiles returned the favor by selling the assembled trappers and Indians "much liquor" with predictable drunken behavior.

May, impressed by the excellent state of Walker's health, typical of the mountain dwellers he had met, felt that it was attributable to diet, exercise, and the absence of politics and lawyers. He suggested that a year in the mountains would give the same benefits to any of his ailing contemporaries back in Missouri. This positive view of mountain men was untypical of emigrant diarists, with the prevalent prejudice against white men who had "gone native" and married Indian women, seeing them as outcasts who had sunk to the level of being at ease in a savage wilderness.[145]

On the first of August they were west of the Bear River, one of the major tributaries of the Great Salt Lake lying to the south. Two days later they were at Steamboat Spring, one of many hot and soda springs in the area. Not far down the trail, Chiles's wagon suffered a shattered wheel, but such was the level of trailcraft by this time that it was fixed on the spot in short order. On 7 August they spent the day at Ft. Hall. May visited Captain Grant, his wife, and another lady of the fort, finding them "intelligent and quite accomplished."[146] Having left the Fort and followed the Snake for four days, on 12 August they reached the divide of the trail, California to the left and Oregon to the right. In an atmosphere of cheerful optimism, they camped on Raft Creek early that afternoon, committed to following the California trail.

They now had the company of the Paiute or Shoshone Indian tribes who were much in evidence, sometimes selling mountain blackberries and other times looking for the opportunity to make off with horses. On the seventeenth they encountered Samuel Hensley and his pack train that they had last seen at Independence

---

[145] Bagley, *So Rugged and Mountainous*, p. 75.
[146] Richard May Diary, p.35.

Rock about six weeks earlier. Going by way of Ft. Bridger and Salt Lake City, Hensley had tried to pioneer a cutoff west of the Lake and had faced disaster after an unseasonal downpour had turned the salt flats into a quagmire. Having exchanged pleasantries and trail information, Hensley's train pressed on towards a significant encounter with a group who were among the most important pioneer trail builders. This was the Mormon Battalion, heading east from California with momentous news.

While Chiles, May, and the others were rolling across the plains, events were stirring in the Sierra that would impact their experience of the most difficult part of the journey. A party of Mormons, enlisted by the US government to fight in California the year before, had arrived too late to participate in the battle for southern California and were mustered out. Thereafter they went north and found work with John Sutter, and some of them were at his mill on the American River when gold was discovered. Like most of the others present at that momentous event, they then passed their time digging gold nuggets out of rock crevices along the river, although they never really succumbed to gold fever in its most virulent form. The lure of home and hearth back in Salt Lake City had a stronger hold, and they decided to set out for their homesteads on 1 June. In the event, they started more than three weeks later, sending out scouts to find a possible wagon route over the mountains that would be easier than the known trail, following the Truckee River with its many crossings.

By mid-July, as Chiles's party was just west of South Pass, the Mormon Battalion was steadily making progress in road building, finding a usable way on the divide between the American and Cosumnes Rivers. They hacked out a route across the summit and moved their wagons over the divide on 29 July. In this they were utilizing the natural advantage of the traveler crossing the Sierra west to east: the availability of inter-stream ridges that lead steeply but steadily toward the Sierra summit. Westbound travelers must try to choose a likely descent, only to find in some cases that the chosen path ends in a canyon deep within the mountains. The Battalion were now a mile and a half down the eastern slope and camped in a place they christened Hope Valley. From here they followed what became known as the West Fork of the Carson River, emerging from the mountains south and east of Lake Tahoe on 5 August. Following the river, they could now move rapidly until they judged that they had avoided Truckee Canyon. On 12 August they left the river and after a day struck the emigrant road at about the place where the westbound wagons encountered the Truckee River. They could congratulate themselves on pioneering one of the most successful achievements in California Trail road-building, later to become known as the Carson Route, which would benefit every future emigrant train heading west. One of the first of these was led by Joseph Chiles.

On 14 August the Mormon group started across the Forty Mile Desert from the west, and by marching through the night they reached the Humboldt Sink about dawn and made camp. They rested through the heat of the day and toward evening were joined by 18 wagons arriving from the east. This was the vanguard of that year's California migration led by James Clyman, and predictably there was an exchange of news. Clyman had nothing particular to report, which was not surprising. As one of the most accomplished and experienced guides, to him the entire journey across the continent up to that point had been unremarkable.

For their part, the Mormons had their two pieces of news, both of which were to be highly significant—first there was the discovery of gold at Sutter's Mill, and second, there was now a new route to get there. This marked the opening of a new road, across the Forty Mile Desert to the Truckee River. From there the directions were to head south to pick up the Carson River which would lead them into the mountains and the path that the Mormons had just constructed. This in turn would take future emigrants directly to Sutter's Fort via the Placerville gold diggings. The Mormons were anxious to get home, and one member of Clyman's party informed them that he had just recently blazed a trail from Salt Lake City to Ft. Hall. This bit of news greatly interested the Mormons, and they decided to try this route rather than go even further east to Ft. Bridger before turning south.

The two groups parted company on 16 August, the Mormons meeting 25 more westbound wagons, though this new group had little to impart about the trail that was not already known. The Mormons continued along the valley of the Humboldt for ten days without incident. On the twenty-sixth they met another ten wagons, probably led by Peter Lassen, who was unmoved by their news of a new route. The next day they met Samuel Hensley and his company of ten men with packs and horses. Hensley had news from Salt Lake City, and just as important, directions for a route that would possibly save the Mormons eight or ten days on their return journey. This route took off from the California Trail at Cathedral Rocks, turning east and south across the Bear River to curve around to the east of the Great Salt Lake. Hensley wrote down in a "waybill" directions for the route he had described, and the two groups parted company.

The Mormons continued east and two days later met the 48 wagons under Chiles's leadership. He was excited by the news of a new easier route across the Sierra Nevada and his party was rejuvenated by the tidings of the gold discovery. Any tiredness they might have felt was dissipated, to be replaced by an enthusiastic eagerness to get to the gold fields as quickly as possible. As they described the diggings, one of the Mormons, indulging in a bit of theater:

> ... poured into his hand perhaps an ounce of gold and began stirring it with his finger. One aged man of probably over three score years and ten, who had listened with intense interest while his expressive eyes fairly glistened, could remain silent no longer; he sprang to his feet, threw his old wool hat upon the ground, and jumped upon it with both feet, then kicked it high in the air, and exclaimed, "Glory hallelujah, thank God, I shall die a rich man yet!"[147]

In return for the good news, Chiles gladly gave the Mormons some advice, a waybill that he said showed a route to their destination that was even shorter than Hensley's. They assumed that Chiles had gone that way himself, which he might have done in 1841 or 1843, but not this year. The two groups parted and the Mormons sent scouts to find Chiles's trail while the main party

---

[147] James Clyman Diaries, William Camp, ed., San Francisco, CA, California Historical Society, Special Publication, No. 3, 1928, p. 239.

with the wagons continued up the Humboldt River. After nine days the eastbound Mormons met the scouts near the head of the river with the news that they had not been able to find any trace of Chiles's cutoff trail to Salt Lake City. They continued to search for a spring noted in Chiles's waybill, but not finding any water had decided to return to the main trail and go on to Hensley's cutoff before turning south, likely with some questions in their minds about where the confusion had occurred.

The whole incident is somewhat mysterious. From what we know of Chiles's character and experience, he would not have sent anyone off on a wild goose chase in that dangerous country, but he was a Missourian, and there was no love lost between Missourians and Mormons in years gone by. Nevertheless, it would have been entirely out of character for him to perpetrate a hoax of this kind. It seems likely that he based his directions on geographical experience from 1841, when his and Bartleson's wagons were fifty miles from the Humboldt, so in his own mind Chiles was giving the Mormons helpful information. For the Mormons, by going ahead on 15 September they were sure that they had found Hensley's route and with little fanfare they arrived in Salt Lake City on 28 September to be reunited with their families. For the final leg of their journey, from Cathedral Rocks to Salt Lake City, they had pioneered a new route, which became known as the Salt Lake Cutoff, hugely important for many of the emigrant trains in the years to come.

Meanwhile, Chiles's train was following the dusty margins of the Humboldt River toward the Sink in good spirits, but engaging in violent clashes with the local Indians over attacks on their stock. From the Sink they followed the established trail westward for a few miles then turned south into the desert skirting the western edge of the Carson Sink. It was a route he would have remembered from the 1841 crossing, and one taken by the Walker contingent of Chiles's party in 1843. After 30 dry miles of heavy pulling they reached the abundant water and grass of the Carson River. Historians note that this section of trail was later sometimes called the Chiles Route. It was comparable in distance to the more famous Forty Mile Desert, but judged by some to be marginally easier as it was flatter, though it had no boiling springs in the middle to use as a convenient resting place.[148]

There was regular skirmishing with the local Indians—probably Northern Piutes, but possibly Shoshone or Washoe—which began to take its toll. On 11 September, Chiles found four arrows in his bull and four other wounded animals. On the fourteenth, the party lost four oxen and eleven cattle. When

---

[148] George Stewart, *The California Trail*, p. 206.

Indians killed a horse belonging to Chiles, some members of the party followed their tracks and exacted revenge, killing the first Indian that they saw. [149] The aggressive behavior on the part of the Indians was unusual at this stage of the development of the trail. Conflict between whites and Indians really began only after 1860 when whites stopped just passing through and began to settle the area, entering into competition with the local tribes for scarce resources.

Various elements of the train fell to bickering among themselves. One member of the party was particularly unhappy that a fellow emigrant with a broken wagon, who was unable to continue with 600 pounds of trade goods for the gold settlements, was forced by Chiles to accept the bargain of supplying him with transport in exchange for a wagon and team which would fetch a high price in the gold country. It was a hard bargain based on the fact that without Chiles's help, the man might lose everything and die in the mountains. [150] The incident recalled another earlier in the trip when the family of Martha Williams Reed ran out of food in Idaho. "There wasn't much to cook, as we were very short of

---

[149] Edward Smith, A Journal of Scenes and Incidents on a Journey from Missouri to California in 1848, Copy at CS 68 C34 v. 4, California State Library. Entries for September 14-21, 1848.

[150] Edward Smith, *A Journal of Scenes and Incidents*, 1845-46, cited in Bagley, p.384.

rations," she recalled. One man in the party (identified by the historian Will Bagley as Chiles) had supplies to sell, "but he sold them so high and Father hadn't much money, so he couldn't afford to buy much, and as a result we went hungry a good deal of the time."[151] This was the hard, pragmatic side of Chiles the entrepreneur, the man who on many occasions looked to create benefits for himself and his family. He was known for using valuable wagon space to transport alcohol into the mountains, knowing that it would claim a high price from mountain men and their Indian cohorts. On all his crossings, he drove livestock which he hoped to sell in California or along the trail. Sometimes these plans worked to Chiles's benefit. On other occasions he was accused of acting recklessly, for example in 1843, by taking too little food in favor of trade goods. Whatever the case, in a fast-changing world of opportunity, where fortune would favor the bold, Chiles was a man with his eye on the main chance.

Before their assault on the difficult Sierra crossing, the party rested by what was sometimes called the Salmon Trout River, (to be renamed by Fremont that year as the Carson River), and then turned upstream toward the southwest. After breaking trail for two days, they found the tracks of the other wagons following the

---

[151] Reed, "Old California Pioneer Passes Away" *The Fallbrook Enterprise*, 12 January 1917, cited in Bagley, p. 99.

Mormon road. Chiles's route to this point then replaced the Mormon route, even though it was not comparatively easier or shorter. As George Stewart observes:

> Here as elsewhere, the decision was determined more by accident and prejudice than by any survey or rational comparison of the two ... Chiles must thus be credited with reopening thirty miles of trail and opening another thirty miles. This section became an integral part of the Carson Route, which remained for some years the chief entry into California. This pioneering must thus be put down as another of Chiles numerous achievements.[152]

Following the Carson River, they made reasonable distances each day, given the ruggedness of the terrain. While they were struck by the great natural beauty with which they were surrounded, their appreciation was tempered by the heavy work required to continue climbing westward into the mountains. At the end of September, they were encamped by a small lake with abundant grass for the stock. Next was the steep elevation of the pass itself. This was much more difficult for the westbound travelers, having to lift their wagons over the high point, than the eastbound Mormons lowering theirs. On this arduous route, the

---

[152] Bagley, p. 206.

small glacial lakes that punctuated the mountains made welcome stopping points for the emigrants. By early October Chiles's party was over the highest of the mountains and dropping down on the other side. The temperature became noticeably warmer and when they arrived in Placerville on 4 October they could consider that they had achieved their objective.

George Stewart summed it up:

> The men of '48, eastbound and westbound, had thus succeeded in establishing the Carson Route, the second entry for wagons into California. It may be compared with the Truckee Route, which presented its fourfold barriers—desert, canyon, pass and downslope. On the Carson Route, desert and pass remained equally arduous, but the difficult canyon was largely eliminated, its river crossings being cut to only three ... the Carson route offered definite advantages.[153]

The 1848 Chiles westbound crossing was also notable for the first delivery of mail across the plains. Thomas Bayley, a school teacher from Mississippi, had arranged with the Independence postmaster to deliver 300 letters addressed to pioneers in Oregon which had been piling up in the post office. His recompense for

---

[153] Stewart, *The California Trail*, p. 207.

his trouble was to be empowered to charge as much as he could get over and above the official price of 40 cents to be paid to the postal service. Bayley and his four sons planned to accompany the Chiles party as far as Fort Hall and then strike off for the Oregon territory, but the news when they approached the fort was that the Snake Indians were on the warpath. Bayley heeded the advice to stay with Chiles and make his way to Oregon via California, so the Chiles company has the distinction of being the first train to carry mail to California via the Carson Pass.

Bayley arrived in the gold fields to find that a large number of the addressees had come down from Oregon to try their luck as miners, and such were the economics of the region, flush with cash and the eagerness of the miners for news from home, that there were no quibbles about the charge of $2 a letter, about $61 in today's currency. It had taken just short of six months for the mail to travel from Missouri to California, but according to Baley's son, "There was not a man that ever made any complaint about the price."[154]

---

[154] Bayley, *The First Overland Mail Bag to California*, Bancroft Library, cited in Bagley, So Rugged and Mountainous, p. 375.

CHAPTER 10

Joseph Chiles, Frontier Entrepreneur

By the end of October 1848, Chiles and his party were at Sutter's Fort, having pioneered another route over the Sierra. Although the Fort was well and truly infected with gold fever, Joseph Chiles was apparently immune to it. He waited there only long enough to rest his stock and set off as soon as possible for his ranch with his children—the two teenagers, James and Elizabeth, and the two younger girls, Fannie and Mary. He had left the reliable Billy Baldridge in charge of the homestead, but had received very little news during the treks east and west about how things were going, so he was anxious to see for himself. As soon as the animals were ready, he was off across the Sacramento River, heading south and west, via the Berryessa rancho and up Cache Creek toward the Catacula.

He was delighted to find everything in order on their arrival. The mill was in operation, grinding wheat and corn, the mules and cattle were in good shape, and the trees he had planted around the adobe were beginning to cast some shade. In the vineyard on the hillside above the adobe, the few remaining clusters of grapes showed that it had been a good harvest.

Although records are sketchy, as noted earlier, it is likely that the bulk of the labor to accomplish the tasks of land husbandry came from the Indians of the locality—Wappo or Patwin—or perhaps members of other tribes who had been drawn in from nearby counties. It was widely noted at the time that the local Indians were skilled with crops and animals—seeding and harvesting, herding and shearing. At the time of the grape harvest in the nearby Napa Valley, Indians from Lake County were regularly drafted in as seasonal hands, so it seems likely that Chiles used the same labor pool for his harvests.[155]

His delight at congratulating Baldridge on a great job turned to sadness when Billy revealed his excitement for setting off for the gold fields. As resistant to the gold bug as Chiles was, Baldridge was seemingly equally vulnerable, heading for the Sierra foothills as soon as he could. It would appear that he did all right in the diggings because two years later he was living comfortably on 165 acres of good farmland near the Oakville Grade, on the west side of the Napa Valley, where he settled down for a number of years.[156]

---

[155] Sherburne Cook, *The Conflict Between the California Indian and White Civilization,* Berkeley, University of California Press, 1943, p. 63-64.

[156] *History of Napa and Lake Counties*, California, San Francisco, Slocum Bowen and Company, 1881, p. 379

With Chiles back on his beloved Catacula, the year 1848 drew to a close, and the famous year of the 49ers dawned. Although they are less celebrated than the gold-crazed miners, it was men like Chiles who were more likely to have found prosperity in the gold rush. By now, the hand-hewn gearing of the mill had been replaced by a set of steel shafts, driving and beveled gears from the east coast imported on sailing vessels that had come around Cape Horn. The addition of a fan room and linen sifters for winnowing the grain added to the efficiency of the operation.[157] The huge influx of gold seekers caused demand for anything they needed, including food and whiskey, to skyrocket in price. Chiles traveled to San Francisco to sell his cattle and produce, and his mill ran full-time turning out flour and wheat whiskey under the Catacula label. The small collection of shacks that he remembered from his first sight of the scruffy little hamlet of Yerba Buena by the bay in 1842 was now recognizable as the city San Francisco, and becoming more so every day, the streets choked with wagons and the Bay a forest of masts. These were the ships whose crews had abandoned them and run off to the gold fields. But from wherever the miners had come, all of them

---

[157] John P. Chiles, Chiles papers in the author's possession.

needed to eat and drink, and Chiles was in a very good position to supply both these needs.

Prices for agricultural products began rising in San Francisco in early 1849 and soon reached the stuff of legend. Cattle, which had been the backbone of the California ranching economy for decades, valued at about $1 each [$32 in current values] for their hides and rendered tallow were suddenly selling for as much as $75 [$2,400] on the hoof.[158] The vast cattle ranches of the *Californios* in the southern part of the state struggled to meet the demand. The *rancheros* drove large herds up the coast or central valley to reap the inflated profits. These temporary riches set off a wave of consumption that eventually helped spell the end for many of the profligate ranchers.[159] At the same time, smaller ranchers like Chiles had fewer cattle to sell, but they were close to the market and could get their products to consumers much more easily, claiming top prices.

The experience of this boom continued to influence Chiles's thinking. In his final crossing from the east in 1853, he herded several thousand sheep that he hoped to sell into the California

---

[158] William Heath Davis, *Seventy-five years in California*, San Francisco,1929, p.323 Cited in Robert Glass Cleland, *The Cattle on a Thousand Hills*, San Marino, Huntington Library, 1941, p. 106.

[159] Charles Nordhoff, *California: For Health, Pleasure and Residence, A Book for Travelers and Settlers*, New York, 1873, p.153, Cited in Cleland, p. 106.

market, though by this time many other suppliers were working their way west from Missouri or north from New Mexico and Texas with much the same idea, soon to overwhelm the market and have prices plunge. In the meantime, Chiles was doing so well that he sent for his brothers, hoping to entice them out to California to help him in his enterprise, especially since Baldridge had deserted him for the gold mines. He also poached his brother Joel's eldest son. At the time, Isaac was 21 and had been running his father's substantial warehousing operation for six years. It was located near Independence, serving the Santa Fe Trail, but Isaac was ready for adventure. He responded positively to the invitation from his uncle to see what his fortune could be in California.

Soon after the arrival of brothers Kit and William Chiles, and nephew Isaac in 1849, there was enough help to manage the Catacula, and Chiles moved his family to Sacramento, where further commercial opportunities beckoned. He leased a 360-acre farm on the north bank of the American River and set up several ventures in partnership with fellow pioneer Jerome C. Davis.

Davis, an entrepreneur in the same mold as Chiles, hailed from Ohio. He had arrived in California with Fremont's survey expedition in 1845. The following year, Davis was promoted to the rank of captain in the California Battalion in the Bear Flag rebellion of 1846, and was assigned to return east with dispatches announcing the state of the conflict late that year. Like Chiles, Davis was summoned to give evidence at Fremont's court-martial, though his testimony would have been that of an eye-witness, rather than the character witness which was the role proposed for Chiles.

After the court-martial, Davis returned to Missouri. He remained in St. Louis for almost two years before setting out for California once again in spring 1849 with a small and fast-moving company of nine young men. He arrived in the gold fields later that year, but failed to strike it rich, and eventually made his way to Sacramento, where he ran into Joe B. Chiles. There was more than one way to get California gold, and Chiles and Davis sensed greater opportunities in supplying the miners rather than doing the digging themselves.

Seeing that milk sold for as much as $1 a quart in the gold fields, Davis partnered with Chiles to establish the area's first dairy to supply the local population. At about the same time, the two entrepreneurs constructed a rope ferry across the Sacramento River to accommodate would-be gold seekers on their way to the mines. Run by Kit and Isaac Chiles, it was a simple flatboat connected to a cable strung across the river. It could accommodate two wagons at a time and there was usually a queue waiting to pay the $6 fare for the crossing.[160] There are no records to check, but a similar rope ferry that operated on the American River four miles above Sacramento is said to have cleared an astronomical $11,000 [$341,000] in its first 11 weeks of operation. This was at a time when annual wages were around $350 per year, and the average worker was paid a dollar a day, though in Gold Rush California wages for manual workers were said to be double that rate.

Of course, this was still the frontier, and the conditions of business rewarded those who were ready to confront the attendant challenges. Chiles's and Davis's right to operate on the west bank of the river was questioned by a settler from Kentucky named James McDowell, who had bought some acreage on the river, and who lived a backwoods life in a riverbank cabin with his wife and nine children. In his angry belief that he should share the takings from the ferry, he took to hanging around by the landing, making threats against the operators and passengers alike. All involved largely managed to ignore McDowell until one morning, in one of his rages, he attacked two teamsters who were maneuvering their wagons on to the ferry, killing one and wounding the other. An unarmed passer-by attempted to intervene and McDowell turned

---

[160] Larkey, *Davisville 68, The History and Heritage of the City of Davis*, Davis CA, 1969, p. 161.

on him. In the melee, McDowell was killed. When informed that the dead man lived with his family in a nearby shack, the killer was filled with remorse and offered to submit to whatever punishment the witnesses thought was proper. They reassured him that he had acted in self-defence, and it was noted by one of the witnesses that the regret expressed by McDowell's family was very muted, giving rise to the supposition that he was a violent man who had often taken out his anger on his wife and children. It was said that the widow remarried a short time later.[161]

In the meantime, the ranch on the north bank of the American River occupied by Chiles and his family created social opportunities to his three lively teenage daughters. The ranch was reachable by another rope ferry that charged prices similar to the one he and Davis operated on the Sacramento. It is said that the income of this ferry was enhanced by the fares paid by suitors of Joe Chiles's three daughters. The young swains, among them Jerome Davis, reportedly paid the ferryman the night-time rate of $16 [almost $500 in current values] for transport in order to press their suit at the Chiles house. The payments for ferry crossings to woo Mary Chiles cut into Davis's profits from his and Chiles's joint ventures, but from his perspective, it was worth the money

---

[161] Heinrich Leinhard, *Pioneer at Sutter's Fort 1846-1850, Life and Death of James McDowell*, West Sacramento Historical Society, West Sacramento, CA.

and effort, as he claimed the 15-year-old Mary as his bride early in 1850. He briefly moved into the Chiles household before the couple set up one of their own.

Given the fact that brother Kit and nephew Isaac were both diverted from the Catacula to Sacramento, it is clear that with so many economic opportunities beckoning, the ranch was taking a back seat in Chiles's thinking at the time. The San Francisco market for his wheat and whiskey was assured, though who kept the Catacula running in Chiles's absence is unrecorded. The income from the ferry proved rewarding, if temporary, with both it and the dairy farm subject to regular flooding. The surging waters of the winter of 1852 destroyed the ferry and all but washed the dairy farm "out to sea." But help was at hand, and Chiles was able to offer his two married daughters, Mary and Fanny, and their husbands, Jerome Davis and Gabriel Brown, land that he had bought on the north bank of Putah Creek, about 11 miles to the west of the burgeoning city. Chiles had, by that time, decided that the land in the Sacramento Valley, although rich, and with good transportation links to fast-growing markets, was too flood-prone for his tastes, but he was happy for his sons-in-law to see what they could make of it.

As early as 1850 Chiles had diverted his attention from directly making money from miners anxious to get to the gold fields, and had begun buying up some of the rich farmland west of Sacramento. In the vicinity of Putah Creek he bought 160 acres from William Matthews and his wife Josefa Martin. Later that year, Chiles paid the Baca (Vaca) brothers $10,000 [$303,000] for 4,327 acres of the Rancho Laguna de Santos Callé Mexican Land Grant. It was in a house on that land, on 24 December 1850, that he hosted the wedding of his eldest daughter Elizabeth to Kentuckian Leonard Tulley. Two years later Chiles built a two-story family home close to where the Mace Ranch House now stands near the town of Davis. The property description in the Yolo County Recorder's Office included:

> Beginning at a stake at the water's edge of Putah Creek or River, running north twenty-one degrees ... having two large oaks on the line, one near the creek and one 130 poles [0.4mile] from the beginning place, having for its bearing the gap between the highest and next highest peaks of the highest of the three Buttes on the Sacramento River ...".[162]

What Chiles had bought was part of the Baca Grant, Rancho Laguna de Santos Callé. As far as prospective buyers were

---

[162] Book of Deeds A, p.306-07, cited in Larkey, Davisville, 68, p. 21, Doc. 411, US Land Commission, Bancroft Library, n.d., also cited in Giiffen, p. 79.

concerned, the grant had been issued by Governor Pio Pico in the last hectic days of California as a Mexican province. The grant was a large, rich, and valuable tract running from the ranch of William Wolfskill up near Berryessa Creek on the west side of the valley, to Cache Creek on the east, and north to the swampy edges of the Sacramento River. But the grant was based on a document written for an earlier age of a few ranchers sharing a vast amount of range and farm land, and in this particular case on documents forged by the devious secretary of Mariano Vallejo, Victor Prudon.[163] It was by no means untypical of many of the old land grants in the description of its boundaries, and serves as an illustration of the larger picture across California that plunged the old *Californio* grandees and optimistic early American settlers like Chiles into years of confusion and litigation in which no one was clear where they stood. When he made his original inquiries about the property in 1846, Chiles was at first suspicious, but was later re-assured that the Bacas were the true owners and that their grant was solid. Then, just as he and the Bacas were about to proceed, the war broke out between Mexico and the United States. After the war, with the Gold Rush in full flow, Chiles again went after the property, aware that he was now in competition with a

---

[163] Larkey, Davisville 68, p. 17, *Vaught, After the Gold Rush*, Baltimore MD, The Johns Hopkins University Press, 2007, p. 49.

much larger group of prospective buyers. Convinced that the deal was legitimate, he concluded it in 1850 on the assumption that the new government would protect the rights of property owners from the previous regime.

The Treaty of Guadeloupe Hidalgo of 1848, which ended the war with Mexico, had guaranteed property rights in the conquered territories, but the Gold Rush had multiplied the population of California ten times in three years. The process of deciding on the legitimacy of the claims of the *Californio* grandees, the newly arrived American ranchers, and the squatting post-Gold Rush smallholders was bound to be complicated, and the flood of new settlers made it well nigh impossible.

The nub of the problem stemmed from the fact that the settlement of California had happened so quickly that there was no time for the organization of titles, as in other states on the frontier. The orderly process of the conversion of territorial lands in the public domain being sold by the federal government in 160-acre parcels was superseded by thousands of emigrants confronting a patchwork of large land grants from a previous era. As we have seen in the case of Chiles's Rancho Catacula, the vast majority of the grants that had taken place in the Mexican era reflected the internal *Californio* politics of the 1830s and 1840s, a political culture that had been swept from the scene by the war concluded by the Treaty of Guadalupe Hidalgo.

The California Land Act, passed by Congress in 1851, was meant to interpret the treaty "on the ground." Its aim was to provide a way of resolving the fact that much of the desirable land in California was legally in the hands of a very small number of *Californios* and early arrivals. There was a huge and increasing demand for smallholdings that were more typical of the American settlement pattern. Under the terms of the Act, the claimants to the grants—about 700 in all—were required to have their titles confirmed by a three-member California Land Commission. There were only two possible outcomes. It was either confirmation of the claim and ownership, or rejection, with the land then becoming part of the public domain. The verdict could be appealed to the appropriate Federal District Court and then to the US Supreme Court, if the claimant had the deep pockets and the time to pursue the appeal. The Land Commission heard more than 800 cases between 1852 and 1856. The average length of time for the claimant to get a patent was 17 years, and costs varied wildly, with some law firms charging two and one-half cents an acre and others charging flat fees that varied from $50 to $1,700.[164]

As one legal expert put it:

> Ultimately that struggle pitted those who had objections to the concentration of land in a few hands against those who believed in the sanctity of vested interests; those who recognized the letter and spirit of treaty obligations to Mexico, against those with an antipathy toward Hispanics; those concerned with protecting the public's welfare against real estate speculators; and the civil law against the common law tradition. [165]

Unfortunately for both the *Californios* and those desirous of clear titles in California, the decade of the 1850s was one of turmoil in the growing national conflict between the north and the south. Questions like land titles in faraway California were allowed to drift. The price paid for Congressional neglect was a mass of difficulties that endured for decades.

The California Land Commission began hearing the Baca claims in 1853. The case of the validity of the grant to the Baca's

---

[164] Paul Gates, "Adjudication of Spanish-Mexican Land Claims in California", *Huntington Library Quarterly*, Vol. 21, No. 3, May 1958, pp.234-235.

[165] Fritz, Christian G., *Politics and the Courts: The Struggle Over Land in San Francisco 1846 -1866* (November 4, 2010). Santa Clara Law Review, Vol. 26, No. 1, 1986.p. 127.

and their subsequent land sales to Chiles and others was as messy as it could be. It exemplified the difficulties of adjudicating ownership of grants across the state. In the years between the Gold Rush and the empowering of the Land Commission, the Baca's had sold off various portions of their grant, and some of those purchasers had re-sold their interests. Beyond that, questions were raised about the legitimacy of the approval by the Mexican Departmental Assembly from the origin of the grant by Mariano Vallejo in 1845. This would have to have been ratified by the Governor in Monterey and the Provincial Assembly, which was meeting in Los Angeles. On closer inspection the Commission decided that Pio Pico was not the Constitutional Governor until after he had signed the grant, and that a messenger could not have traversed the distance between Sonoma and Los Angeles before the Assembly adjourned in October 1845. Questions were also asked about the validity of Pico's signature.[166]

Early in 1856, the Commission ruled that, "the documents (of the Baca's) were spurious and that the claimants' right to

---

[166] US Land Case 411, US Land Commission, cited in David Vaught, *After the Gold Rush*, Baltimore, The Johns Hopkins Press, 2007, p. 49

confirmation cannot be sustained."[167] But well before this, in early 1854, probably in the knowledge that the struggle to obtain clear title would be long and expensive, Chiles conveyed his interest in that western part of the grant to Jerome Davis and his wife Mary Chiles, for which Davis paid $4,000 [$114,000], and the eastern part of the grant to Gabriel Brown and his wife Fanny Chiles, for which they paid $5,000 [$143,000].

Now in his mid-forties, Chiles decided that these ranches represented more complications than he wanted in his life. By selling his landholdings in the Sacramento Valley, he had recouped most of the outlay, in straight cash terms, on the $10,000 he had paid the Vaca's, and was happy to be out of the legal quagmire that titles in this part of the Sacramento Valley were becoming. Not for him were the complexities of the emerging California statehood, where government commissions, businessmen, developers, and lawyers held sway. One can imagine Chiles thinking that it was best to pass these holdings in the Sacramento Valley on to the next generation, who would have the energy to fight for them.

---

[167] US Land Case. 411 n.d. US Land Commission, Bancroft Library, Cited in Giffen, pp.80-81.

CHAPTER 11

The Final Crossings 1853-1854

As the 1850s wore on, Chiles returned to the business he knew best, working with his elder brother Joel to profit from driving livestock from Missouri to California. Joe corresponded regularly with Joel over the purchase of sheep, cattle, and his favorite, mules, which he prized from his experience in crossing the country several times with them. The offspring of the mating of a female horse and a male donkey, mules were instrumental in opening up the American West. These sure-footed animals could carry up to 250 pounds, survive on rough forage, did not require feed, and could operate in the arid higher elevations of the Rockies and Sierra. They served as the main cargo carrier to the west from Missouri during the heyday of the fur trade and on through the nineteenth century. In most cases, Joe Chiles relied on the ability of Joel to source livestock, especially when it came to mules. In 1852 he wrote, "It is a matter [choosing a mule] I rely on your judgment but I will only say that I wish to have a good jack [male mule] and had rather wait and get the best or find a good two-years-old, and another afterwards."[168]

In the early 1850s, having seen his three daughters well married, Chiles might have hoped that his son James would find a way to settle down, but that did not appear to be happening, so Joseph decided that perhaps a return to Missouri and a few more years of schooling might give James the maturity he needed. Joe consequently wrote to the ever-helpful brother Joel to ask if he would take James in again and supervise his schooling. Joe sent some money to cover costs and James went east in the spring of 1852.[169]

With his son back in Missouri, the following year Chiles began to think of making another trip himself. In the spring of 1853 he prepared himself for the now-familiar journey that he had helped to establish. There is no record of the route, but we can assume that it was via the Carson River, the Forty Mile Desert, the Humboldt Sink, Salt Lake City, up to Ft. Bridger, South Pass, and eastward following the trail that was now virtually a road. In less than four months he was back in Independence.

As usual, he stayed with Joel and his sister-in-law Azuba in his hometown of Independence. By this time Joel was one of the

---

[168] Letter from J.B. Chiles to J.F. Chiles, San Francisco, Jan. 31, 1852, Society of California Pioneers.
[169] Ibid.

most substantial citizens of Jackson County, a highly successful frontier entrepreneur. He was a wealthy shopkeeper, who also made loans and speculated in frontier commodities, along with having an interest in the freighting and warehousing business of the Santa Fe Trail. When he died suddenly in 1855, his estate was valued at $75,000, a substantial sum at the time, which would have made him a multi-millionaire ($2.1 million) in 2015 dollars.[170]

A regular visitor to the house of Joel and Azuba that autumn of 1853 was a close friend of Azuba's, Margaret Jane Garnhart, who was visiting from Harpers Ferry, Virginia. Joseph, a widower of almost 20 years standing, was smitten with the twenty-seven-year-old Margaret. She returned the feelings, but Joseph's plans for a return to California were already firming up and necessitated that the courtship be of short duration. Within two months, on Christmas Day 1853, they were married in a small family ceremony at Joel and Azuba's house.

Chiles was forty-three-years-old and had crossed the 2,000 miles of plains six times. Margaret had no experience of the overland crossing of the western half of the continent but must

---

[170] Joanne Chiles Eakin, *Walter Chiles of Jamestown*, Independence MO, Wee Print, 1983, p.p. 105-107.; Samuel H. Williamson, "Seven Ways to Compute the Relative Value of a U.S. Dollar Amount, 1774 to present," *Measuring Worth*, 2017.

have known that once married to a man like Joseph she soon would. The newlyweds made their plans for a May departure. By the time spring rolled around, Margaret was five months pregnant, but she and her new husband were not setting out into the great unknown that had confronted the emigrants of the early years. When they departed with their wagon train on 1 May, the trail was now a road in all but name, and the sight of wagon trains accompanied by as many as 2,500 sheep, oxen, and cattle was commonplace. One diary of the time describes the trail as being 100 feet wide, with the grass killed by the constant procession of wagons, and not a stick of wood available with which to make a fire.[171]

Chiles's entrepreneurial bent and access to capital meant that he would be traveling with a sizable herd and wagonloads of goods for sale. Many others had taken commercial goods and herds overland to the west coast successfully, arriving with their wagons intact and most of their animals alive. At the same time, there were no guarantees that all, or any, of the livestock would make it all the way across the plains to claim the high prices that they could command in California. For all its familiarity, there

---

[171] Lydia Waters, Account of a Trip Across the Plains in 1855, Quarterly of the Society of California Pioneers, Vol.VI, No. 2, June 1929, p. 64.

were many rivers to ford and dry grassless stretches to cross that would tax the survival and health of all the animals on the trail.

All the same, many of the river crossings that had vexed earlier emigrants were now bridged or had ferry service, which made travel easier, at least for those with the money to pay the tolls. There was, for example, a new bridge across the Platte made of hewn timbers, reported to have cost $14,000 [$401,000] to construct. For individual wagons the $1.50, or perhaps more, for crossing on a bridge or a ferry was worth the money for the time it saved, but with a herd of livestock, one had to make a calculation.[172] Ever the optimist, Chiles attempted to swim his herd across the Platte, and ended up losing half of his 2,000 sheep in the fast-moving current. This was a setback, but as was his custom, Joseph was traveling with wagons loaded with goods for sale or barter as well as his livestock, so he could still anticipate covering his costs for the overland crossing and perhaps making a profit. To cut costs further, he pioneered a new route to the west of Fort Laramie by staying on the north bank of the Platte, thereby avoiding an expensive river crossing, a route which came to be

---

[172] John D. Unruh, *The Plains Across*, Urbana: Univ. of Illinois Press, 1993, p.289.

called Chiles' Cutoff, outflanking the bridge and ferry profiteers.[173]

Although he departed later than most of the other trains that spring, Chiles proceeded at his usual leisurely pace. His train was following the well-worn trail toward their destination. Surrounded by his herd, the Chiles party were similar to many other trains on the way west that year. It is said that the numbers of cattle and sheep totaled 100,000 head. As historian George Stewart put it:

> In the old days the idea of driving cattle to California would have been a coals to Newcastle notion. But the demands of the greatly increased population had depleted the herds of the ranchos. Besides, the American farmers wanted something better than the Mexican longhorns. Similarly, better breeds of sheep were needed. So a great business of droving suddenly developed, highly speculative, since a single stampede might ruin all your prospects. Though the losses on the road were considerable, the venture as a whole was successful.[174]

Chiles was only one of many who saw the Gold Rush-fueled market for livestock in California as a huge opportunity. Word of

---

[173] National Park Service, National Historic Trails, Auto Tour Route Interpretive Guide, 2011, p. 9.
[174] Stewart, *California Trail*, Berkeley p. 307.

high prices on the west coast had made it back to Texas by the early 1850s. With thousands of miners pouring into the California gold mines from all over the world, the local meat supply could not keep pace with demand, and Texas ranchers found that cattle bought for $5-$15 a head in San Antonio brought $60-$100 in Sacramento or San Francisco. Cattle breeders from other western states like Arkansas seized on the opportunity as well.[175]

Even though Los Angeles County alone was supplying 25,000-30,000 head of cattle during the boom, it was not enough for the hungry miners, and thousands of animals were trailed overland from Missouri as well as from Texas to the Sacramento Valley.[176]

From Texas the cattle-drive trail began at San Antonio, struck west to Franklin and El Paso, and then headed for the Gila River and the Colorado River by way of Tucson, Arizona. The route crossed the Colorado Desert into California, then the herds were trailed to Warner's Ranch southeast of Los Angeles to recuperate. From there, they were driven into Los Angeles or San Diego, and from these cities they were driven north to the major

---

[175] J. H. Atkinson, "Cattle Drives from Arkansas to California Prior to the Civil War", *Arkansas Historical Quarterly* 28, (Autumn 1969) pp. 275-281.

[176] Richard H. Dillon, ed., *California Trail Herd*, Los Gatos CA, Talisman Press, 1961, cited http://.ancestry.com/~crow2000/california_trail_herd_intro.htm

population centers of San Francisco and Sacramento. On the northern route, which Chiles was following, the Los Angeles *Star* estimated that 90,000 head of cattle had passed Fort Kearny, Nebraska, that year *en route* to California, and the governor of California reported at the start of 1855 that 62,000 head had entered the state.[177]

California sheep production, also unable to keep up with demand, was supplemented by livestock from out of state, notably New Mexico, as prices rose from $1 a head to $15 in the months after the discovery of gold. The first flocks in 1849-1850, totaling 25,000 head, entered via the Mojave Desert and turned north up the Central Valley toward the markets of the northern population centers.[178]

The migration of 1853 had been the largest since the year of the 49ers, and much of the increase was women and children, who now made up almost a third of those on the trail. One of those westering women, Sarah Sutton, in her diary described the scene around her train on 12 May 1854:

> ... there was about 30 wagons in sight and about 1000 cattle there appeared to be a string about a mile long.

---

[177] Ibid, introduction.

[178] Edward N. Wentworth, *The Mississippi Valley Historical Review,* Vol. 28, No. 4 (Mar., 1942), pp. 507-538

Roads very hard and dusty there is about 10 thousand head of cattle campt near us, and 100 wagons, mostly bound for California. Our cattle mix together and makes a great deal of trouble. We hear more noise than if we were in the bustle of town, the men hoy hoy hoying, the cattle bawling and the bells rattling. Oh what a time.[179]

The Indians, too, were becoming more commercially minded. Tribes at the eastern end of the trail were likely to pester emigrants, not with threats of violence, but by charging tolls for their bridges or payments for the pasturage of animals. There were also reports that year of a party driving 4,000 sheep that had a man murdered and 1,000 sheep driven off. It was also said that some of the depredations, although committed by local Indians, were instigated by white renegades.[180]

The emigrant numbers in 1854 were reduced from the previous year but still totaled about 12,000. What was striking was the speed of their crossing, with parties starting to arrive in California in August. One of them included an 81-year-old woman who claimed to have recovered her health on the trail. The

---

[179] Sarah Sutton, Diary entry, May 12, 1854, Holmes and Leckie, eds., Univ. of Nebraska Press, 1998, p. 38.

[180] Sarah Sutton, A Travel Diary In 1854, entries April 26 and April 30, published in *Covered Wagon Women*, Lincoln, Univ. of Nebraska Press, 1987, p. 34-35; Stewart, p. 311.

same month noted the arrival of a party in the Sacramento valley with 400 head of cattle, having made the crossing in three and a half months. Meanwhile, Chiles, having lost half his herd on the Platte, detoured southwest to Salt Lake City with the aim of bartering his goods to make up the numbers of his livestock.

The year 1854 was also noteworthy as marking the end of the long, relatively peaceful conditions on the plains after almost a decade and a half of travel by whites. That year a lame cow from a Mormon party wandered into a camp of hungry Lakota Sioux awaiting the delivery from their US Indian agent of their annual annuity goods outside Fort Laramie. The hungry Indians slaughtered the stray cow for food. This was the source of a complaint made by the Mormons to the Fort, and an insistence that the Sioux pay $25 rather than compensate the owner with a horse or one of their own cows. Into the ensuing stalemate, in the middle of the large Sioux camp marched a hot-headed and inexperienced young officer, Lt. John L. Grattan, along with his drunken interpreter, 28 soldiers, and a cannon. The soldiers used their cannon to wound two warriors and kill the chief, who was trying to negotiate a settlement. The enraged Indians, following years of acquiescence, turned on the soldiers and within minutes the lieutenant and all of his men lay dead. This was the opening skirmish of the wars that would grow in intensity over the next three decades, finally resulting in the reduction of the proud plains tribes to reservation-bound remnants, decimated by alcohol, disease, and privation.[181]

In 1854, even with all the improvements of the trail and the knowledge of what to expect, how quickly a wagon train made the crossing was still a matter of luck and timing. Thunderstorms, flooded crossings, and early snows in the Sierra could still spell disaster. That year the early trains made record time. Those who came later were unlucky in encountering early snows. As we have seen, one of these unfortunates was "that veteran of veterans" Joseph Chiles. He left Independence on 1 May, and went by Salt Lake City hoping to make up some of his losses through barter of trade goods for the livestock he had lost on the Platte. From Salt Lake City, he crossed the desert and took the Carson Route, which he had helped open in '41 and '48. Unfortunately, as was his custom, he had taken his time. Caught by a snowstorm on the pass, he was forced to abandon several loaded wagons, and lost about 100 cattle. Finally, as he had done so often before, he made it through. He arrived in California with 115 head of fine cattle, including a thoroughbred Durham bull. Whether the remainder of

---

[181] Unruh, John, D, *The Plains Across*, Urbana, Univ. of Illinois Press, 1979, p. 214-215; Stewart, California Trail, p. 312.

the sheep were bartered in Salt Lake City or herded across the mountains was not recorded.

Isaac Chiles, Joe B's nephew, described the California end of the trail in a letter to his brother back in Missouri. From Sacramento in September 1854 he wrote:

> Jim Crow Chiles got in to the [Sacramento] valley a few days ago. He said he left Uncle Jo on the Humbolt and did not think he would get in with his stock for two or three weeks yet. Gabriel Brown started out to meet him about ten days ago, he said he thought he would stay with the stock and let Uncle Jo come in ahead as they are a little fearful of having snow before they get in, so the boys report. Jim says that [Joe] had lost when he left about a thousand head of sheep mostly drowned swimming south Platte.[182]

This letter gives the first mention of the name Jim Crow in connection with the California Chiles. The 21-year-old Jim, who had been working in the family business as a freight wagon master on the Santa Fe Trail, succumbed briefly to the lure of California and the opportunity to accompany his uncle out west. It

---

[182] Letter, Courtesy of Jackson County, [MO] Historical Society, cited in Giffen, p.89.

would appear that, having achieved his goal of crossing the plains and "seeing the elephant", Jim decided that California was not enough to his liking to keep him there and he returned to Missouri not long thereafter.

According to contemporaries, Jim was very handsome, and an agile, graceful dancer. These attributes earned him the nickname Jim Crow, in direct reference to his moves in the popular dance of the 1850s called the "Jim Crow Set." Unfortunately, Jim's positive attributes were offset by a hot temper and a willingness to see differences of opinion, particularly those about slavery, settled at the point of a gun. The year following his return from California, 1856, he became involved in the violence between the pro and anti-slavery factions that were coalescing across western Missouri and eastern Kansas in anticipation of the national intersectional violence to come. In the semi-lawless conditions, violent men came to the fore. In 1855, Jim Crow Chiles had been tried and acquitted for his first murder in Independence, and rather than settling down after marrying one of prettiest girls in Jackson County in 1859, he became more and more involved in the violent behavior that was roiling Missouri and Kansas. In the murderous prelude for the war that was to follow, Missouri and Kansas became a fierce and ill-defined theater of conflict along the border. It was a world of cruelty and senseless violence, and Jim Crow Chiles stood out for his fearsome and brutal reputation. In the latter stages of the American Civil War, along with several of his relatives, Jim rode with William Quantrill's infamous guerrillas, spreading havoc and destruction, and although many of them were killed, Jim survived another eight years, only to find his end in an argument with a deputy marshal on the courthouse steps in Independence in 1873.

But this was years into the future and 2,000 miles away from the California life that his uncle Joe was building. It would appear that the 1854 crossing was a financial disaster, with the loss of 1,000 head of sheep crossing the South Platte, and the loss of wagons and cattle crossing the high Sierra. At the end of 1854, the ever-sanguine Joe Chiles summed up his final trip in a letter to his brother and business partner Joel:

Brother Frank, [Joel Franklin] I write you from San Francisco all well … I had a fare trip to the sink of the Humbolt River. From there I lost one third of my stock in number and at least one half in value. I thought several times I would loose all, the cause I cannot give any account. They died day and night. I got through with the mare and colt from Hambrite and 8 mules. The balance died, the cow and calf from Sanders died. What I have looks well. I did well with my goods in exchanging for cattle [in Salt Lake City] but they all died. I think I have 3 or 400 steers out of 2000 yoke I bought at the lake. The cattle that worked all the way stood it best. I lost over half of my sheep of the fine sheep I have one buck and one ewe … I write this to inform you about money matters. I shall send you a thousand or 2500 dollars by the next mail and want you to pay it out for me. I shall send directions with it. The times are hard, we have no rain yet … Myself and Davis bought 11 hundred head of cattle for 11 thousand dollars cash. The cattle were Spanish so you will see it is a bad time to drive cattle to this market. We sell beef at 12.5 cts American [stock] and 10 Spanish…[183]

With this optimistic tone, Joe B. Chiles summarized a four month trip in which he had walked 2,000 miles, losing the better part of two herds of sheep and cattle, and fought his way over the crest of the Sierra in early snows with a new wife and newborn child. Having covered the business issues of the trip, Joe sent news of family matters, announcing the birth of a son on the trail, near present-day Winnemucca, Nevada. He well knew that things could have turned out far worse and chose to focus on the positives.

---

[183] Letter, Courtesy, Jackson County [MO] Historical Society, cited in Giffen, p.88.

We have a fine boy and call him William. We found him on the Humbolt on our way out. Not bad luck. All well. I cannot write about all hands but will just say all is well as far as I know. I have a [law] suit in Sacramento for the money I lost some years ago and a good chance to get 20 thousand dollars of it and maybe more. We have a large lot of fat cattle on hand and expect to sell as soon as it rains.[184]

This was probably the last communication between the two brothers. Joel died suddenly at home on the 1 February 1855 and was buried in the Chiles family cemetery in Jackson County the next day, breaking the strongest connection Joe Chiles had with the state he had long considered his home, but to which he never returned.

---

[184] Ibid, pp. 88-89.

CHAPTER 12

A California Family

Joe B was gradually homing in on the life he wanted to lead in California, as head of a family on a substantial 8,500-acre land grant in his own small valley. Shortly before Joel died, Chiles had relinquished all interest in his lands north of Putah Creek in the Sacramento Valley. As we have seen, he sold the western half of his original purchase from the Vaca brothers to his son-in-law Jerome Davis for $4,000, together with all stock and improvements; with the eastern half of the purchase going to his other son-in-law, Gabriel Brown, for $5,000.[185]

This was excellent and highly valuable land that produced large acreages of wheat and barley, and the farms were well stocked with cattle, horses, and mules, all of which were much in demand in the mining operations in the Sierra. For these holdings, Joe Chiles paid almost $1,300 ($37,000) in state and county taxes that year.[186] It seems clear that he wanted to be rid of them in order to focus on the Catacula and other parts of Napa County

---

[185] *Davisville '68, City of Davis*, CA, p. 22.

[186] Joseph B. Chiles papers, San Francisco, Society of California Pioneers Library. Samuel H. Williamson, "Seven Ways to Compute the Relative Value of a U.S. Dollar Amount, 1774 to present," *Measuring Worth*, 2017

while setting up his two daughters and their husbands with good agricultural properties that would produce a comfortable living. At the same time, he was well aware of the legal battles being fought by his son-in-law Jerome Davis who, with co-appellant Champ Hutchinson, in April 1858 sent him an urgent letter from San Francisco, telling him:

> It is absolutely necessary that you be here tomorrow night or next day, as things now stand we shall be very likely to lose our case unless you get here at once ... The Court meets on Monday morning here, must have you here some time beforehand in order to get ready for Court when it meets ... Don't delay a moment.[187]

It is possible that four years earlier, when he sold the ranches that had formed part of the Rancho Laguna de Santos Callé to his sons-in-law, Chiles would have known that the titles were not as solid as they might have been. Perhaps he wanted to put them in the hands of a younger generation who would have the energy to fight for them, and who shared his optimism about rising land values and constantly expanding local markets for agricultural products, particularly beef and wheat. Chiles certainly shared this optimism with Jerome Davis, whose two decades of struggle,

---

[187] Letter, Courtesy of Henry Lee Chiles, cited in Giffen, p. 82.

litigation, and negotiation would be emblematic of the problems of California landowners without clear title. That lay in the future and in the 1850s Davis aggressively expanded his holding to the point where it was the economic and agricultural center of the district and comprised a slaughterhouse, a steam flour mill, a dairy, and two large "manufacturing shops."[188] In this, Jerome had the assistance of various other Davis family members who joined him from Ohio, and a favorite nephew of Joe B, Isaac S. Chiles, who worked on the Davis farm as superintendent for several years.

By 1863 the Davis farm had expanded to 7,000 acres and was valued at $21,000, [$414,000 in today's values] even though that year its owner was $40,000 in debt, including a note to his father-in-law for $15,000 at an interest rate of 1.5% per month. In the wake of the tempestuous rainfall that year, he had to engage in a slight-of-hand with his father-in-law to hide his personal property from his creditors and the county assessor. Joe B. had survived the raging weather better on the high ground of Chiles Valley and agreed to assume the payments of Davis's debts in exchange for his livestock. This was a paper transaction only,

---

[188] Vaught, *After the Gold Rush*, p.60.

meant to shelter Davis's assets from his creditors, and it seems to have worked, at least in the short term.[189]

In spite of Chiles's and Davis's optimism that things would eventually right themselves, there remained the unresolved question of clear title to the land. Their hopes rose in 1862 when two northern California members of the House of Representatives, encouraged by syndicates of land speculators, introduced a bill to "quiet land titles" in California. Their legislation directed that, as long as grantees had acted in good faith, and settled and improved their properties, the purchasers of questionable Mexican land grants could buy the land at the legal minimum of $1.25 an acre without regard to the usual 160-acre maximum. When the bill finally passed in 1863 it promised windfall profits for the San Francisco-based investors in Mariano Vallejo's old Rancho Suscol. The gracious land grants of the Mexican period had become the object of speculation for syndicates of investors for whom they were merely financial instruments. The bill to quiet land titles in its final form applied only to Suscol, but Davis was greatly encouraged. If the principle was now established, he felt optimistic that he could request the same special legislation for the claimants of the Rancho Laguna

---

[189] Ibid. p. 93.

de Santos Callé. In the summer of 1863, he and his wife Mary set out for Washington DC to pursue Davis's goal of settled title to his ranch. Helped by the junior senator from California, John Conness, Davis petitioned Congress in March 1864 to pass a law that would enable him to purchase clear title to his land at $1.25 an acre. This eventually occurred at the end of June, which delighted Davis, though the costs of staying in wartime Washington had necessitated the sale at auction of most of his personal property from the ranch, from farm implements to furniture. Jerome and Mary stayed on in Washington until December the following year, when they returned to Sacramento to defend his claim against squatters who had marked off a number of 160-acre parcels. The following July, Congress, exhausted by fifteen years of argument and influence peddling, passed "An Act to Quiet Land Titles in California," surrendering the ultimate fate of the ownership of the land to the state.[190]

In the meantime, Davis was successful in his struggle with the squatters, and he was eventually notified in March 1867 that his claim was in order and he had three months to make his payment of almost $10,000. To raise the money, he had to sell the last of his prized possessions, his herd of horses, which followed

---

[190] Thirty-ninth Congress, Session 1, Chapter 219, 1866.

the furniture and farm implements under the auctioneer's gavel. Davis paid for his acreage on 16 May 1867, and this should have ended the matter satisfactorily, but negotiations were held in abeyance over almost 3,000 acres, in other words, almost half his holding, that was put into doubt as "Swamp and Overflowed lands" claimed by both Davis and the state of California. There would be a decision about this issue made by the US Government Land Office pending further investigation.[191] Davis returned to Washington in August 1867, convinced that the best way to deal with the federal government was in person. He was also happy to be away from his ranch which was now a mere shadow of the vibrant enterprise it had been. Beset by creditors, he had even transferred title to his father, so he did not technically own the land for which he had fought so hard.

His presence in Washington did not ultimately guarantee his success in the pursuit of title to all of his land. After yet more representations, the state was given priority over Davis for title of the 2,900 acres of Swamp and Overflow land. He had spent almost two decades in pursuit of title to the ranch that he had bought from his father-in-law. When he finally received his

---

[191] *Solano Press*, March 13, 1867; May 8, 1867; *Woodland News*, March 30, 1867, May 18, 1867, cited in Vaught, *After the Gold Rush*, Baltimore, The Johns Hopkins University Press, 2009, pp. 98-99.

special act granting title early in 1869, the money he realized from the sale was already committed to satisfy his creditors. The year before, most of the ranch had been sold for $80,000 to promoters of the town of Davisville, and to provide a right of way for the California Pacific Railroad, which was about to become the first transcontinental railroad.[192] After the sale, from which he netted little, Davis and his wife Mary moved to Sacramento, where he became involved in local politics until his death in 1881, leaving an estate of less than $2,000.[193]

Unfortunately, his brother-in law, Gabriel Brown, was not a good or lucky businessman either. His ownership of the ranch also coincided with the decade of adverse weather. Climatic conditions in the1850s were extremely variable, something that climate scientists now identify as a marked shift, from the abnormally cool and moderately dry conditions of the previous two centuries (the "Little Ice Age"), to the relatively warm and wet conditions that have characterized the region in the modern period.[194] In 1858, after a run of bad years, Brown was forced to mortgage his ranch to Sacramento banker Benjamin Hastings.

---

[192] *Davisville '68*, pp. 49-51.

[193] *Davisville '68*, p. 162.

[194] Stine, *Climate 1650-1850*,
https://pubs.usgs.gov/dds/dds/43/VOL_II/VII_CO2.Pdf

Unable to maintain that mortgage, two years later he turned to his father-in-law, and Joe B. took over the debt payments. Brown hung on by leasing out a large portion of his land to neighboring farmers. But his run of bad luck was not finished. The winter of 1861-62 was marked by almost continuous rains, and snow at higher elevations between November and January. Then on 9 January the heavens opened and a record level of rainfall blanketed the entire west coast, falling as huge amounts of snow in the mountains. The farmers of the Central Valley had struggled to survive the rain, but their troubles were far from over. A warming trend followed the inundation, with predictably large amounts of snow melt swelling the rivers even further.

Across the entire affected area, any farms or businesses near rivers or watercourses were devastated, with houses, dams, mills, fields, and farm animals swept away. Property damage was put at a conservative $10 million, [$200 million] with a quarter of the taxable real estate in California destroyed, bankrupting the state.[195] The great flood of 1862 established a rainfall record in California and washed away Brown's hopes, along with the farmers to whom he was renting his land. He sold his interest later that year to his cousin by marriage, Isaac Chiles, for a mere

---

[195] Up and Down California in 1860-64, Journal of William H. Brewer, New Haven, Yale University Press, p. 243.

$2,000. The Browns moved to Napa County, presumably to take advantage of the proximity of Joe B. Chiles, before eventually moving to Los Angeles and disappearing from the story.[196]

Isaac Skinner Chiles, Joel's eldest son and a favorite of his uncle Joe B, was prospering in California, partly with the help of his uncle. Though he arrived in 1849, the lure of easy riches in the mines somehow never touched him. Isaac had a look around northern California, doubtless including his uncle's Rancho Catacula, before he settled down in a job that suited his steady temperament, as telegraph operator for the California Stage Company, which ran lines to most points of California, with connections to transcontinental stages and the Oregon Territory.[197] Isaac worked on the Sacramento and Napa line for about two years, then became a cattle buyer for a slaughterhouse in Sacramento. In the early 1860s he became superintendent of Jerome and Mary Davis's farm. After two years in this role, he had saved enough to buy part of Gabriel Brown's 3,200 acre tract. From a modest beginning in the post-war depression years of the 1860s, Isaac developed a large farming operation, including

---

[196] Chiles Family Papers, *Davisville '68*, p. 29.

[197] Sacramento Daily Union, Vol 20, No. 3047, Jan 1, 1861, p. 4; *Davisville '68*, p. 154-55.

raising stock and grain, and became a highly respected member of the new community of Davisville.

Now in his thirties, Isaac had for years resisted the blandishments from his family about marrying, but he finally succumbed in 1863. The object of his affection was Bridget Dee, an Irish girl in her early twenties from County Waterford, whom he had gotten to know when she was working as the housekeeper and companion of his cousin, Frances "Fanny" Brown. Isaac and Bridget were married by the bishop of San Francisco in February that year and quickly began a family. Before the end of the year, their first son, James Franklin, was born, followed by another son, William, in 1868. Isaac continued to develop his farming and property interests in the area. To meet expenses in the difficult years of the 1860s he apparently rented land to two neighbors in exchange for a share-cropping arrangement. Isaac also did thriving business pasturing cattle and horses at $1.50 a head per month. He also raised his own cattle, as well as crops of peaches and pomegranates. Chiles sold produce to travelers on the road to Sacramento, and dairy products and cattle in the city. As his situation improved, he invested in business lots in the new town of Davisville, named after his aunt's husband, purchasing one of the first business sites in 1869, and later acquiring some twelve city lots. Their prosperity and parental concern were manifest after their son James contracted infantile paralysis (polio) in 1865 at age two. After trying the local medical advice, in 1869 Bridget boarded the newly completed transcontinental railroad to head to the east, seeking help for her son's condition in New York and Philadelphia.[198]

With the birth of a second son William, in 1868, in spite of their worries about the health of James, the future looked promising for Isaac and Bridget, but five years later, in the days before antibiotics, Isaac suddenly succumbed to pneumonia. The devastated Bridget faced the prospect of trying to manage what had become a successful and complex farming operation while raising two small boys. But help was at hand in the form of Isaac's younger brother Phineas, who was summoned from Missouri to help with the managing of the estate. A widower, thirteen years younger than Isaac, Phineas had already worked for the government on the frontiers of both New Mexico and Colorado, which included several skirmishes with the Navajo, and found employment on frontier stock farms before settling down on a farm in Missouri.

Phineas had traveled to California to take up management duties on his brother's ranch, but it was not long before the

---

[198] Chiles Family papers in the author's possession.

relationship of the widower and the widow became more than a business arrangement. Phineas disposed of his Missouri property and looked forward to a permanent existence in California. He and Bridget were married early in 1877 by Bishop Alemany of San Francisco. They continued to develop the prosperous foundations laid by Isaac, and Phineas became a loving father to his brother's sons.

A document from 1879 is testament to Phineas's prosperity built on the platform established by his older brother. In the latter part of the 1870s, salesmen for "illustrated histories" of various counties called at the ranches in the Sacramento Valley, offering to immortalize these pioneer families and their land holdings through drawings, biographies, and photographic portraits. The *Illustrated Atlas and History of Yolo County* was one such publication.

Phineas, as the new master of the ranch, spared no expense in buying the entire package. In 1879 he bought the two lithographic drawings of the ranch, an extended 600-word biography (at two-and-one-half cents a word), and a full-page family portrait of himself, his new wife, and his two stepsons—for what must have been at least $1,000 [about $25,000]. The top lithograph is of the farm and residence [built in 1852 for Gabriel and Fanny Chiles Brown] against the backdrop of the coast mountains. The perspective is looking west, toward the town of Davisville, with two locomotives departing from the depot. "The detailed drawing of the ranch exudes order, neatness and comfort."[199]

In the illustration, large oak trees shade the house. A buggy proceeds up the lane to the residence, drawn by two matched horses. Also visible are walnut and fig trees. Included in the drawing are the barn, carriage house, corrals, chicken yard, and grape arbor. The other lithograph of the stockyards facing south was equally striking. The illustrator depicts the ranch's prize-winning cattle, horses, hogs, and sheep with stunning clarity.[200] The ensemble represented a conscious attempt to bring an economic and historical solidity to "the old Chiles ranch", distancing it from the get-rich-quick, boom-and-bust nature that formed the background of much of California economic life at the time.

Isaac's and Phineas's development of the family ranch was continued by Isaac's sons, particularly the elder, James Franklin (Frank) Chiles. Because of his childhood illness, he was educated privately on the ranch for several years before being sent in 1876 to the newly opened St. Patrick's Institute in Sacramento, run by the Catholic order of the Christian Brothers. Apparently

---

[199] Vaught, p. 180.
[200] *Davisville '68*, pp. 29-31.

dissatisfied with the education there, Bridget sent James down to Santa Clara College to try the Jesuit educational regime for two years. As James was still dogged by ill health including asthma, it was thought that the drier air of the Chiles Valley might provide the cure, and he was sent to Napa County in 1881 for three years. The inland climate seemed to agree with the young man, and after 1884 he finished his education by "traveling widely" for several years before taking charge of the main part of the ranch.[201]

Once in charge of ranch operations, Frank oversaw the transition from the wheat-and-cattle culture of his father and step-father, to a fruit-and-nut agriculture, principally involving the development of almonds as one of the predominant cash crops of the region. Almond trees had flourished in the area since the early days of Jerome Davis, but their popularity took off after the invention and local manufacture of the first successful almond huller by a local farmer in 1893. This was followed by subsidiary inventions to extract almond by-products, and local ranchers, most of them second-generation agriculturalists, found themselves responding to a worldwide market. Fifteen of them formed the Davisville Almond Growers Association, an early grower's cooperative, in 1897. They constructed warehousing and shipping

---

[201] Chiles Family papers.

facilities to meet the demand. Frank Chiles was a charter member of the Association and elected as its first secretary-treasurer. Success followed success, and the organization shared out $75,000 [$2.2 million] between its members in 1902. They gained worldwide attention with a prize at the St. Louis World Fair in 1904. In 1910 the Davisville cooperative joined with several other California associations to form the California Almond Growers Exchange—today's Blue Diamond cooperative.[202]

Frank Chiles continued the development of the ranch that he inherited. He raised purebred, prize-winning stock and became one of the elder citizens of the town of Davisville, and one who claimed the first telephone in the county, the first electric line into his house, and the role of first promoter of sugar beets as a crop in the Valley. Chiles was also the first to hire Japanese pickers for his almond crop, helping to integrate the agricultural labor market. He was respected as an officer of the Almond Growers Association, and his family's social position was secure, particularly after his marriage to Maude Buneman, a San Francisco socialite, in 1897. Active in civic life and local Democratic politics, in 1900 Chiles was elected State

---

[202] David Vaught, *Cultivating California*, Baltimore, Johns Hopkins University Press, 1999, p. 13; Vaught, *After the Gold Rush*, Johns Hopkins University Press, 2007, p. 217.

Assemblyman for the Yolo County district, and in 1913 he sat on the Board of Directors of the Bank of Davis, ensuring the continuing presence of the Chiles family in this part of the Sacramento Valley.[203]

But what of the patriarch? By the 1860s he had distanced himself from his connections to the Sacramento Valley, and here the documented thread of Joe B. Chiles's life begins to unravel, or at least the colors start to fade. Never a great one for writing or keeping records, in the 1870s Chiles now focused on settling himself into the fabric of daily California rural life, as it was lived in Napa and Lake counties, particularly in the towns of Rutherford and St. Helena. His days of exploring, of leading companies of migrants across great distances, were over. The records and mentions of his name become more episodic. He was well known in the small communities where he lived, but for the most part he lived quietly.

The mill in Chiles Valley continued to add to his prosperity. In 1874 the concern milled 400 tons of wheat with an output of nine barrels of flour a day. Whether it was all Chiles's wheat, we do not know, but with a barrel of flour selling at $12-$15, this would have represented a handsome income, likely to have been

---

[203] Chiles Family papers; Vaught, *Cultivating California*, p. 92. *Davisville '68*, pp. 64-65.

in the neighborhood of $40,000--$50,000, or more than $1million in modern currency.[204] And flour was not the only source of income from the mill. The previous decade, with the help of his son-in-law Leonard Tulley, married to Chiles's eldest daughter Elizabeth, the mill was producing wheat whiskey, and in 1864 paid taxes on 2,142 gallons of proof spirits sold.[205]

The details of Chiles's life that we are able to glean from family correspondence and the occasional newspaper reference from these later years reflect the great events and trends shaping the new state of California more so than Chiles's impact on them. Never one for politics, the only office Joe B would accept was the first Vice-Presidency of the Society of California Pioneers, from 1851 to 1853, recognition by his peers of Chiles's pivotal role in the making of California. The Society was formed in 1850 and open to all men who had lived in California for at least three years. It aimed to "cultivate social bonds, to collect and preserve information related to California history, and to perpetuate the memory of early pioneers."[206] Funded by San Francisco

---

[204] Helen Giffen, p. 84; Samuel H. Williamson, "Seven Ways to Compute the Relative Value of a U.S. Dollar Amount, 1774 to present," *Measuring Worth*, April 2017

[205] Napa Family History Center, IRS Tax Assessment List, April 1864; Excise Taxes 1866. St. Helena *Star*, June 17, 1904.

[206] http://www.californiapioneers.org/home/history/.

millionaire James Lick, at one time the richest man in California, the Society grew and ultimately occupied a permanent home, Pioneer Hall in downtown San Francisco.

The fact that there was now a society to celebrate and maintain the memory of those who had arrived before 1850, spoke volumes about how quickly California was changing. Beyond mid-century, most of the members of Joe Chiles's generation of pioneers had largely moved away from the center of the stage. The skills and attitudes that had led them to leave "civilization" and cross largely uncharted territories were not the ones in demand now that civilization had caught up with them. Having said that, Joe B still had one last trip across the plains left in him.

On the trip west in 1854 with his bride of nine months, Joe B had welcomed the first son of a new family, William Garnhart Chiles, born, as mentioned, on the trail near present-day Winnemucca, Nevada. Five more children followed—Amelia Jane, Susan Anna, Dixie Virginia, Joseph Ballinger Jr., and Henry Lee. All of these children except William, the oldest, and Henry Lee, the youngest, were born in a house in Rutherford that Chiles built on a 1,000-acre plot he bought for $12,000 from the Bartlett-Vines family, who had come west with him in 1843. The house was later incorporated into the Inglenook [Coppola] Vineyard.

With the disruption caused by the Civil War and the unprecedented floods that had deluged much of northern California, by 1862 Joe B and Margaret were experiencing "hard times", according to a friend of Margaret's who was staying with them in Rutherford. While some sections of California were profiting from the wartime economy, the strains of the Civil War were being adversely felt throughout the Napa Valley, though the Chiles family could take comfort from the presence of like-minded neighbors. "Home to whiskey-drinking pioneers ... there was a strong Southern faction [in the Napa Valley]." [207] They were prepared to give a good hearing to the noisy minority segment of the general population throughout the state that was agitating for California to join the Southern cause. Some of the early pioneers, many of whom had come from the South, were sympathetic enough to have the pro-Union Napa County *Reporter* publish frightened warnings about the rebel sentiment.[208] According to the census of 1840 in Missouri, some members of the extended Chiles family were slaveholders, but Joe Chiles seemingly was not, and there are no records of him having slaves

---

[207] Lin Weber, *Old Napa Valley*, p.171.
[208] Weber, *Old Napa Valley*, p.171.

in California.[209] Yet, in deference to his heritage, he, like others in Napa County, held on to his Southern sympathies.[210]

Incidents like the one reported at Joe Chiles's place in Rutherford might have helped spark some of the Napa newspaper's anxiety. At some point a prankster hoisted a Confederate flag on Chiles's porch. It would have been easily visible from the main road, and a neighbor, a Union supporter, took offense and asked Joe B to remove it. Now it was Chiles's turn to stand on his dignity, saying that as he hadn't put it there, he wouldn't remove it. The Stars and Bars eventually came down, but when a local Union supporter called Chiles a rebel behind his back, he was knocked down by some of Joe B's friends for his loose tongue. Rebel or not, if the presentation of the Stars and Bars on the front porch were not enough of a demonstration of where his sympathies lay, the names of his two last children—Dixie Virginia born in 1862, and Henry Lee born in 1864—demonstrated further his devotion to the Southern cause.

The loyalty of his friends reflected both the Southern sympathies of part of the population, but also for the general

---

[209] Bancroft in his *History of California* quotes Vallejo remembering years later that Chiles was accompanied by a black man when he went with Baldridge to discuss his mill with the General in 1843, but there is no other reference to this occurrence.

[210] U.S. Census Bureau, 1840 Census, Missouri.

popularity of Chiles's character, fleshed out in stories about him that made the rounds in the valley. One story in particular demonstrates his leniency and toleration for the foibles of others. A mule skinner on the Catacula was given the job of driving the wagon loaded with the modest production of Chiles Valley whiskey for distribution to various saloons in St. Helena. It was not a complicated task, and for a time the wagon and its driver came and went with expected regularity. Then suddenly the wagon was returning later and later and the driver was reported as being very drunk. The suspicion was that he was being treated to some of the cargo by the saloon keepers on his route. This was investigated by Joe B and all whom he questioned claimed that they had never served the driver so much as a drop and he that was cold sober when he made his last delivery. Joe B came to the conclusion that the answer must lie somewhere along the trail between St. Helena and the Catacula. Unannounced, he followed the wagon into town and waited until all the deliveries had been made. Sure enough, the teamster was sober as he set off through the canyon between the town and the ranch, with Joe B following at a discreet distance, though within earshot of the harness bells of the mules. Suddenly the bells fell silent. Chiles dismounted and crept along the trail. There in the creek that ran through the canyon was the wagon with the driver nowhere in sight. From a vantage point behind some bushes, Chiles settled down to wait for the reappearance of the driver who soon came into view stumbling along on unsteady legs. He slowly pulled himself into the wagon seat and the mules, long practiced, pulled the wagon across the ford in the direction of the ranch. As soon as they were out of sight, Chiles followed the faint path of the mule skinner leading up the hillside and there, half-concealed in the bushes, was a partially empty whiskey keg. The driver was never sent on that errand again, but neither was he fired. Not much of a drinker himself, Chiles was nevertheless tolerant of the tastes of others— or maybe good mule skinners were hard to find.[211]

The distant war rumbled on, and the likelihood of California joining the Confederacy receded, but closer to home Joe B and Margaret's situation was compounded by other financial reverses, like a friend defaulting on a note for which Joe B had gone surety. Suddenly he was in debt and forced to sell his own Rutherford house and its 1,000-acre parcel to raise some capital to pay off his unexpected obligation. Sources are sketchy as to why Chiles negotiated this bad bit of business, other than his loyalty to friends, but we do know that it necessitated a return to live in the adobe house in the Chiles Valley in 1862.

---

[211] Giffen, pp. 91-92.

This was also the year in which he responded to the entreaty from his son-in-law Jerome Davis, in dire financial straits, to help hide his personal property from his creditors and the county assessor. Chiles agreed to assume the payment of Davis's debts in exchange for all the livestock he had remaining after the unprecedented floods of that year. It was largely a fictitious transaction and no actual exchange took place. Both men were exhibiting their faith that the greatly diminished supply of beef due to the floods would drive up prices and restore their fortunes. Instead, the climate continued its gyrations, and the searing drought that followed the floods parched the grazing lands and, "for the time being, beef all but vanished from the diet of Sacramento Valley residents."[212]

The paper transaction with Davis yielded nothing to help Joe B's finances, and it was ten years before he had recouped enough of his assets to afford a move back to the Napa Valley, this time to St. Helena, where Southerners were still in abundance. This was particularly for the sake of his fast-growing children of his second family, who wanted to be near their contemporaries. Part of his home in St. Helena still stands and is intermittently used by the St. Helena Baptist Church.

---

[212] Vaught, *After the Gold Rush*, pp. 93-94.

If the move back to the St. Helena house was part of a strategy to have his and Margaret's children find friends and life companions, then it was a successful plan. Within a few years, all three daughters, Amelia, Susan, and Dixie Virginia, had found husbands in the Napa Valley. But for Chiles himself, while he clearly enjoyed family life and seeing his children launched in Napa society, the valley was perhaps becoming too civilized and tame. Like many of his pioneer contemporaries, his passion was acquiring land. In the 1870s he bought two ranches in the country that he had traversed in 1843, the Fish Creek Ranch in southern Oregon and a ranch in Modoc County, in north-eastern California. Before the end of the decade both properties were gone in financial setbacks attributed to helping out relatives.[213] It was also in the 1870s that he sold off three peripheral parcels of the Catacula grant to the Priest, Sievers, and the Whittle families.[214]

As the state and the county continued their intention of myth-making about the first settlers, it is difficult to imagine that Chiles relished the role of local hero that others were bestowing on him. In the 1880s he bought a portion of the Guenoc ranch in the Coyote Valley of Lake County bordering northern Napa County.

---

[213] Chiles Family Papers

[214] *Memorial and Biographical History of Northern California*, Chicago, Lewis Publishing Co., p. 520, 813.

This was in the rugged hill country near the source of Putah Creek which flowed into the Sacramento Valley where it formed a border of Isaac Chiles's ranch.[215] The "History of Napa and Lake Counties" published that year said:

> ... it affords us great pleasure to present to our readers the portrait of this most excellent and worthy pioneer of pioneers, for be it here noted that he is the oldest living American settler in Napa County. He is still hale and hearty, and the prospects are good for him to spend many years yet, ere he is called hence to meet the reward of a well-spent life. It is a rare treat to sit and listen to his reminiscences of the days now long gone by. He is particularly noted for telling wonderful bear stories, all of which are "true to life," and we regret that our space forbids the reproduction of a few of his best.[216]

As Joe B. Chiles slipped into old age, what of the founding fathers of California that he had counted among his personal friends and acquaintances?

Billy Baldridge remained a friend and neighbor through the intervening years. He sought the excitement of the Bear Flag

---

[215] History of Napa and Lake Counties, 1881, transcribed by genealogytrails.com/napa.
[216] Ibid.

Revolt and was elected Lieutenant of Company C. of the Bear Flag Battalion. He was present at the surrender of the *Californios* to Fremont in 1847 at Cahuenga, near Los Angeles. Returning to civilian life, he earned enough in 1849 from mining gold to acquire some acreage in the Napa Valley near the town of Oakville, and settled down to a life of farming and stock raising for the next 40 years. A lifelong bachelor, he was a much-respected member of the local community, outliving his old friend Chiles by 17 years, dying in 1902.[217]

Charlie Hopper had returned east with Chiles in 1842. He resumed his life in Missouri, but the urge to settle in California never left him and in 1847 he formed up a wagon train with his family, bringing them out west and serving as captain of the party he led. Once there he settled in the Napa Valley near his old friends, Chiles and Yount. He had five children, and was considered a leading citizen of the area, spending the rest of his life there and dying in 1880 at the age of 81.[218]

George Yount, another friend from Missouri whose influence had been so useful to Chiles on his first arrival in California, was a neighbor in the Napa Valley, occupying two land grants, both of

---

[217] History of Napa and Lake Counties, California, San Francisco, Ca, Slocum, Bowen & Co.,1881, page 379-385.
[218] Nunis, p. 158-159.

which were patented by the Land Commission. Yet in spite of their history together and the proximity of their ranches, in 1847 Chiles and Yount were involved in the first libel suit in California over some cattle dealings. The jury could not reach a verdict, and the trial wrecked the friendship that went back to the Missouri days. After Chiles published a retraction of the charge that Yount had stolen some of his cattle, the two never spoke again, with Yount dying in 1865 at the age of 71.[219]

John Marsh, the business associate of Chiles in Missouri whose letters had lured him and the others of the first party to California in 1841, was among the first to go. In the years after Chiles and the others of the first emigrant party arrived at his rancho on the back side of Mount Diablo, his "medical degree" meant that by charging fees payable in cattle, he grew his herd to be one of the largest in northern California. The Gold Rush spelled huge opportunity for a well-established rancher like Marsh, who made a fortune from his 17,000 acres, supplying beef and grapes to San Francisco and to the mining towns of the Sierra. By 1851 Marsh was a wealthy man, with his ranch producing $20,000 a year. He was introduced to a New England school teacher who was the principal at a girls' school in San Jose and

---

[219] California *Star,* June 25, 1847, Sonoma District Court Records.

the two were soon married. Back at the adobe house on the rancho, they began work on a 7,000- square-foot home in the fashionable Gothic Revival style, made of local stone and topped by a 60-foot tower. Marsh's ranch was now valued at $500,000, but the huge influx of gold seekers had brought with it rustlers and squatters, who constantly challenged the ownership of his land grant and preyed on his cattle. Marsh took a more confrontational approach than Vallejo or Sutter, which earned him enemies and death threats. In addition to these worries, Marsh's wife suffered a return of a respiratory ailment that was exacerbated by the valley summer heat. She died in August 1855. A year later the great stone house was nearing completion when the annual roundup took place. It ended in acrimony with Marsh claiming that his *vaqueros* were overcharging him for work that they had done for a fixed price over several years. They disputed his claim and insults were exchanged. A few days later they met Marsh on the road between Pacheco and Martinez and in a botched robbery attempt, the doctor was killed. In response to the public outcry at the cold-blooded murder of one of the state's leading citizens, the governor offered a $1,000 reward for the capture of his killers. Two of the killers were eventually brought to justice, one of them pardoned and the other serving 25 years at San Quentin prison, from which he emerged in 1891.[220]

John Sutter, with his vast holdings in the gold-bearing Sierra foothills, was one of the first victims of the Gold Rush. His land holdings were slipping away by 1850 and his Fort was in ruins by 1854. He was forced to spend increasing amounts of time and money to fight squatters all the way to the Supreme Court, a fight that cost more than $300,000 and reduced his holdings by two-thirds. By 1860, he was reliant on funds from the Society of California Pioneers and the California legislature for his livelihood. Driven from his home at Hock Farm on the Feather River by arson, with all of his clothing, relics, art works, and documents destroyed, he sailed for the east coast in 1865. He had hopes that Congress would reimburse him for his losses at the hands of American immigrants. When a "Bill For the Relief of John A. Sutter" died in committee in the forty-first Congress (1869-70) Sutter moved from his Washington hotel to the village of Lititz near Philadelphia. He was still receiving his pension from the California legislature, and in spite of the support of Mark Twain, William T. Sherman, and various Pioneer Associations, he could not get the Congress to reimburse even part of his losses.

---

[220] George Lyman, *John Marsh, Pioneer,* New York, Charles Scribner's Sons, 1930. Details of the last days of Marsh pp.314-323.

After 14 years of disappointment and frustration, he died on 18 June1880, the thirty-ninth anniversary of his New Helvetia grant from Governor Alvarado. John C. Fremont delivered the graveside eulogy to the fellow pioneers who had assembled in Washington to send off one of their own.[221]

Another victim of the Gold Rush, and of the Americanization of California, was Chiles's friend and early patron, Mariano Vallejo. As military commander of Northern California, he was the most powerful man in the region at the arrival of the Bidwell-Bartleson Party in 1841. Yet, by the end of the decade he had endured incarceration during the Bear Flag Revolt, loss of power and prestige, and struggles with squatters on his extensive holdings to the north of San Francisco Bay. In spite of these troubles, Vallejo continued to believe in the American future of the state. He was elected to the first session of the State Senate in 1850 and donated 156 acres of his land for the location of a new state capital near Sonoma. Planning work commenced but after much wrangling the state capital was fixed at Sacramento. The Treaty of Guadalupe Hidalgo had guaranteed the existing property rights of great landholders like Vallejo, but years of legal

---

[221] Richard Dillon, *Fool's Gold*, Sanger CA, The Write Thought, 1967, pp. 278-94; Albert Hurtado, *John Sutter*, Norman OK, Univ. of Oklahoma Press, 2006, pp.337-340.

challenges cost him thousands of dollars, and although he supported himself by leasing out small plots of land, eventually his holdings of tens of thousands of acres were reduced to 224 acres called Lachryma Montis, just west of the Sonoma plaza. He lived out his final days there and in spite of his reversals of fortune, he never lost his faith in the Americanization of California. He told his embittered son, "Let the wound heal. I brought this upon myself. I did what I thought was best. It was best for the country and so far as I am concerned, I can stand it."[222] Vallejo died at home in January 1890. Flags flew at half-mast throughout the state, and local dignitaries gathered in Sonoma for the funeral. A military band was sent up from the San Francisco Presidio, and the State Legislature sent a silken flag to be unfurled at the graveside of one of the fathers of California.

John Bidwell, whose friendship Joe B shared in Missouri before the start of their adventure in 1841, remained on amicable terms with him for almost the next two decades, though it is likely that Chiles's Southern sympathies and Bidwell's anti-slavery convictions would have created some distance between the two men. After Bidwell's marriage to Annie Kennedy, an ardent

---

[222] Emparan, Madie Brown, *The Vallejos of California*, San Francsico, The Gleeson Library Associates, 1968, p.345, Cited in Rosenus, *General Vallejo*, Berkeley, Heyday Books, 1995.

prohibitionist, in 1868, a greater coolness was created between teetotal Bidwell and whiskey-making Chiles. Bidwell served on the committee that drafted the declaration of independence from Mexico in the Bear Flag Revolt, and in the Mexican War that followed he advanced to the rank of brevet major. Bidwell succumbed to gold fever briefly in 1848, discovering gold on the Feather River, but when his Rancho Chico grant, 22,000 acres north of Sacramento, was confirmed, he returned to agriculture. In 1849 he was elected to the State Senate and in 1854 and 1860 he was vice president of the state Democratic convention. His was a strong voice for the Union in the Civil War, and he was elected to Congress on the Union ticket in 1864 but then ran unsuccessfully for governor on the Republican ticket in 1867. When the Bidwells were married in Washington in 1868, serving President Andrew Johnson and future president Ulysses S. Grant were in attendance, and when the couple returned to Rancho Chico, they played host to political and social luminaries of the day. President Rutherford B. Hayes, Gen. William T. Sherman, Susan B. Anthony, and John Muir were among the visitors in those years. With time, Bidwell's politics went farther toward the fringe. He ran on the Anti-Monopoly ticket in 1875 and for president on the Prohibition ticket in 1892, winning little more than two per cent of the vote. He spent his last years at Rancho Chico, concerning himself with agriculture and attempts to direct California Indians toward the white man's civilization. He saw off his fellow pioneer, Joe Chiles, and he saw out the century, dying in April 1900.[223]

Veterans of 1841, Nancy and Ben Kelsey, followed their first trek across the continent with a half century of wandering California and the West. Having squatted in Napa County in 1842, they moved to Oregon the following year, returning to Napa a year later driving a herd of cattle to start a ranch. Both legs of the journey were plagued by hostile encounters with Indians. The negative attitudes of the Kelseys' toward the Indians played a major part in these violent clashes. In 1845 Nancy gave birth to a second daughter at Sutter's Fort. Her role in the Bear Flag Revolt was to contribute her sewing skills in the making of the flag, while Ben rode off to support Fremont. After the conclusion of the war with Mexico, Ben went into partnership with Mariano Vallejo to build and operate a saw mill, but the enterprise was largely abandoned with the news of the discovery of gold. Kelsey went to present-day El Dorado County with 60 Pomo Indians he had commandeered from his brother's ranch, and in two days mining he amassed $10,000, but shortly afterward found that he could make even more money selling supplies and meat to miners

---

[223] Gillis and Magliari, *John Bidwell and California*, Spokane, Arthur H. Clark, 2004; John Bidwell Biography, *Spartacus Education. 2006*

rather than panning for gold himself. With the profits, he and his brother Andrew bought land in Lake County from Vallejo's brother, though the title was later rejected by the Land Commission. The ranch was abandoned in late-1849 after Andrew was killed by enraged Pomos who had been badly mistreated. The following year the Kelseys moved to Humboldt County, though the experiment proved unsuccessful and they returned to Sonoma, only to move to Oregon once again, living there for some of the 1850s before moving back to various locations in California. By now, Ben was troubled by ill health and the couple sought a drier climate as a solution, moving first to northern Mexico in 1859 then to Texas in 1861. Finally, after several episodes involving fights with local Indians, they returned to California, residing at Lompoc, Fresno, Inyo County, and Los Angeles. Ben died there in 1889 and Nancy moved to the wilder parts of Santa Barbara County where she supported herself by acting as a midwife and herbalist, talents much appreciated by the locals. She summed up her life for an interviewer, "I have enjoyed riches and suffered the pangs of poverty. I have … baked bread for Fremont and talked with Kit Carson. I have run from bear and killed most other smaller game." She had borne ten children, eight of whom survived. She died in 1896 at age 73.[224]

Of all the friends and acquaintances of Joe B. Chiles from the 1840s, John C. Fremont was the one who enjoyed the largest national reputation across five decades. After his court-martial and pardon by President Polk in 1848, he was encouraged by his father-in-law, the powerful senator Thomas Hart Benton, to mount two more expeditions. These aimed at both furthering the American claims of Manifest Destiny and exploring railroad routes to connect the west coast with the rest of the United States. He redeemed his reputation in California as one of its two first US senators, and his land holdings at Mariposa in the Sierra foothills made him hugely wealthy and enabled a lavish lifestyle lived among the elite of New York. He stayed in the public eye, running for re-election in 1851 in California as a Free Soil Democrat, but he was defeated largely because of his opposition to slavery. The reputation he gained from his principles led to a run as the 1856 presidential candidate for the fledgling Republican Party. Coming in second to James Buchanan, he won more than 40 per cent of the popular vote and 114 Electoral College votes. The Fremonts returned to California, where they

---

[224] Cited in Nunis, p. 197.

enjoyed a place at the pinnacle of San Francisco society. With the start of the Civil War, Fremont was appointed army Commander of the Department of the West, based in St. Louis, but his command was revoked after five months amid a welter of insubordination and corruption claims. He was later given another command, but resigned after four months for personal reasons and his inability to accept his place in the chain of command. A largely impractical man, he was forced to sell his Mariposa estate to pay debts and returned east to get embroiled in dubious railroad bond schemes while enjoying a life of wealthy privilege. In 1865 he returned briefly to San Francisco for the fifteenth anniversary of California's statehood, leading a parade down Market St. with Mariano Vallejo. His final stint of government service was as governor of Arizona territory from 1878 to 1881. He spent little time there and was asked to resign. With virtually all their wealth gone, the Fremonts relied largely on the earnings from the writings of Jessie Benton Fremont. By now largely forgotten, John C. Fremont died alone in an inexpensive rooming house in New York in 1890.

When Bidwell died in 1900, Nicholas "Cheyenne" Dawson was almost the last surviving member of the Bidwell-Bartleson party. As a young Pennsylvanian in 1838 he determined that he would spend at least six years seeing the world and he set off for the frontier of Missouri. His travels took him down the Mississippi River and along several of its tributaries, working his way, laboring, and teaching. In 1841, he joined Chiles and the others in their trek west and stayed in California for almost three years. The urge to travel seized him again, and he set off for Mexico. From there he took a ship to New Orleans, and thence to Arkansas, where he married a former pupil. Marriage did not prevent Dawson from heading back to California to join the Gold Rush in 1849. In the goldfields, he was able to build up a sizeable nest egg by freighting cargoes, and with this he returned east via the Isthmus in 1851 to rejoin his wife. The following year they settled near Austin, Texas, and Dawson became a staunch supporter of the Confederacy. An inheritance enabled him to buy a farm near Austin where he put down roots. He corresponded with Bidwell in the 1890s and kept tabs on several of the other survivors of the 1841 party until his death, but he was not the last of the 1841 adventurers. That distinction fell to Michael Nye, who became a naturalized Mexican and was given a large land grant near Marysville in recognition of his support of the *Californios* against Governor Micheltorena in 1845. The grant of "Rancho Willy" was later disallowed by the Land Commission. In 1847 Nye married one of the Donner Party widows, Harriet Pike. They moved to Cook County Oregon and lived there until his death in 1906, 65 years after the first crossing.

While these diverse lives were playing out, Chiles lived quietly in remote Coyote Valley, Lake County, for four more years, leaving his home there in early 1885 because of failing health. He was almost 75 when he returned to the St. Helena house. By this time, the town and the Napa Valley were a far cry from the rough and ready community of early settlers that he had first encountered four decades earlier. The valley had experienced an influx of Europeans during the post-Gold Rush period, and the landscape was dotted with their wineries, 16 of them near St. Helena alone. Their output was gaining acceptance and recognition far beyond Northern California. The rush to plant vineyards was yet another manifestation of the boom-and-bust cycle evident in other parts of California. In the process, it transformed the landscape of the Napa Valley and much of the rest of the state.

Overall, it was a different world for Joe Chiles, and it was one that had moved beyond him and the skills that had taken him so far from Missouri. Winter became spring, then summer, and the town prepared itself for its annual Independence Day July Fourth celebrations. But before they could take place, a shock rippled through the valley with the news that "Colonel" Joe B.

Chiles had died on 25 June at home on Spring Street in St. Helena. The funeral to mark his passing took place the next day, one of the largest ever held in Napa County. The local paper noted:

> ... the many hundred spectators, with the sorrowing relatives, took a last view of the mortal remains of the old hero, who in life had been such a conspicuous figure in our history.[225]

The florid tributes came from all quarters for the devoted father, the generous husband, and the true friend. Probably the old Colonel himself would have been one of the first to raise a quizzical eyebrow at all this fulsome praise. He had lived a long time and been down enough hard trails to not be all things to all men, but there was no denying his achievements. The community gathered for the last salute to a part of their history—to bid farewell to one of their founding fathers. Joseph Chiles's body was borne on a horse-drawn carriage from his home at 1343 Spring St. down the road to the cemetery. More than 100 carriages followed as the leading citizens of the Napa Valley and beyond paid their respects to "the Adam of a generation of

---

[225] Napa Valley *Register*, June 25, 1885, cited in Giffen, p. 95.

California pioneers," [226] a man who could unreservedly be called a trailblazer of the Old West.

---

[226] Webber, Old Napa Valley, p. 42.

APPENDIX I

Road Trip Diary 2015—In the footsteps of Joseph B. Chiles

This is a story of visionaries, fools, and mid-size rental cars on the 174th anniversary of the 1841 trek.

> We knew that California lay west, and that was the extent of our knowledge—John Bidwell

The air ticket is booked. The rental car is booked. The maps are spread out on the floor, along with background reading, interpretive guides, illustrations. You name it, I've got it. We just have to get there and do it. Has it been done before? You bet. Has it been done by Joe B's California descendants? I doubt it—and it's about time somebody did. 2016 is the 175th anniversary of that first company of wagons across the plains. Let's shine a new light on that memory and see what it can teach us.

Lots to learn, particularly about the lay of the land. For left coasters, this is the bit that we fly over. This is the supposedly flat, uninteresting bit which is nothing but corn and cowboys. It might be that this view changes over the next weeks …

The Rendezvous: 27 August 2015

It's all set for the afternoon of 27 August. Brother Jim flies in from Connecticut and I fly in from London via Chicago. Time to fold up all those maps that cover the floor in the spare bedroom. It's an early flight from Heathrow, so I'm hitting the road at 4.30 in the morning. Yikes! This is going to be an exploration on more than a few levels. Doing a road trip together as brothers for the first time in about 40 years—will our nerves stand it? Then, there is the physical exploration of a part of the country about which we know nothing. Bidwell says that their company's ignorance was almost total about the land that they had to cross—so no change there. My ignorance is virtually as pristine as Bidwell's and Joe B's, though I have the advantage of having seen lots of movies featuring horses, cows, corn, and gunslingers, which is not reassuring.

There is also the discovery of the route, as we follow in Joe B's footsteps. The early pioneers like him were embarking on a landscape which was nothing like what they had experienced before. Searing deserts, soaring mountains, narrow defiles for which they had no descriptive word, and had to borrow the word "canyon" from the Spanish. But that was to come—this part of the trip for the pioneers was all about pushing out on to the rolling prairies and crossing streams, creeks, and rivers—some by pulling, some by pushing, some by floating. We'll be saddling up our mid-size rental car at Kansas City Airport and heading out on to the wide open spaces of Interstate 435, a prospect that Joe B would surely have found more daunting than meeting up at the big oak tree outside of Independence. But never mind. We're committed to head on out …

Thursday 27 August 2015

After the Rendezvous

First touchdown on the great plains—Chicago. Not much of the old west here, at old O'Hare Airport though, I was treated to an auspicious view of a plane from Frontier Airlines, so that was a good start. Not only that, there were two Indians in the departure lounge for the flight to Kansas City, except that one of them was wearing a sari, so that didn't count for much. On the other hand, there was someone else in a big black hat-—a cross between a cowboy hat and a sombrero, with a moustache to match, so I knew we were headed in the right direction.

Then on to another plane for the hour flight to Kansas City, an uneventful if bumpy ride through tall thunderheads building up in the sultry sky with many miles of Missouri and Kansas spread out below us, a largely tamed landscape, with only the old watercourses of the Missouri River, the Kansas River and the

Little Blue giving us a hint of the landscape crossed by the early trailblazers.

And there in the arrivals hall, awaiting my appearance as he had been for several hours, was brother James, looking distinguished in his straw pork pie hat. He was ready to hit the trail, having walked the length of the airport concourse more times than he could count and sampled something from all the food vendors he could stomach. We grabbed my bag and got over to the Hertz desk to see what they had in the way of wagons, and found not a station wagon with wood on the sides, but a respectable Toyota Carolla, built for service, if not for speed and style. We shunned the Satnav—how could we follow in those pioneering footsteps with that bumptious lady telling us every twist and turn? It was unthinkable.

From the rolling wooded hills on the east side of the Missouri, we followed the major roads west to our first stop, Topeka Kansas. This is where we began to see hints of the great plains which so impressed the pioneers, where they would be trespassers on Indian lands, beyond the protection of the government—without shops, hospitals, or laws. They were in a land with no second chances.

As one of them put it in *The Emigrants' Guide to Oregon and California*:

Here we were, without law, without order, and without restraint, in a state of nature ... Some were sad, while others were merry; and while the brave doubted, the timid trembled.

But they had been told by newspaper editor, John L. O'Sullivan:

We are the nation of human progress and who will, what can, set limits to our onward march? Providence is with us and no earthly power can.

He later shortened this to proclaim that it was, "Our Manifest Destiny to overspread the continent allotted by providence for the free development of our yearly multiplying millions." That's been the line around here ever since.

"Setting up camp" in the dusk, surrounded by the screeching of the cicadas, we'll head down to the chuck wagon to recruit ourselves with a local beverage or two ... while the big, muddy Missouri and the Kansas Rivers are still rolling along, with the traffic roaring over them in a way that would have baffled our pioneers.

Friday 28 August 2015

From Topeka Kansas to Kearny Nebraska

Greater Topeka:

About last night—the outlook on arrival wasn't propitious—we found the hotel off the strip mall, behind a Hooters bar, within earshot of the Interstate, but on closer inspection, it was clean, friendly, and quiet. Though quiet refers to man-made noise only, for as we sat by the pool [waterhole?] drinking a complimentary beer [who says this isn't a great country?] the noise of the cicadas in the surrounding trees was deafening—like an orchestra of hair dryers tuning up. Their noisy efforts to deter predators forced our conversation to the level of a low shout. In noticing their noise we were in company. They have been featured in literature since Homer's Iliad. The local dining offerings did not include deep fried cicadas as they do in other parts of the world, but the franchised fare of the strip mall included, Jack-in-the-box, McDonalds, Pizza Hut, and the rest, supplemented by some locals—a Mexican, a Freddies Steakburger, and another establishment offering a deep fried Oreo cookie, a churro-like object, capable of clogging your major arteries at a distance of 10 yards.

Flat and straight through Kansas

The next morning, we were wiggling our way through Kansas to Nebraska then up and across Nebraska toward the great Platte River. Here is where the plains really come into their own. The rolling, semi-wooded nature of western Missouri now becomes the big-sky-far-horizon, with corn, sorghum, and soybeans as far as the eye can see. In the far distance, the grain elevators stand out on the horizon like ocean liners at sea.

Some didn't make it

The road passes plaque after plaque, commemorating watering holes, meadows, fords, and springs used by the emigrants. Scattered along the road are also isolated graves, left for the emigrants whose adventure to California ended not with the pot of gold at the end of the rainbow, but with the rapid onset of cholera, the biggest killer on the trail. There were other hazards besides. In Joe B's company, the unfortunately aptly named Mr. Shotwell, carelessly pulled his rifle, barrel first, out of his wagon. The trigger snagged on something and Shotwell was well-shot in the chest and died within the hour. He was buried on the spot with as much ceremony as they could muster, and the wagon train moved on.

Today, at the likes of Alcove Springs, there is a boarded nature walk down to the creek, and a plaque with a flagpole commemorating this welcome and popular spot on the trail. We walked to a roughly-carved obelisk standing in the middle of a field to see the tombstone of a cholera victim and on the hill opposite we could see the faint trace of wagon ruts—an infrequent moment of connection between the present and the past.

Saturday 29 August 2015

Up the Platte Emigrant Highway

Today was all about the Platte River and finding a cup of coffee in something that wasn't a Styrofoam cup.

First, the Platte—a wide, shallow, east-west river, providing a corridor which drew Joe B and those who followed him westward. Starting in the uplands of central Wyoming, it snakes eastward 800 rugged miles to the Missouri River. Some of the Indians called it the Great Medicine Road as they roamed along it with the great herds of buffalo on which much of their culture was based. Various emigrants called it the Oregon Trail, the Pony Express Route (about which more later), The Mormon Trail, or the California Road.

This was a western river. "Too thick to drink, too thin to plow, too pale to paint." "A mile wide and an inch deep." It was like no other that they had encountered east of the Missouri, but it provided a route into the continent, first for the trappers of the Hudson's Bay Company, then the first settlers bound for California, then for the flood of emigrants, adventurers, and gold-seekers who followed, turning the trace of the faint tracks of the Indians and the trappers into a trail, "nearly a quarter of a mile wide—that is, a row of wagons fifteen hundred feet across, and extending in front and to the rear, as far as we could see ... a vast sea of white flapping wagon covers, and a seething mass of plodding animals", as described by an emigrant from 1852.

Now about that cup of coffee. We had been on the road for over two days, and as lunchtime approached I realized that every cup of coffee that I had been served was presented in a styrofoam cup, which as anyone can tell you, is not a proper cup of coffee. The economics of modern food service—at a certain price level in America—seems to point the way towards completely disposable plates, crockery, and utensils. An ecological and gastronomic disaster. Fortunately, the ladies running the Julesburg Cafe in dusty little Julesburg Colorado, just over the state line from Nebraska, had not yet been copied in on that memo and we were able to obtain lunch and a passable cuppa in a heavy china mug. Out on the interstate, trucks and cars barreled along fueled by caffeine from Styrofoam, unaware of their benighted status.

Wagon trace in the foreground, caffeine junkies in rear

Julesburg, and a cathedral of the plains

The rest of our time was spent roaming on both sides of the river, following the National Park Service Auto Tour Guide, looking for emigrant wagon ruts and swales (whatever they might be—I don't travel with a dictionary) and they were there, where we were directed to look.

Faint tracks, but still visible

Some of the other roadside historical notices highlighted tracks of the emigrants. Others indicated burial places of the unlucky who never made it further than the Platte Valley. Yet other places commemorated wrongs done to the native inhabitants that would culminate in bloodshed in the 1860s. As early as 1841, a Sioux chief was complaining to a trader:

> The white man takes our property without paying for it!
> He kills our game, he eats our meat, he drinks our water,
> and he travels our country, and what does he give the red
> man in exchange for all of this?

This was not going to end well, as more and more emigrants and settlers piled in to the plains.

But for our purposes, we reveled in the footsteps of Joe B. Chiles who had followed this route in both directions, seven times. Especially striking were the landmarks of Chimney Rock, and Courthouse Rock with its accompanying Jail Rock. Perhaps the emigrants might have been anticipating Elvis in calling it Jailhouse Rock. At any rate, from the time of the very first travelers through this land, these striking rock formations were indications of progress they were making on their way west at the rate of 15-20 miles a day. And the romance of the landscape is still readily available today, even without a covered wagon.

Chimney Rock was another mark
of progress along the trail

Jailhouse Rock

Sunday 30 August 2015

Approaching the Rockies

After about eight weeks on the trail, or three and a half days in our case, the emigrants were about to leave the easy bit behind. They had sauntered by the Big Blue, the Little Blue, and the Platte. There was abundant water and usually feed for the animals. But this was about to end. The country grew rougher and the scenery more spectacular as they rumbled past Chimney Rock and Scotts Bluff. As they crossed into what would become Wyoming, the rubber was about to hit the road—although rubber hadn't yet been invented—but you get the idea. One of the first milestones that would tell them that they were in a new phase of their journey was Fort Laramie, and that was our stop too.

Part of what we saw was this. The old barracks have been re-built and the Indians are gone

When Joe B stopped by in 1841, the fort was a simpler privately-run affair, where Indians, trappers, and commercially-minded people could meet and bargain. By the time he made his last crossing, 13 years later, buildings like the one above were beginning to be built by the new owners, the US government. Though life was still very colorful, as described by one visitor; "We were visited by about two hundred Cheyennes and Sioux, who danced a little, stole a little, eat a great deal, and finally went their way rejoicing.

The next stop after Ft. Laramie was about ten miles up the North Platte, where many of the emigrants stole away from their chores for a few minutes to carve their names in the soft stone face of Register Cliff, for posterity and for friends who might be following behind, letting them know they were still alive.

Joe B, is that you?

They were still in pleasant country, and some of the emigrants even took some time to visit another natural wonder, even though it was about a mile from the trail, the natural stone bridge spanning a nearby creek.

The stone bridge

There were a number of hard miles to be crossed before the emigrants could tick off another marker. It was Independence Rock, first named by trappers because they camped near it on July 4. In the following years, if emigrants made it there by Independence Day they celebrated by carving their names in the rock, reading the Declaration of Independence and having a few drinks. So many did this that they began running out of space. One emigrant in 1852 complained, "Came to Independence Rock about ten o'clock this morning. I presume there are a million of names wrote on this rock."

We enjoyed a walk around Independence Rock, until we got to the back side—the furthest distance from the car—and a squall hit. Then we got a little taste of pioneer "suck it up" medicine—and some damp clothing in the bargain.

The emigrants could enjoy the Sweetwater River for the next few days, but they were now venturing on the way to South Pass and the country was turning into something that was unlike anything they had seen before.

Independence Rock on the horizon

As we stopped for our umpteenth roadside information board, I was struck by the number of mentions received by the Pony Express—so here's a little rant about the Pony Express. They get a lot of attention, some might say an inordinate amount of attention, in this part of the world. Their entrepreneurial effort to deliver express mail to California from St. Joseph, Missouri, in ten days by using young men riding in relays on good horses as fast as they could is the very stuff of cowboy adventure. Very romantic and colorful, but it only lasted from 3 April 1860 until 24 October 1861, before going out of business with the arrival of the transcontinental telegraph in 1861. Yet on a plenitude of wayside plaques, its ephemeral existence is celebrated from St. Joseph to Sacramento. Without wanting to be too curmudgeonly, let me put this into context. "The Pony" lasted about 18 months on the trail between the Missouri River and Sacramento. Joe B. Chiles, in seven crossings of approximately four months each, spent 28 months on the trail between Independence Mo. and California. So take that, Pony Express. He wasn't as romantic, but Joe B knew how to walk and navigate and negotiate with the people he met on the trail. And where are his wayside plaques?

Monday 31 August 2015

South Pass and the Continental Divide

Before we leave the Great Plains and the buffalo too far behind …

South Pass? What is it south of? Turns out it is south of whatever is north of it; the name was given by Indian tribes from the northern Rockies, a name that they shared, along with directions, with the first trappers who roamed the area in the 1820s.

Buffalo on the plains

Heading up to South Pass

What's in a name—that's where we're going ... to the part of the country where you can see the bones of the earth exposed, as in this view over the road up to the pass, where you can look down and still see the tracks of the wagons etched in the terrain.

The route the guide Broken Hand Fitzpatrick took the party of 1841, following the Platte, then the North Platte into Wyoming, along the Sweetwater and up to the Pass, became the combined corridor for all the trails—California, Oregon, Mormon, and Pony Express. The Pass, 20 miles wide by 80 miles long, looks much as it did when the wagons were pouring over it, with the emigrants nervous about its startling appearance—a gray-green ocean of sage brush. At the same time, they were heartened by the fact that the streams that they walked along were now flowing west.

The Continental Divide—it all flows west from here

The going was increasingly tough, bouncing over sage tufts and sandy soil, but they could still mostly hold to their 15-20 miles a day, though the experience of being in a thunder storm "caught between heaven and earth" was an experience never forgotten. The companies that came after 1841 were approaching a point of decision where they would have to choose between various trails or cut-offs. As more knowledge spread from emigrant parties that had gone before, more and more shortcuts began to be proposed, many of them more difficult than the main trail that they were trying to shorten. But particularly in the Gold Rush, the emigrants were desperate for anything that would shave off a few miles and a few days, convinced that their fortune depended on it.

The early far West, where all the women were strong,
and all the men were good looking—weren't they?

Another pioneer descendant, brother James,
out strolling the trail in the South Pass

Heading west out of South Pass and following the route taken by the Company of 1841, we dropped down near the Utah border before heading north toward south-eastern Idaho, stopping in Soda Springs, named for the naturally carbonated springs for which the town is justly famous. The pioneers learned to add flavorings to the water to make it even tastier—the Kool Aid of the California Trail.

This happens every hour on the hour

In 1841, at the springs, they were approaching the point where the company was going to have to take leave of their guide, as he had contracted with the missionaries in the party to get them to the Oregon Territory, which made up the two modern states of Washington and Oregon. The guide, Fitzpatrick, believed that Joe B and the others were foolish to tempt fate in the Great Basin deserts without any experience or maps. He persuaded about half of them to give up their dreams of California and follow the

Snake and Columbia rivers to Oregon with him. The others, including Joe B, were willing to disregard the advice and strike out on their own. One of them later remembered, "We were now thrown entirely upon our own resources. All the country beyond was to us a veritable *terra incognita*, and we only knew that California lay to the west." They were going to pay a harsh price for their arrogance.

Tuesday 1 September 2015

Down the Valley of the Bear

No one of the party knew anything about mountaineering and scarcely anyone had ever been into the Indian Territory, yet a large majority felt that we were fully competent to go anywhere no matter what the difficulties might be or how numberous [sic] and warlike the Indians.

So said John Bidwell, whose diary forms the main record of the 1841 expedition in which Joe B played a major part. Ignorance and self-confidence are always a potent mixture, and up to this point they had enjoyed their great stroke of luck in joining with the expedition of the missionaries and their guide, Broken Hand Fitzpatrick.

Fitzpatrick then guided them thus far with no great dramas, during which time there had been two weddings and a funeral, after a self-inflicted death. But now, in present-day southeast Idaho, following the Bear River in a north-westerly direction, past Soda Springs to Sheep Rock where the river curls around the north end of the Wasatch Mountains and turns back to the south, he had some strong words of advice. He believed that to try and carry on to California, where no other wagon train had ever gone, was foolhardy in the extreme, but the 34 who wouldn't be persuaded, including Joe B, turned their oxen south with the Bear River heading for the Great Salt Lake. They sent four men on horseback to Ft. Hall, four days ride away, to see if they could purchase some supplies and ideally a guide who knew something of the route they should take to California.

In the meantime, the remainder of the California-bound emigrants went slowly down the valley of the Bear, which was reminiscent of their travels along the other rivers with which they had become familiar. They crisscrossed the river, waterway, enjoying the late-August sun and the availability of feed for their animals. But some severe challenges lay ahead. The four horsemen returned from Ft. Hall after ten days with the news that there was nothing to buy and no guide who could lead them. But they pressed on nonetheless. Bidwell and another man even found time to explore the neighboring mountain where they had seen snow glinting in the sun. They entirely misjudged the distance and were forced to sleep under a tree high up on the mountain, returning the next day to a mixture of relief and opprobrium from their fellow travelers who were convinced that they had been killed by Indians. The party now got under way in earnest, shortly arriving at the northern edge of the Great Salt Lake where their trials would truly begin.

The valley of the Bear as it looks today

Still as crowded as ever

Our little present-day party is now three—the three Chiles brothers—joined today in Pocatello, Idaho by youngest brother John. We might be fewer than Joe B's company, but our technology is mighty, even here in The Big Empty of the Great Basin. Of course, this encourages lively discussion about directions as the two who are not driving consult with maps and smartphones to help us most closely map our route on to that of Joe B, from Sheep Rock to the Great Salt Lake. Up to this point, the route of the 1841 expedition had been blended into the same California Trail followed by all the others who came after, but beyond south-eastern Idaho, their route was almost unique to these first emigrants across the continent, in large part because it was so difficult and tiresome that virtually everyone who followed found an easier route.

We ate tonight in a Mexican restaurant, largely because it was the only place we could find that served alcohol in the form of beer. Utah is a famously dry state because of the influence of the Mormon Church, so there we sat, ready for beer and Mexican cuisine. And it was all worthwhile when we examined the menu to find one of their signature dishes was called *'Los Tres Chiles'*. Job done.

Wednesday 2 September 2015

Salt Lake Saga

The riders returned from Fort Hall, overtaking the main group including Joe B in what is today northern Utah, bringing second-hand information from trappers at the fort who had heard about the country that lay in front of them. The advice was, don't go too far south before turning west toward California because there was an immense desert with no water and no feed for livestock. They were further warned not to turn too far north because they would get lost in a maze of streams and canyons where they would wander, confused and starving. But if they would head west at the right place, they would eventually strike the Mary's River [later named the Humboldt] which they could follow to the heart of the

Great Basin between the mountain ranges and eventually to the rivers flowing west. As the party continued down the Bear River, looking down for the place where they could turn west toward the Mary's River, they noticed that the stream was growing increasingly salty.

The far side of the Salt Lake riding on a mirage of water

They toiled in the August temperatures; the oxen and horses could not eat the grass which was covered in salt. The heat waves shimmered, turning clumps of bushes into well-watered groves of trees. Confused, the company followed mirages across the mud flats north of the Great Salt Lake.

John Bidwell recalled:

Thus misled, we traveled all day without water, and at midnight found ourselves on a plain, level as a floor, incrusted with salt, and as white as snow ... This plain became softer and softer until our poor, almost famished, animals could not pull our wagons. In fact, we were going direct to Salt Lake and did not know it.

Try driving a wagon through this stuff

They looped around, crossed their own tracks, struggling through sagebrush so dense that it tipped some of the lighter wagons over. In their blundering along the north end of the lake, they at last found a source of good water and sent out scouts to try and find the Mary's River. They sat in camp for over a week waiting for them to return, which they did with the news that the river was about five days march ahead. They toiled onward with their wagons, until near the present western border of Utah, one of the more forceful characters in the company had had enough. Ben

Kelsey unyoked his oxen, emptied his wagon and loaded what belongings he could on his animals' backs. On their horses he put his 18-year-old wife Nancy and their toddler daughter. The wagon would stay where it was and they would pack to California driving their oxen. Within a few days, the rest of the party had copied their example.

With this, they were no longer a wagon train, but a starving group of increasingly fractious stragglers with the dream of California in their minds. If it could be anywhere along the line of our pursuit of our ancestor, this was the place where my brothers and I would be able to see exactly where he had gone and what he had faced. The road was unpaved and the dust billowed up behind the car as we rumbled over the gravel toward the town of Lucin, Utah. The thermometer in the car showed that the outside temperature was topping 90 degrees. It was a good day to be together—three brothers whose great-grandfather's uncle had done challenging things.

The road north of the Great Salt Lake

So, we were able to accomplish one of our goals—to walk in Joe B's footsteps—in the shadow of one of the landmarks that guided Joe B and the other emigrants who came this way, Pilot Peak.

Pilot Peak

And along the way, quite by chance, in a tiny town that vanished into the landscape, we came upon another relic of more recent times—an establishment that referenced the overland trail, on our little bit of it, though so far off the beaten track of the interstate that it never had a chance.

Brother John, is he welcoming us, or warning us off?

Thursday 3 September 2015

Nevada Nightmare on the Humboldt

Having made good their escape from the Salt Lake Basin, the company of 32 men, one woman and a child, now wagon-less, footsore and hungry, trudged wearily west. The menacing drama of the landscape could only have heightened the tension of being lost in the desert. It was mid-September. The days were still hot, but the temperature dropped ominously at night to freeze the water in the buckets. Ben and Nancy Kelsey abandoned their wagons near present-day Lucin, Utah. The others followed suit four days later at Oasis, Nevada. As they tried to fashion packsaddles for their mules, horses, and oxen, they were visited by an ancient Indian who told them by gestures that he had dreamed of their coming. While they set aside the goods they could not transport, they gestured that he should help himself—to which the elderly man responded with a lengthy prayer of thanks. It was a meeting marked by an unusual level of good will, sadly not reflected in many other exchanges in the years to come.

We signed to our aged host that the wagons and everything abandoned were his, all his, and left him circumscribing the heavens—the happiest, richest, most religious man I ever saw—Nicholas "Cheyenne" Dawson, 1841

The old Indian must truly have thought he had happened on to some strange beings as he watched them depart with their animals, unused to being saddled with goods, twitching, and bucking under the weight of their burdens. The first few miles toward the Ruby mountains saw loads being shed and much re-packing accompanied by significant profanity.

Bidwell noted in his diary, "It was but a few minutes before the packs began to turn; horses became scared, mules kicked, oxen jumped and bellowed, and articles were scattered in all directions." Dawson added grimly, "There was one thing we had no trouble to pack—our provisions."

East of the Ruby Mountains

The company tacked anxiously south, west, and south again until they found themselves at the foot of the Ruby Mountains. They had been warned to not go too far south—or north. Blindly, they pushed on into the mountains, over Harrison Pass, following the creek at the bottom of the twisting canyon which led to a west-flowing river. Although they did not know it, this was the south fork of the Mary's River [soon to be renamed the Humboldt] that they had been seeking.

Entry to Harrison Pass through the Ruby Mountains

Up over Harrison Pass *through the Ruby Mountains*

But no sooner had they started to follow the river, then it appeared to be dwindling and drying up. They had been expecting it to swell with tributaries and guide them, said Nicholas Dawson, "to the plains of California and on to the Pacific, where our troubles would end, and where we could eat, eat, eat..."

The slow-moving Humboldt River

Here, their solidarity began to seriously fracture. The owners of the horses and mules could move faster than the oxen, but the oxen were all the food remaining. After a few days of tracking the winding Mary's River, eight men of the party seized the lion's share of the meat from one of the freshly butchered oxen, mounted up and made for the mountains, leaving their companions staring after them in the desert. The remaining 26 emigrants had found some local Paiute guides who had a limited knowledge of the desert ahead. The party plodded onward with the remaining cattle, past the place where the river disappeared into the sands. Next, they made their way across the desperate Forty Mile Desert and turned south toward the west fork of the Walker River, running parallel to the wall of the Sierra Nevada mountains. On 15 October, with the winter advancing day by day, they camped at the foot of the Sierra, hoping to get a foothold into the mountain fastness. During the night, their Indian guides, unable or unwilling to take them any further, slipped away into the darkness ...

Friday 4 September 2015

Humboldt hell

We can leave Joe B and the others at the foot of the Sierra for the time being and consider the fate of those who followed in his wake along the Humboldt where my brothers and I drove today. Where Joe B's company had the disadvantages of being the first and not knowing where they were going or how much time or distance would be involved, the followers in later years, particularly during the Gold Rush of 1849-50, experienced all the difficulties in competition with thousands of others, all trying to get food and especially water in this desert which bordered the Humboldt River. This was a journey that Joe B also completed in 1848 and 1854.

If all went well, they reached the Humboldt in late-August or early-September, after the hot dry summer had reduced its flow. The emigrants expected a typical river from the eastern US, and instead found a stream that meandered, warm and soapy with alkali, down weaving channels, twisting and turning along loops and turns called oxbows because they resembled the yoke that fitted over the necks of the oxen who pulled the wagons on the trail. The river was constantly creating new oxbows and cutting off old ones, leaving standing water in oxbow lakes, called sloughs by the emigrants. Wary companies did not allow their animals to approach the dangerous river bottoms to drink, but instead took water and feed to them. Many an ox or mule sank into the muddy margins of the river and drowned trying to reach the murky, soapy water for a drink.

A Humboldt slough

The channels were lined with their bloated bodies, combining their smells with that of carrion and waste to create an odor that tortured the emigrants—along with the exposed, dreary landscape and the caustic alkali dust that burned the skin and eyes.

The heat is fiery, intense, sultry, oppressive, suffocating, parching and scorching earth, and water and air and every green thing —Israel Shipman Lord, 1849

Forty Mile Desert

Discomfort, hunger, annoyance, and exhaustion sharpened the emigrants' nerves to a razor edge. In one of the better documented episodes, this was the place where James Reed of the Donner Party of 1846 killed a fellow emigrant and was banished into the desert. From Winnemucca Nevada, where we stayed last night, the Humboldt begins to arc southwest into 45 miles of trail with worse water, more dreary brown hills, deeper dust, and diminishing forage for the animals. Emigrants who had been disgusted by the local Indians' diet were now hunting for the same lizards, coyotes, squirrels, or whatever they could find to eat.

I killed and skinned and gutted about fifty frogs an inch and a half long and fried them with our hawk this noon and eat them … shot a fisher [heron] and had him and his gravy for dinner with burned-biscuit coffee very good. — Charles Darwin, 1849

I have noticed several dead horses, mules and oxen by the roadside, that had their hams cut out to eat by the starving wretches along the road. —Eleazer Ingalls, 1850

The farther we traveled the worse [the river] became. During the last eight or ten days it seems to have been mixed up with everything nauseous ... This is the end of the most miserable river on the face of the earth. Margaret Frink, 1850

More Forty Mile Desert

But now the emigrants started across something even worse, the Forty Mile Desert, a hot griddle of dry expanse, with no shade, and a crust of salt and silt crunching underfoot. The emigrants would start into it in the evening, hoping to cross the main part before the sun came up. On moonless nights they would light their way with burning abandoned wagons, whose illumination reflected the eyes of the dead oxen, mules, and horses who lay still attached to their traces.

At intervals could be seen wagons ... with two to four yoke of cattle lying dead, with the yokes on their necks, the chains still in the rings, just as they fell and died, most of them with their tongues hanging from their mouths. — Gilbert Cole, 1852

But no one stopped to gaze or help. The living procession marched steadily onward, giving little heed to the destruction going on, in their own anxiety to reach a place of safety. — Margaret Frink, 1850

The final stretch was the Carson or Truckee dune fields, a dozen or fifteen miles of deep, loose sand that sucked at hooves and wheels, while the animals scented water and desperately strained to reach it. California traders hauled water out from the Carson River and sold it to frantic immigrants for a dollar [$30] or more a gallon. Some emigrants, having reached the rivers, transported water back to struggling family, friends, and strangers. For most the worst was now over, and they had only to breach the high Sierra which rose in their path like a towering wall of rock.

Dune fields

Today, an endless succession of 40-60-foot trucks, and countless cars, roll along the interstate at seventy or eighty miles an hour, covering the same distance and terrain that cost the emigrants so dearly, in less than an hour.

Saturday 5 September 2015

Into the Mountains

We left Joe B and the others standing in the Nevada Desert, open-mouthed at the treachery of Bartleson and the others riding off with the last of the good ox meat, determined to save themselves by getting over the mountains before the winter set in. The remainder of the party had to face up to the Sierra, a mountain-range the like of which they had never encountered before. It would be their greatest physical and psychological challenge of the journey, demanding route-finding and mountaineering skills of the highest order. To get to their destination—the ranch of John Marsh—east of San Francisco bay, they had to navigate their way through mile-deep canyons and soaring snow-capped mountains. And it was mid-October—they had to do it before the snows came. In the meantime, Bartleson and his companions had eventually returned, hungry, sorry, and footsore. They had failed to find a way over the mountains and had used up all their food. Now they were going to be served up a generous portion of humble pie. Needless to say, they were coolly received, but another ox was slaughtered to feed them, and the party proceeded into the mountains together.

Into the Sierra

It's hard to imagine that any of us would be so forgiving, but they had all come a long way together, and probably realized that there was strength in numbers, even if some of those numbers had shown themselves wanting in the solidarity department.

The precise point of entry into the Sierra is unclear from the diary entries of the two principal diarists. It is generally agreed that they followed the west fork of the Walker River to the foot of the eastern Sierra, and the mountains can be entered two different ways from this approach.

Rather than debate which canyon they entered, I can quote from the two diarists in the party as my brothers and I tried to follow their progress from the roads that exist today, carrying motorists from the eastern Sierra across the mountains via the Sonora Pass.

This morning we set forth into the rolling mountains, in many places it was so steep, that all were obliged to take it on foot. Part of the day we traveled through vallies between peaks where the way was quite level ... encamped on the side of the mountain, so elevated that the ice remained all day in the stream—but we had not yet arrived at the summit. Killed another ox this evening—made 12 miles. —John Bidwell

Rolling mountains

"Many of the pines were 12 feet in diameter and no less than 200 feet high"

From here, they intersected the East Fork of the Carson River, which had some grass for their animals. They were desperate to supplement their stock of food, but were unable to find any game. The rock walls of the canyon of the Carson River became so steep that they were forced to dismount and look for a side canyon. They explored several before selecting Golden Canyon and making camp on 17 October.

The "frightful prospect" for the footsore

The next morning, "Having ascended about a half mile, a frightful prospect opened before us: naked mountains whose summits still retained the snows of perhaps a thousand years ... the winds roared—but—in the dark deep gulfs which yawned on every side, profound solitude seemed to reign."

On 18 October, they climbed 2,300 feet up Golden Canyon and at an elevation of 9,425 feet they crested the Sierra Nevada, but although they were pleased at having located a pass over the summit, they were now faced with the chilling prospect of snow-capped mountains in every direction.

Today, 174 years later, in the fourth year of the California drought, we were short on snow-capped mountains, but the towering peaks above the deep stream-cut gorges were very daunting. It was hard for us to understand how Joe B and the others had held their nerve—except that they had no alternative. In later years, Joe B recalled how the sight of Nancy Kelsey, with her toddler in her arms, marching resolutely along with the others, had inspired him to carry on when he felt like quitting.

For the emigrants, the next days were spent in even greater challenges in getting down from the peaks that they had conquered, with virtually all their food gone. We pondered this by one of the streams that they crossed while we ate our twenty-first century sandwiches ...

Through to the San Joaquin

Little Antelope Valley, where they started.

Then this?

Are you sure it's not this way?

Wandering dazed and confused—and that's us, not Joe B— we set out this morning with the best of intentions to find the company's starting point from Antelope Valley, near Topaz Lake on the California-Nevada border. It all seemed reasonably clear when the large-scale topographical map was laid out on the bed in the hotel, but somehow when we drove toward the mountains, all the cross-referencing between the map and the territory in front of us fell apart. Looking for the actual trail, as opposed to the one on the map, as described in the diaries was like a semiotic conundrum, and when we three brothers—two holding the map and one holding the steering wheel—began to interact, it was a rerun of ancient history to the time when we were growing up. Freud would have had a field day, Gregory Bateson would have been nodding sagely, and a glance at the gas gauge showed that we were heading toward empty. It was all a metaphor for the road trip. And all this was in an air-conditioned car with full stomachs. Take away the air-conditioning, the food, the car, and the map—it's no wonder that the company of 1841 began to fall apart

In the previous chapter, we left our company contemplating the menace of the High Sierra, with snow-capped mountains in every direction. They descended quickly from the high pass where they crested the Sierra—down 3,000 feet in six miles of trail. By the next day, 19 October, they were at the Middle Fork of the Stanislaus River.

Bidwell wrote:

> Descending the stream, we found several oak scrubs which confirmed us in the hope that we were on the waters of the Pacific. But the route became exceedingly difficult—the stream had swelled to a river—could not approach it—could only hear it roaring among the rocks … The roaring winds and hollow murmur of the dashing waters conveyed in the darkness of the night the most solemn and impressive ideas of solitude.

They camped overnight, and looking around the next morning, they began to fear that they were descending too deeply into a canyon that was narrowing impossibly. The next morning, they sent out scouts to see if there was an alternative route. Bidwell wrote:

> Men went in different directions to see if there was any possibility of extracting ourselves from this place without going back ... Capt. B [Bartleson] also tired of waiting for the explorers to return, started down the stream, which so jaded his animals that he was obliged to wait all day to rest them before he was able to retrace his steps. In the meantime the rest of the Company, suffering for water were obliged to travel. We proceeded directly N. up the mountains about 4 miles, found a little grass and water - here we killed one of the 2 oxen.

They were now down to one scrawny travel-worn ox as their only food supply. Bidwell went out hunting and became separated from the rest, found nothing to shoot for food, but managed to acquire some acorn mush from an Indian boy he met on the trail. He was still desperately hungry and now completely unsure of which direction the rest of the company had gone. When darkness fell, he curled up under a fallen tree with a small fire to make up for the lack of a blanket or coat. Come morning he found that he had spent the night in a grove of giant sequoias, and later in life claimed that he was the first white man to see these amazing trees.

He soon found the rest of the party and although the exact route they took is unclear, they worked their way down to the river and eventually crossed to the south bank, then traveled south down the South Fork canyon before crossing north-westerly to the North Fork to follow the drainage of the North Fork into the San Joaquin Valley. It was while they were working their way out of the canyon lands that they had their only violent encounter with native Americans of the whole trip. They had taken on a guide who, in their opinion, was mis-directing and deliberately confusing them in order to have them abandon all their goods for his companions to ransack. They became aware that Indians were shadowing them, looking for abandoned valuables in their vacated campsites and dismissed the guide. Convinced that he had been trying to kill them, one of the party, Grove Cook, determined to mete out justice.

As the rest of the company broke camp on 27 October, Cook stayed behind, hidden, to see if their former guide would turn up to lead his companions to ransack the former campsite. When he appeared at the head of a small band of local Indians, Cook shot him and fled. Fortunately for the company they were almost out of the mountains, and within three days they emerged into the great valley of the San Joaquin River, before the Indians could launch a retaliatory raid.

On the last two days of October, to their relief and delight, they found themselves traveling down the valley of the Stanislaus River where it opens into the central valley. They saw the tracks of large herds of elk, and flights of wild fowl. When they finally reached the lower Stanislaus they saw thousands of antelope. On the first of November they stopped to hunt, bagging antelope and fowl. Bidwell wrote, "My breakfast, this morning formed a striking contrast with that of yesterday which was the lights of a wolf", while Chiles recalled, "…every man wept that night as they feasted," safe in the knowledge that they were out of the mountains and out of danger.

It was near the end of the dry summer season in California and they observed a parched, sere, landscape. But it didn't matter to them. There was game, there were wild sweet grapes, and they were in the land that they had sacrificed so much to reach. Nothing they would do later in life would be so memorable as being in the first company across the plains to California, establishing a route that would be followed by one of the biggest overland migrations in history. Joe B. Chiles made six more trips across the plains, but this was the one that stood out in his memory.

Monday 7 September 2015

End of the Trail

Joe B. Chiles and the rest of the party reveled in the warmth of foothills with their lower elevations. Overnight, they had gone from eating wolf guts to roasting antelope steaks, and from hopeless desperation in the cold trackless mountains to an optimistic feeling that their journey was almost at an end. Cheyenne Dawson, who had been almost forced to his knees from thirst and hunger, rejoiced with the others. "…and we decided to tarry, kill and eat… Bidwell says there were 13 deer killed and eaten, [by 32 people] and as we remained there only two or three days, there must have been some tall eating." Vegetarians, look away now.

The first night in the valley of the Stanislaus River they gorged on as much deer and antelope as they could, overcome to the point of tears with relief and delight as they ate their fill. Wild grapes still hung on their vines, sweet and thirst-quenching. After almost seven months on the trail, the first party of American settlers to cross the continent was in sight of their goal.

The next day the Bartleson group remained in camp to dress the meat that they had killed the day before, while the rest of the party set off down the river. As they followed the watercourse they were startled by the sudden appearance of Thomas Jones, one of the hunters who had been gone for just over a week. He explained that he had descended from the mountains looking for game a few days before the main party and by the greatest stroke of good fortune had run into an Indian whose one word of English was, "Marsh, Marsh."

The Indian had indeed been sent out by John Marsh, who had heard that a party of fellow Missourians was struggling through the mountains, to give them supplies and guide them across the San Joaquin all the way to his rancho on the slopes of Mt Diablo. A most welcome item was farina meal for Nancy Kelsey, who a few days before had become too weak to travel on until her husband shot a deer and brought her some meat to revive her.

They waited for Bartleson and his men to catch up and then all proceeded together to Marsh's rancho, crossing the San Joaquin River whose width they estimated at about 100 yards. The promised land of the San Joaquin looked like anything but a paradise to the new arrivals. The drought had left the land depressingly parched and sere, but Marsh cheered them up with a feast of a fat hog accompanied by some of his California brandy. Their welcome was warm, as he happily showed off his surroundings and family, consisting of his wife from one of the local tribes, and several children, who slept most nights out of doors unless it was raining, in which case they unrolled some skins on the dirt floor and slept inside.

Afterwards, some of the travelers took up Marsh's offer to sleep under a roof after so many months under the stars. Dawson and some of the others tried this novelty, but found that between the fleas and the rushing for the outhouse by their companions whose digestion could not cope with the fat pork that they had eaten so eagerly, they hardly slept.

For Chiles, Hopper, Dawson, and Bartleson, two days with Marsh was enough. They wanted to get on and see the territory. So, it was off to the nearby pueblo, San Jose for passports, by way of a night in jail over a little misunderstanding as to how they had arrived in California. But once that had been cleared up, and with the payment of $5, they were visitors in good standing and off to Monterey, the provincial capital, to see the lay of the land. More exploring followed, and on a visit to a former Missouri neighbor in Napa County, George Yount, Chiles saw the valley that would excite his imagination and industry. He also called on Gen. Mariano Vallejo, military governor, who wholeheartedly supported his plan to establish a mill in the region. It was the start of the adventure that would last the rest of his life.

[The majority of the text above is taken from the MS of my next writing project—Forgotten Trailblazer – Joseph B. Chiles and the Making of California]

Speaking of adventures, here are some statistics from our transcontinental junket:

Miles—approximately 3,010 miles

States visited—8: Missouri, Kansas, Nebraska, Wyoming, Colorado, Idaho, Utah, Nevada, California

Number of cups of coffee served in something other than Styrofoam—5

Tanks of gas—approx. 14

Number of motels stayed in—12

Memorable meals—few

Memorable meals for the wrong reasons—too many

Discouraging words—few

Good company—priceless

Index

Selected Bibliography

Primary Sources

Alvarado, Juan, *Historical and Personal Memoirs Relating to Alta California* [*Recuerdos Historicos y Personales Tocante a la Alta California*], 1875, San Francisco, Book Club of California, 1982, (Original MS at the Huntington Library)

Applegate, Jesse, "A Day With the Cow Column, 1843", *The Quarterly of the Oregon Historical Society* Vol. 1, No. 4 (Dec., 1900)

Baldridge, William, *Days of '46*, MS Bancroft Library, Univ. of California, Berkeley, p.32

Belden, Josiah, Letter to his sister Mrs. Eliza M. Bowers, Dec. 21 1841, Coe Collection, Yale Univ. Library, quoted in Nunis. Ed. 1992.

Belden, Josiah, "The First Overland Emigrant Train to New California," *Touring Topics* 22 (July 1930): 14-18; 56

Bidwell, John, *Across the Plains*, pub. C. 1843, publisher unknown

Bidwell, John, "Fremont in the Conquest of California," *Century Magazine* 41 (February 1891) p.518 - 525

Bidwell, John, "Life in California Before the Gold Discovery", *Century Magazine* 41, (December 1890) p.163, cited in Gillis and Magliari, 2004

Bidwell, John, *Echoes of the Past*, ed. Milo Quaife, Chicago 1928

Bidwell, John, "A Rendezvous on the Green River", reprinted in Gillis and Magliari, *John Bidwell and California*, Spokane WA, The Arthur H. Clark Co., 2004

Bidwell, John, Dictation from *General John Bidwell: An Autobiography*, p.10, Dictation for HH Bancroft Collections, Bancroft Library, Univ. of California

Bidwell, John, Translation of Bidwell's original passport, Courtesy of California State Library

Brannan, Samuel, *Scoundrel's Tale: The Samuel Brannan Papers*, Will Bagley, ed., Spokane WA, Arthur H. Clark, 1999

Brewer, William H., *Up and Down California in 1860-64: The Journal of William H. Brewer*, Berkeley, University of California Press, 1966

Book of Deeds A, p.306-07, Doc. 411, US Land Commission, Bancroft Library

Bryant, Edwin, *What I Saw in California*, New York, D. Appleton & Co., 1848

Chiles, Henry Lee, Letter from Jerome Davis to Joseph Chiles 1858, Chiles Family Papers

Chiles, Joseph B. papers, San Francisco, Society of California Pioneers Library

Chiles, Isaac, Letter to Joel Chiles 1854, Courtesy of Jackson County, [MO] Historical Society

Chiles, J.B., Letter from Joseph Chiles to Joel Chiles 1854, Courtesy, Jackson County, [MO] Historical Society

Chiles, J.B., A Visit to California in 1841, MS, Bancroft Library, Berkeley CA

Chiles, J.B., Letter from J.B. Chiles to J.F. Chiles, San Francisco, Jan. 31 1852, Society of California Pioneers

Chiles, John P., Annotations of Chiles papers in the author's possession

Chief Marin, Letter May 5 1833, Santa Barbara Mission Archives 3414, cited in Goerke, Betty, *Chief Marin, Leader Rebel, and Legend,* Berkeley, Heyday Books, 2007

Clyman, James, Diaries, Charles L. Camp, ed., San Francisco, CA, California Historical Society, Special Publication, No. 3, 1928

Dana, RH, *Two Years Before the Mast,* New York, D. Appleton & Co, 1899

Davis, William Heath, *Seventy-five years in California,* San Francisco,1929

Dawson, Nicholas "Cheyenne", *Narrative in Camp,* San Francisco, 1933; also in Nunis, *The Bidwell-Bartleson Party*

DeSmet, Pierre Jean, *Life and Sketches: With a Narrative of a Year's Residence Among the Indian Tribes of the Rocky Mountains*, Philadelphia, 1843

Farnham, Thomas Jefferson, *Travels in the Californias, and Scenes in the Pacific Ocean*, New York: Saxton & Miles, 1844

Fremont, J.C. Lieutenant, "A Report on the Exploration of the Country, Lying Between the Missouri River and the Rocky Mountains, on the Line of the Kansas and Platte Rivers", Senate doc. 243, Washington 1843

Hastings, Lansford W., *Emigrant's Guide to Oregon and California*, 1845, Reprint, New York: Da Capo Press, 1969

High Court of Admiralty: Instance and Prize Courts: Examinations and Answers, National Archives, UK, Kew, London.

Hopper, Charles, "Narrative of Charles Hopper a California Pioneer of 1841", written by RT Montgomery at Napa 1871 [dictation for HH Bancroft]

John, James Diaries, Himes, George H., ed., "The Diary of James John", *St. John* [Oregon] *Review*, March 16, 30; April 6, 13,20,27, 1906

Johnson, Overton, and William H. Winter, *Route Across the Rocky Mountains*, Angela Firkus, ed., West Lafayette IND, Notabell Books, 2000

Jones, Mary A, Personal Diary n.d., Bancroft Library, Berkeley CA

Kelsey, Nancy, "Nancy Kelsey's Own Story of Her Life", Pomo Bulletin (Feb. 1983) Lake County Historical Society, Lakeport CA., Manuscript, Mattes Library.

Larkin, Thomas O., *The Larkin Papers: Personal, Business, and Official Correspondence of Thomas Oliver Larkin, Merchant and United States Consul in California*, George P. Hammond ed., Berkeley, Univ. of California Press, 1951–1968

Leinhard, Heinrich, Pioneer at Sutter's Fort 1846-1850, "Life and Death of James McDowell", West Sacramento Historical Society, West Sacramento, CA

Letter May 5, 1833, Santa Barbara Mission Archives, 3414, cited in Goerke, Betty, *Chief Marin, Leader Rebel, and Legend*, Berkeley, Heyday Books, 2007

"List of Officers, Sailors and Marines of the Virginia Navy in the American Revolution." *The Virginia Magazine of History and Biography*, vol. 1, no. 1, 1893

Marsh, John, Letter from Marsh to Commodore Thomas Ap Catesby Jones, Nov. 24, 1842, MS Bancroft Library

May, Richard Martin, "A Sketch of a Migrating Family to California in 1848", reprinted Fairfield WA, Ye Galleon Press, 1991

May, Richard Martin, *The Schreek of Wagons: 1848: The 1848 Diary of Richard M. May*, edited by Devere Helfrich and Trudy Ackerman, Rigel Publications, Hopkinton, MASS, 1993.

Memorial and Biographical History of Northern California, Chicago, Lewis Publishing Company, 1875

Mengarini, Gregory, "Recollections of the Flathead Mission", Translated and edited by Gloria Lothrop, Glendale, CA, 1977

Napa Family History Center, IRS Tax Assessment List, April 1864; Excise Taxes 1866

Napa Valley Register, June 25, 1885

Norris, Frank, *The Octopus*, New York: Doubleday, Page and Company, 1901

Parkman, Francis, Jr., *The California and Oregon Trail: Being Sketches of Prairie and Rocky Mountain Life*, New York: George Putnam, 1849

Reading, Pierson B., Journal written during his journey from Westport, Missouri, to Monterey, California in 1843, Society of California Pioneers, Vol. 7, No. 3, San Francisco, 1930

Reed, Martha Williams, "Old California Pioneer Passes Away at Fallbrook. Martha Williams Reed, Age 87, Crosses the Plains by Ox-Team in the Early Gold Excitement of California.", *The Fallbrook Enterprise,* 12 January 1917

Sacramento *Daily Union,* Vol 20, No. 3047, Jan 1, 1861

Smith, Edward, "A Journal of Scenes and Incidents on a Journey from Missouri to California in 1848", CS 68, C34, California State Library

Solano *Press*, March 13, 1867; May 8, 1867

State of Missouri, Soldiers' Records: War of 1812–World War I, Missouri Digital Heritage, Missouri State Archives.

Supreme Court of California, *Report of Cases Determined in the Supreme Court of the State of California,* Vol. 69, San Francisco: Bancroft-Whitney, 1906

Sutton, Sarah, Diary entry, May 12, 1854, Holmes and Leckie, eds., *Covered Wagon Women,* Univ. of Nebraska Press, 1998

United States Census Bureau, 1840 Census, State of Missouri

United States Congress, Thirty-ninth congress Session 1, chapter 219, 1866

United States Land Case 411,n.d., US Land Commission, Bancroft Library

United States Senate, 30th Congress First Session Document No. 33, Proceedings of the Court-Martial of Lieutenant Colonel John C. Fremont

Vallejo, Mariano, *Historical and Personal Memoirs Relating to Alta California* [*Recuerdos Historicos y Personales Tocante a la Alta California (1875)*], Vol. 2,3,5, 1875

Waters, Lydia, "Account of a Trip Across the Plains in 1855," Quarterly of the Society of California Pioneers, Vol.VI, No. 2, June 1929

Williams, Joseph, Narrative of a Tour from the State of Indiana to the Oregon Territory in the Years 1841-2, Cincinnati, 1848

Woodland News, March 30, 1867; May 18, 1867

www.tn.gov/regimental-histories-during-war-1812

Published Sources

Atkinson, J. H., "Cattle Drives from Arkansas to California Prior to the Civil War", *Arkansas Historical Quarterly* 28, (Autumn 1969)

Bagley, Will, *So Rugged and Mountainous, Blazing the Trails to Oregon and California 1812 – 1848*, Norman OK, University of Oklahoma Press, 2010.

Bancroft, Hubert Howe, *History of California*, Vol IV and Vol V, San Francisco, The History Company, 1886 - 1890

Bancroft, "Sacramento Transcript", May 21, 1850, cited in Nunis, p. 267

Barry, Louise, *The Beginning of the West: Annals of the Kansas Gateway to the American West, 1540 – 1854*, Topeka KS, Kansas State Historical Society, 1972

Bayley, Thomas S., "The First Overland Mail Bag to California," Bancroft Library

Bean, Walton, and Rawls, James J., *California: An Interpretative History,* New York: McGraw–Hill, 1983

Billington, Ray Allen, *The Far Western Frontier, 1830 – 1860*, Albuquerque, NM, Univ. of New Mexico Press, 1956

Bigler, David L., and Will Bagley, eds., *Army of Israel: Mormon Battalion Narratives*, Spokane, WA, Arthur H. Clark, 2000

Boorstin, Daniel J., *The Americans: The National Experience,* New York, Random House, 1965

Burcham, Levi T., *Historical Geography of the Range Livestock Industry of California,* Berkeley, Univ. of California Press, 1956

Burke, Diane Mutti, *On Slavery's Border—Missouri's Small Slaveholding Households 1815-1865,* Athens GA, Univ. of Georgia Press, 2010

Camp, Charles L., ed. *George C. Yount and his Chronicles of the West, Comprising Extracts from his "Memoirs" and from the Orange Clark "Narrative",* Denver, Fred A. Rosenstock, The Old West Publishing Co., 1966

Camp, Charles L, *James Clyman, American Frontiersman, 1792 – 1881,* San Francisco, California Historical Society, 1928

Camp, William Martin, *San Francisco, Port of Gold,* New York, Doubleday & Co., 1947

Caughey, John W., *California,* New York, Prentice Hall, 1954

Churchill, Charles B., *Adventurers and Prophets: Autobiographers in Mexican California, 1827 – 1847,* Spokane WA, Arthur H. Clark, 1995

Clark, Chris, *Untold History, The Survival of California's Indians,* Link TV script, September 26, 2016, www.linktv.org.

Cleland, Robert Glass, *The Cattle on a Thousand Hills,* San Marino, Huntington Library, 1941

Cleland, John, *Pathfinders*, Los Angeles, Powell Publishing Co. 1929

The Conference on Research in Income and Wealth, Trends in the American Economy in the Nineteenth Century, Princeton NJ, Princeton Univ. Press, 1960

Cook, Sherburne, *The Conflict Between the California Indian and White Civilization*, Berkeley, University of California Press, 1943

Cureton, Gilbert, "The Cattle Trail to California, 1840–1860", *Historical Society of Southern California Quarterly*, 35 (June 1953) 99 – 109

Dary, David, *The Oregon Trail*, New York, Knopf, 2004.

Davis, Virginia Lee Hutcheson, *Tidewater Virginia Families*, Baltimore MD, Genealogical Publishing Co., 1989

Davis, Virginia Lee Hutcheson, *Tidewater Virginia Families, Generations Beyond,* Baltimore MD, Genealogical Publishing Co., 1998

Davis, William Heath, *Seventy-Five Years in California: Recollections and Remarks by One Who Was a Resident from 1838 Until the end of Long Life in 1909,* Edited by Harold A. Small, San Francisco, John Howell Books, 1967

Denhardt, Robert M., *The Horse of the Americas,* Norman OK, Univ. of Oklahoma Press, 1946

De Voto, Bernard, *The Year of Decision 1846*, Cambridge MASS, The Riverside Press, 1942

Dillon, Richard H., ed., *California Trail Herd*, Los Gatos CA, Talisman Press, 1961

Dillon, Richard H., *Fool's Gold*, Sanger CA, The Write Thought, Inc., 1967

Dillon, Richard, *Humbugs and Heroes: A Gallery of California Pioneers*, Garden City, N.Y. Doubleday, 1970

Dippel, John V H, *Race to the Frontier: "White Flight" and Westward Expansion*, New York, Algora Publishing, 2005

Eakin, Joanne Chiles, *Walter Chiles of Jamestown*, Independence, MO, 1983.

Emparan, Madie Brown, *The Vallejos of California,* San Francisco, The Gleeson Library Associates, 1968

Faragher, John Mack, *Women and Men on the Overland Trail,* New Haven, Yale Univ. Press 1979

Fellman, Michael, *Inside War, the Guerilla Conflict in Missouri During the American Civil War*, New York, Oxford Univ. Press, 1989

Fremont, John C., *Memoirs of My Life,* Chicago, 1887

Fritz, Christian G., "Politics and the Courts: The Struggle Over Land in San Francisco 1846-1866", (November 4, 2010), Santa Clara Law Review, Vol. 26, No. 1, 1986

Gates, Paul, "Adjudication of Spanish-Mexican Land Claims in California", *Huntington Library Quarterly*, Vol. 21, No. 3, May 1958

Gates Paul W., *The Farmer's Age: Agriculture, 1815– 1860*, New York, Harper & Row, 1960

Giffen, Helen S., *Trail-Blazing Pioneer, Colonel Joseph Ballinger Chiles*, San Francisco, CA, John Howell Books, 1969

Gillis and Magliarii, *John Bidwell & California*, Spokane WA, The Arthur H. Clark Company, 2004

Goerke, Betty, *Chief Marin, Leader Rebel, and Legend*, Berkeley, Heyday Books, 2007

Graebner, Norman A., ed., *Manifest Destiny*, Indianapolis, Indiana, Bobbs Merrill, 1968

Heath, Minnie B., "Nancy Kelsey–The First Pioneer Woman to Cross the Plains," *The Grizzly Bear Magazine* XL (February 1937): 3, 7

Haley, J. Evetts, *Life on the Texas Range*, Austin, Univ. of Texas Press, 1952

Hardeman, Nicholas Perkins, *Wilderness Calling, The Hardeman Family in the American Westward Movement, 1750 -1900*, Knoxville TN: University of Tennessee Press, 1977

Harlow, Neal, *California Conquered, The Annexation of an American Province, 1846–1850*, Berkeley, University of California Press, 1982

Heidenreich, Linda, "This Land Was Mexican Once", *Histories of Resistance from Northern California*, Austin, University of Texas Press, 2007.

Hickey, Donald, *The War of 1812,* Urbana, Univ. of Illinois Press

History of Napa and Lake Counties California, San Francisco, Slocum, Bowen & Co., 1881

History of Solano and Napa Counties, San Francisco, California 1912

Holliday, J.S., *Rush for Riches: Gold Fever and the Making of California*, Oakland and Berkeley, Oakland Museum of California and University of California Press, 1999

Holmes, Kenneth, *Covered Wagon Women, Diaries and Letters from the Western Trails, 1854 – 1860*, Lincoln, University of Nebraska Press, 1987

Hornbeck, David, "The Patenting of California's Private Land Claims, 1851–1885", *Geographical Review* 69 (October 1979): 434-48

Howard, Thomas, *Sierra Crossing,* Berkeley, UC Press, 1998

Hurt, R. Douglas, *Agriculture and Slavery in Missouri's Little Dixie*, Columbia, Univ. of Missouri Press, 1992

Hussey, John A., "The Origin of the Gillespie Mission," *California Historical Society Quarterly* 19, (March 1940): 43-58

Hurtado, Albert, *Indian Survival on the California Frontier*, New Haven, Yale Univ. Press, 1988

Hurtado, Albert, *John Sutter: A Life on the North American Frontier*, Norman OK, Univ. of Oklahoma Press, 2006

Igler, David, *Industrial Cowboys, Mill & Lux and the Transformation of the Far West, 1850–1920*, Berkeley, Univ. of California Press, 2001

Igler, David, "The Industrial Far West: Region and Nation in the Late Nineteenth Century", *Pacific Historical Review* 69 (May 2000): 159-182

Johnson and Winter, *Route Across the Rocky Mountains*, ed. Angela Fircus, West Lafayette Indiana, Notabell Books, 2000

Kelly, Charles, and Dale L. Morgan, *Old Greenwood: The Story of Caleb Greenwood, Trapper, Pathfinder and Early Pioneer*, Georgetown California, The Talisman Press, 1965

Kelley Robert, *Battling the Inland Sea: American Political Culture, Public Policy and the Sacramento Valley, 1850–1986*, Berkeley: University of California Press, 1989

Kroeber, Alfred Louis, *Handbook of the Indians of California*, Washington DC, Government Printing Office, 1925

Larkey, Joann, *Davisville 68, The History and Heritage of the City of Davis*, Davis CA, 1969

Leek, Nancy, *John Bidwell, The Adventurous Life of a California Pioneer*, Chico CA, ANCHR, 2010

Lancaster, Jane F., *Removal Aftershock: The Seminoles' Struggles to Survive in the West, 1836-1866*, Knoxville, University of Tennessee Press, 1994

Lawrence, Eleanor, "Mexican Trade Between Santa Fe and Los Angeles," *California Historical Society Quarterly*, X (1933):27-39

Lyman, George D., *John Marsh Pioneer*, New York, Charles Scribner's Sons, 1930

Lynch, Robert M., *The Sonoma Valley Story*, Sonoma CA: The Sonoma Index-Tribune, 1997

Magliari, Michael, "Free Soil, Unfree Labor: Cave Johnson Couts and the Binding of Indian Workers in California, 1850-1867", *Pacific Historical Review*, Vol. 73 No. 3, 2004

McWilliams, Carey, *Factories in the Field: The Story of Migratory Farm Labor in California,* Boston: Little, Brown and Co., 1939

Meldhal, Keith H., *Hard Road West: History and Geology along the Gold Rush Trail,* Chicago, University of Chicago Press, 2007

Merk, Frederick, *Manifest Destiny and Mission in American History: A Reinterpretation,* New York, Knopf, 1963

Miller, David E., "The First Wagon Train to Cross Utah, 1841," *Utah Historical Quarterly*, XXX (1962): 41-51

Miller,Robert, *Juan Alvarado, Governor of California 1836-1842,* Norman OK, Univ. of Oklahoma Press, 1998.

Monroy, Douglas, *Thrown Among Strangers, The Making of Mexican Culture in Frontier California*, Berkeley, CA, Univ. of California Press, 1990

Morgan, Dale, ed., *Overland in 1846: Diaries and Letters of the California–Oregon Trail*, Lincoln, Univ. of Nebraska Press, 1963

Morgan, Dale L., *Shoshonean Peoples and the Overland Trail: Frontiers of the Utah Superintendency of Indian Affairs, 1849–1869*, Logan, Utah, Utah State University Press, 2007

Morgan, Dale L. *The Humboldt, Highway of the West*, New York, Farrar & Rinehart, 1943

McLynn, Frank, *Wagons West*, London, Jonathan Cape, 2002

Miller, Robert Ryal, *Juan Alvarado Governor of California*, Norman OK, Univ. of Oklahoma Press, 1998

National Park Service, National Historic Trails, Auto Tour Route Interpretive Guide, 2011

Nordhoff, Charles, *California: For Health, Pleasure and Residence, A Book for Travelers and Settlers*, New York, 1873

Nunis, Doyce B, Jr.,Ed., *The Bidwell-Bartleson Party, 1841 California Emigrant Adventure*, Santa Cruz CA, Western Tanager Press, 1991

Oglesby, Richard, *Manuel Lisa and the Opening of the Missouri Fur Trade*, Norman OK, Univ. of Oklahoma Press, 1963

Paden, Irene, *The Wake of the Prairie Schooner*, New York, The Macmillan Company, 1945

Paul, Rodman, *California Gold*, Lincoln NEB: University of Nebraska Press, 1969

Paul, Rodman, *The Far West and the Great Plains in Transition, 1859–1900*, New York, Harper and Row, 1988

Phillips, George H., *Indians and Intruders in Central California, 1769 – 1849,* Norman OK, University of Oklahoma Press, 1993

Pisani, Donald J., "Squatter Law in California, 1850–1856", *Western Historical Quarterly* 25 (Autumn 1994): 277-310

Pitt, Leonard, *The Decline of the Californios: A Social History of the Spanish Speaking Californians, 1846–1890,* Berkeley, University of California Press, 1966

Rasmussen, Cecilia, *John Marsh*, Los Angeles Times, February 5, 2006

Rice, William B., "Last Days of Gen. John A. Sutter," *Out West* 17 (October 1902): 441-445

Rolle, Andrew, *John C. Fremont, Character as Destiny*, Norman: Univ. of Oklahoma Press, 1991

Rogers, Fred B., *William Brown Ide: Bear Flagger*, San Francisco: John Howell, 1962

Rollins, Philip Ashton, ed., *The Discovery of the Oregon Trail, Robert Stuart's Narratives of his Overland Trip Eastward from Astoria in 1812-13*, Lincoln, Univ. of Nebraska Press, 1935

Rosenus, Alan, *General Vallejo and the Advent of the Americans*, Berkeley CA, Heyday Books, 1995

Silliman, Stephen W., *Lost Laborers in Colonial California: Native Americans and the Archaeology of Rancho Petaluma*, Tucson: University of Arizona Press, 2004

Snodgrass, Mary Ellen, *Settlers of the American West*, Jefferson NC, McFarland and Co., 2015

Starr, Kevin, *Americans and the California Dream*, New York, Oxford Univ. Press, 1973

Stewart, George R., *The California Trail*, New York, McGraw-Hill, 1962

Stewart, George R., "The Prairie Schooner Got Them There", *American Heritage Magazine* 13, No. 2, (February 1962) pp. 7-16

Street, Richard Steven, *Beasts of the Field*, Palo Alto, Stanford University Press, 2004

Stine, Scott, *Climate 1650-1850*, https://pubs.usgs.gov/dds/dds/43/VOL_II/VII_CO2.Pdf

Taylor, Paul S., "Foundations of California Rural Society," *California Historical Society Quarterly* 24 (1945): 193-228

Unruh, John D. Jr., *The Plains Across, The Overland Emigrants and the Trans-Mississippi West, 1840–60*, Urbana ILL, University of Illinois Press, 1979

Vaught, David, *After the Gold Rush,* Baltimore, The Johns Hopkins University Press, 2007

Vaught, David, *Cultivating California*, Baltimore, The Johns Hopkins University Press, 1999

Walker, Dale, *Bear Flag Rising*, London, St. Martins Press, 1999

Walton, John, *Western Times and Water Wars: State, Culture and Rebellion in California*, Berkeley, University of California Press, 1992

Webb, Todd, *The Gold Rush Trail and the Road to Oregon*, Garden City New York, Doubleday & Co., 1963

Weber, David J., *The Mexican Frontier, 1821–1846: The American Southwest Under Mexico,* Albuquerque NM, University of New Mexico Press, 1982

Weber, Lin, *Old Napa Valley*, St. Helena CA, Wine Ventures Publishing, 1998

Wentworth, Edward N., *America's Sheep Trails, History, Personalities*, Ames, Iowa State College Press, 1948

Williams, Jacqueline B., *Wagon Wheel Kitchens: Food on the Oregon Trail*, Lawrence KA, University Press of Kansas, 1993

Williamson, Samuel H., "Seven Ways to Compute the Relative Value of a U.S. Dollar Amount, 1774 to present", *Measuring Worth*, 2017

Wood, Ellen Lamont, *George Yount*, San Francisco, The Grabhorn Press, 1941

www.ingramcontent.com/pod-product-compliance
Lightning Source LLC
Chambersburg PA
CBHW051540030726
47592CB00001B/66